HOME CARE
FOR THE DYING

A Reassuring, Comprehensive
Guide to Physical and
Emotional Care

DEBORAH WHITING LITTLE

THE DIAL PRESS
DOUBLEDAY & COMPANY, INC.
GARDEN CITY, NEW YORK
1985

Library of Congress Cataloging in Publication Data
Little, Deborah Whiting.
Home care for the dying.
Bibliography: p. 300
Includes index.
1. Terminally ill—Home care. 2. Terminally ill—
Family relationships. I. Title.
R726.8.L58 1985   649'.8   84-12709
ISBN 0-385-27750-4 (pbk.)
Published by The Dial Press

Living Will reprinted with the permission of Concern for Dying,
250 West 57th Street, New York, N.Y. 10107.

Manufactured in the United States of America

This is for everyone who helped, for Margaret de Rongé Little, who brought us all together, and for John Ludden, who first said, "Tell me about it" and keeps on listening.

CONTENTS

PREFACE
xi

ACKNOWLEDGMENTS
xv

PROFESSIONAL ADVISERS
xvii

1 WHY HOME CARE?
1

2 WILL HOME CARE WORK?
13

3 CAN I DO IT?
24

4 HOME CARE BEGINS: PREPARE THE WAY
37

5 YOU AND YOUR DOCTOR
45

CONTENTS

6   CREATING A TEAM
64

7   SUPPLIES
80

8   KEEPING RECORDS
101

9   PHYSICAL CARE
113

10   EATING
130

11   CARE OF SYMPTOMS
139

12   PAIN
150

13   HOSPITALIZATION
166

14   A CHILD IS DYING
170

15   SELF-CARE
184

16   FAMILY AND HOUSEHOLD
196

17   VISITORS AND FRIENDS
213

18   BEING WITH A DYING PERSON
220

19   SOME HARD CHOICES
234

20   LIVING ONE DAY AT A
TIME: FOR SOMEONE DYING
246

CONTENTS

21   PRACTICAL MATTERS
     257

22   DYING
     272

23   GRIEVING
     287

24   EPILOGUE
     298

BIBLIOGRAPHY
300

INDEX
307

PREFACE

This book is about caring for someone dying at home. I wrote it because I needed a book like this when I cared for my terminally ill grandmother. In the spring of 1978, I took a leave from my work and moved into her house, responding to my own need to help and to the loyalties of a lifetime relationship. We had been friends for thirty-odd years. Our bond hadn't always been easy, but it was important to us both. We had a long history of standing by each other. I imagined that my being there would cheer her up and keep her mind off her disease, and that she would be back on the golf course by summer.

There was much that I didn't know. I knew nothing about serious illness or about nursing. I was completely unprepared for the routine physical care, disease symptoms, family interactions, moral issues, and personal stresses. I didn't know then that her illness would be fatal. I had never seen death and knew nothing about what dying was like, how she would feel, or how it would affect her family or our friends.

I learned a few skills of caretaking from visiting nurses and two wonderful housekeepers. More information would have been extremely helpful, but I knew so little that I had no idea even what questions to ask. Dr. Elisabeth Kübler-Ross's *On Death and Dying* taught me something about death and grieving. I knew my grandmother and I, family members, and friends were experiencing natural feelings. So, I had a little company and a little information. It made me want more, yet I was so totally involved in caregiving that I did not have the emotional or physical energy to seek and secure help.

The experience changed my life. For six months I lived with and often felt overwhelmed by loneliness, anger, compassion, boredom, fear, grief, uncertainty, and physical exhaustion. Each moment presented the painful juxtaposition of intimacy and loss: we were becoming closer, yet she was moving farther away. I felt hopeless and frightened when my grandmother's physical and emotional needs could not be met. Yet for all its shortcomings this experience gave me what I have heard other caregivers share—that is, my first real hard-won success. I learned that I could take on something very difficult, stick with it, and finish it. I could look back and say, "I did that well—not perfectly, but just fine. I did the best I could at the time." Although after her death I felt I had completed the work for my grandmother, I knew there was something more to do for me.

In the last weeks of her life, Gaga suffered from what her doctor said "couldn't possibly be pain." She was miserable and wanted to die. Neither the doctor nor I was well enough informed to make her comfortable. In the months after she died, I learned that with more skilled attention both to her various sources of discomfort and to her pain medication, she could have been quite at ease. I decided to harness the energy created by my grief and anger, learn what I could about care for people dying, and write about it. I wanted to make terminal care easier for others to provide. I also wanted to support everyday heroes—you, my mother, a friend—who are caring for dying people at home. Most of all I wanted to write the book I needed while I was caring for my grandmother: a book that describes the important factors in making a choice for home care; a book that provides the specifics of medical, practical, and emotional care; a book that gives caregivers access to a community of people who understand what it's like to care for someone terminally ill at home.

Financial, social, and medical support for home care is growing.

Use this book to guide you to resources which no doubt exist and are accessible to you. If you are exploring home care without an immediate need for it, I hope the stories and information will encourage you to hold it as an option for the future. If you are in the midst of caregiving, I pray that the facts and experiences in this book will allay your fears and support your practical and emotional needs.

But inevitably you must set your own course. There is no one correct way to give care or to assemble support, or to be with a dying person. Many of the mechanics of care will be dictated by the patient's disease, symptoms, age, and home situation. Personal history and relationships will work together with available resources to shape the care you can provide. Take what you need from the experiences of other people, what worked and didn't work for them. No one can say exactly what to do or what will work. We can simply tell you what we did.

I will be clear about my biases. First, every dying person has a right to be at home and to have comfort be the first priority of caregivers. With sufficient support most people can be comfortable at home for most or all of the terminal phase of illness. Second, although appropriate institutional alternatives are becoming more plentiful—such as palliative care units in hospitals, terminal care programs in nursing homes, and hospice facilities—they should support, not direct, the course of care. The dying person and caregivers should do their own planning and turn to institutions if or when they see no alternative for medical, social, or emotional help. Third, we need as human beings to do all we can to stay connected to each other. We need to break down our own boundaries and push ourselves to make commitments to others. Providing home care is a real challenge to assumptions we may have about ourselves. It is a real physical, emotional, and spiritual struggle to be that close to another person. Most people who do it say they received immeasurable personal rewards. Fourth, we each have very real and very different limits. But providing home care won't be possible for everyone and we need to forgive ourselves and others when it is not.

This book is addressed—except for one chapter written for the person dying (chapter 20)—to you, the caregivers, families, and friends. I know how difficult your task is, and I know intimately that you may disregard the toll this exacts on you. The truth is that your feelings, physical stresses, and needs are as important as the patient's. Because you will live longer, you owe it to yourself and others who care about you to treat yourself well.

I just want to add one more thought. I asked my mother once how she had decided to have children and she said she didn't think about it. She just did it. This was how I "decided" to care for my grandmother. I just did it. I didn't have any special courage, or planning, or skill. Some of you will "just do it"; others will make a choice. In either case, try not to imagine what may happen. Tomorrow will take care of itself. Do it for just one day at a time.

DEBORAH WHITING LITTLE
Cambridge, Massachusetts

ACKNOWLEDGMENTS

It is impossible to acknowledge all the people who have influenced and contributed to my writing this book. Over the years I have been blessed with teachers whose values, discipline, and skill instilled in me a commitment to pursue ideas and observations in words, to be curious, to listen and study: Mary McGuire, Alice Boyle, Zora Unkovich, and Fran Walker. Over the six years of writing this book, old friends, colleagues, and many new friends helped and reassured me about the value of this project; some of them are listed as advisers. Dying people and their families welcomed me into their lives and told their stories, among them: Sally and Julie Mamolen; Fazal Chowdhry and Zekiye Eglar; Put, Helen, and Martha Livingston; Susan and Mildred Zawalich; Mary and Tom Bross; Elizabeth Digby; Eric Robinson; Beth, Tim, Michael, and Andy Shafer; Sue Longley; Katharine Flindell; Bill, Sam, and Freda Rebelsky; Annette Delaney; Donna Witham; and Cathy, Sarah, and Jenifer Mitchell. Mary Macy helped me prepare the first proposal; Mary Howell propped an early draft on her leg cast, sharpened her pencil, and gave me invaluable criticism; Mary McGuire sat me down at her kitchen table and explained parallel construction and "tightening" in that gentle but sure way so familiar from twenty years ago. Many others read chapters and kept telling me the book was necessary even when I didn't want to hear it, among them: Ann Quenin, John and Susan Putnam, Al Kershaw, Regina Reitmeyer, Karen Hermann, Sarah Arista, Kate Nixon, Alvin Handelman, Chris Coughlin, Sam, Sandy Pilotto, and Effie Shumaker. The Leyre and Lavergne families provided quiet, safe workplaces in their Montélimar, Pradelles, and Paris homes. Anne Perrino and Mary Casey showed me by their special example that with loving, attentive, common sense care—not professional training—you and I can provide exactly what a dying person needs. Judy Feldman kept me afloat by reminding me over and over to "keep one foot in reality." Finally, how can I thank all my friends whose hundreds of gracious invitations have been casualties of this book. Since I wrote in my "spare" time—nights, early mornings, weekends, vacations—carrying file folders wherever I went, I have not been as attentive a friend as I wish. My greatest joy is now to turn with open arms to all those people and say, "I'm finished. How about getting together for a long talk?"

Stories and ideas are taken from interviews, books, articles, personal narratives, and secondhand accounts. The unidentified speakers throughout the book are actual people—some dying, some giving care—who shared themselves hoping their experiences would help others. Several of these voices are now silent. For survivors, the remembering has often been painful. I am very grateful to each one.

PROFESSIONAL
ADVISERS

Many professionals provided ideas, answered questions, and raised issues from their own experiences with terminal care and home care. Their help, given in interviews, telephone conversations, letters, and printed materials, is represented on every page of this book.

Rosemary Ananis, M.S.W., Senior Oncology Social Worker, Deaconess Hospital, Boston

Brenda Attia, R.N., M.A., oncology nurse

Rafik R. Attia, M.D., anesthesiology, Lynn Hospital, Lynn, Massachusetts

Anna Bissonnette, R.N., M.S., University Hospital, Boston; Assistant Professor of Community Medicine, Boston University School of Medicine

Ned H. Cassem, M.D., Associate Professor of Psychiatry, Harvard Medical School; Chief, Psychiatric Consultation Liaison Service, Massachusetts General Hospital, Boston

Don Frederic Colenback, Ph.D., Professor of Christian Ethics, Episcopal Divinity School, Cambridge, Massachusetts

Mary E. Constanza, M.D., Director, Division of Oncology, University of Massachusetts Medical Center; Associate Professor of Medicine, University of Massachusetts School of Medicine, Worcester

Annette M. Delaney, R.N., Director of Quality Assurance, New England Medical Center, Boston

Joan Erikson, artist, author, collaborator with Erik H. Erikson, and volunteer in creative arts for the terminally ill

Corinne S. Ertel, M.D., pediatrician, Weston, Massachusetts

Barbara Farley, R.N., Nursing Coordinator, Oncology-Hematology, Beth Israel Hospital, Boston

Todd Holzman, M.D., Chief of Child Psychiatry, Harvard Community Health Plan, Wellesley; Chief of Psychiatry, HCHP Hospital; Beth Israel Hospital, Boston

Mary C. Howell, M.D., Ph.D., in private home care practice; author of *Healing at Home* and *Helping Ourselves: Families and the Human Network* (Boston: Beacon Press)

Donna Larson, R.N., M.S.N., Adult Primary Care Practitioner, Brigham and Women's Hospital, Boston

Daniel M. Leyre, M.D., anesthesiologist, Clinique Capmal, Montélimar, France

Ann Lovett, R.N., Director, Home Care Division, Beth Israel Hospital, Boston

Agnes Meth, R.N., M.S.N., Adult Primary Care Practitioner, University of Massachusetts Medical Center, Worcester

Martha Scott Perkins, B.S., nutrition educator, Stow, Massachusetts

Samuel Putnam, M.D., School of Medicine, University of Rochester, New York

Freda Rebelsky, Ph.D., Professor of Psychology, Boston University

Dennis Robbins, Ph.D., M.P.H., Fellow in Medical Ethics, Department of Health Policy and Management, Harvard University School of Public Health; National Fund for Medical Education Fellow, Cambridge, Massachusetts

Charles Rosenbaum, M.D., Chief of Clinical Division, Tufts University Medical School Cancer Unit, Boston

Dame Cicely Saunders, D.B.E., F.R.C.P., Medical Director, St. Christopher's Hospice, Sydenham, England

Karen Taft, M.A., Home Care Counselor, Harvard Community Health Plan, Boston

Sigrid Tishler, M.D., Oncology, Beth Israel Hospital; Harvard Community Health Plan, Boston

Rev. Thomas A. Welch, M.Ed., Program Director, OMEGA, Somerville, Massachusetts

Mary Welsh, Social Worker, HCHP Hospital, Boston

1
WHY HOME CARE?

I am dying. I can no longer say I'm sick. There is a difference. I was sick and now have crossed the line. Knowing that I will die, how do I live? What is important for me now? What does my body need? What does my heart need? I want a chance to live this out on my own terms. Dying will take just a moment. The rest is living. Don't argue, I don't have time or strength for that. I just want your help. I want to stay at home. I could be anyone. I could be you, your spouse, child, relative, friend, neighbor. You may want to run from me. Dying is not at all easy, for either of us.

Consider yourself in this person's position for a moment. Imagine getting the news that you are dying. You are the same person you were yesterday, wanting to be loved, loving, worrying about money, excited about a book you are reading, concerned about a friend, annoyed by a losing team or bad weather, confused about your gas bill. But now you are told that the "stomach upset" you have endured for the last few months which has drained your energy and worried the family means you are going to die. In a way, you half suspected it. The doctor's news has had its antecedents in periods of discomfort, maybe hospitalization, and treatment. At times you sensed you weren't getting well. Now the vague fear has been confirmed. But you are not suddenly dead; you haven't stopped living, even though the future as you are accustomed to thinking of it has disappeared. What do you do?

What most often happens is that without much thought, without really considering alternatives or making a choice, a patient either remains in or plans to return to the hospital. And although some patients—especially those who value their independence—may prefer not to remain institutionalized, they do so because they believe that to rely on a family member or friend for help seems irresponsible or beholden. As for the family, keeping the patient in the hospital is their way to ensure the best care.

Over the course of this century, we have come to depend increasingly upon institutions to care for dying people. In 1900, only 5 percent of Americans died in hospitals, while by 1970 that figure rose to about 70 percent. Although four out of five people who responded in a recent study said that they would prefer to die at home, current estimates show that four out of five die in some institution.

The center of health care moved from the home to the hospital as medicine became more specialized, more technological, and—in fact—more successful at correcting and curing people's ills. We live longer and have come to believe that a long life is our right and the medical profession's responsibility. In order to make good on these assumptions, a contract is implied. Patient and doctor agree to try innovative protocols, using all available medication and technology to extend life. This aggressive, state-of-the-art attack on disease serves us well, up to the point when our bodies give out. When *curing* is no longer the realistic goal of health care, someone dying needs to be removed from the curing environment to a caring one.

THE PROBLEM WITH HOSPITALS

Hospital routines are designed for patients who will recover. This function is served through efficiency. Because of the large number of cases they must handle, hospitals are not designed to allow for individual choice, flexible schedules, or personalized, relaxed care necessary for someone dying. While it may be possible to develop a personalized routine with sufficient doses of compassion, privacy, and calm in a hospital, the effort and careful management it requires on the part of the patient and family is energy that can be better spent. Hospital personnel, trained to cure, tend to feel useless when they cannot use their skills and may turn their attention to patients they know will benefit. Even the most sympathetic hospital staff must adhere to a stricter regimen than is comfortable for a dying person.

For those who love the person, seeing him or her in a hospital makes her seem tragically inaccessible, unreal, as if she had already died. When necessary, we make a brief visit, probably with little engagement or conversation with the patient, and a hushed word with the family. A fifteen-minute visit to a favorite uncle with tubes in his arms and a mask on his face can be a terrible shock. All the blinking and bleeping machinery, while we want to believe it is helpful, is frightening to us and probably to him. The distance and fear experienced is even greater if the patient is in pain, confused, or drugged. A hospital visitor does not usually have the opportunity to be natural, nor the ease to stay and share in the considerable variety of the patient's physical states, moods, and activities.

Another problem is that day-to-day life as the patient, family, and friends know it is disrupted. When someone is dying in a hospital, everyone who wants to be nearby must suspend normal activities. Hours can pass with no relief from sitting at the bedside, watching and waiting. Nurses come and go to perform hospital routines not necessary to someone dying, such as taking vital signs, and provide such simple tasks of physical care that it's easy to say to yourself, "I could do that." While some of the staff may become friends, others will be intrusive. Pay phones, the hospital coffee shop, visitors, doctors' rounds, catnaps, and the commute to and from the hospital all contribute stress and a sense of strangeness which amplify the strain of knowing someone you love is dying.

Because of our reliance on hospitals most of us know little about death or dying. We keep illness at a distance—literally, by removing it from the home; figuratively, by assuming it will be cured. Scratch the surface, and many of us admit we believe disease is relegated to people who don't take care of themselves, that to some degree it is unnatural, or unnecessary.

Hospitals satisfy our impulse to isolate a person who is diseased, as though he might infect our way of life. Some of us defend ourselves from the fear of illness by imagining that the patient is somehow responsible, that she did too much of one thing, too little of another. Maybe she smoked a pack a day, or didn't exercise enough. We so fear disease that we look to find fault with the sick person. If he made some mistakes—physically, spiritually, emotionally—then we can avoid them: "I won't do what he did to cause his illness. By any and all means, I will avoid sickness and death."

But denying illness is wasted effort. Everyone gets sick; everyone dies. As friends and loved ones, we need to reconsider how we think about disease. With their impressive technology and capable caregiving, hospitals have allowed us the satisfaction of having illness "controlled," in the sense of having it cured and in separating it from us. In a strange way, what people discover is that getting closer to dying—bringing it home—makes it less frightening.

Most of us do not fear death so much as we fear the process of dying. We are terrified of pain, isolation, losing control over our lives. When a person is told he is dying, his immediate fear is of being left. Patients who feel abandoned or who have lost control of their lives deteriorate rapidly. We can all retell a sad nursing home story. Aunt Sue had a stroke and couldn't stay at home alone, so was placed in a home, where she became depressed and died. People in institutions often die of isolation, depression, and boredom, not of the effects of a stroke.

What is most important in terminal care is the person's spirit. The patient and people in his life must concentrate on reinforcing human bonds. A hospital tends to isolate the patient even under the best circumstances. A patient develops behavior that only isolates him further: childishness, helplessness, and self-pity, which make his family conclude his value to them and to himself has diminished. Some may enjoy being cared for—we all do—but independence and participation are important. Given the choice, most people want to maintain as much of the pattern of daily life as possible.

DECISION FOR HOME CARE

Recognizing the overriding need for support, independence, and stability, as well as the requirements of appropriate care, has led many to rethink the whole question of "proper" ways and places to die. More and more patients and their families are opting for home care.

My husband and I chose to have him be at home because we never wanted to be separated. Nothing would have made up for the loneliness for both of us if he had to be in the hospital. I could not have him be among strangers without the constant love of his own people, in his own environment. I never considered any alternatives.

The decision for home care is easy for some, difficult for others, and for still others, impossible. For the woman above, the decision was simple and immediate. Another widow told a similar story of following her natural instincts.

I think my husband belonged in his home, surrounded by normal activity and a loving, caring family. We were fortunate to have nine children who loved their father as deeply as he loved them. Bringing my husband home to die was his request. He asked me early in his illness not to let him die in the hospital; he wanted to be home with us.

For some families and cultures that traditionally care for sick friends and family members, home care is not a new idea.

I come from a large Italian family, and we all take care of each other. You couldn't be alone if you wanted to be, but no one really likes solitude anyway. When my mother was dying we were all there, cooking, sitting with her, taking turns. We all supported each other, and she knew we were all together. When she died, we were all standing around the bed, maybe twenty of us.

Others reject institutional care on philosophical grounds.

Home care chose me. It was the only response I knew. I was raised in England in a family that stayed to itself, rarely seeking any kind of help. Each family member did his or her share in the household. I have always been independent of others. When I married, I knew my wife was dying and I never thought we would do anything but be at home as much as possible.

Still others seek home care as a natural extension of consumer awareness. Interest in paramedical care, home birth, patient rights, holistic medicine, medical costs, and preventive care are all ways individuals take health care into their hands and homes.

Another social trend—the increasing awareness of social networks and development of community resources—also supports home care. Many individuals—whether members of a traditional nuclear family or not—are conscious of other families and communities from which they can draw support. People develop bonds with friends, church members, or those who share a social concern or activity. Single and married people live in group houses, develop block associations, establish day-care and food cooperatives, and organize car pools. Many have a support group. Dying at home calls for developing similar networks.

But no matter how possible it seems or how much someone wants to be at home, how do we turn our backs on the most technologically advanced system of medical care in the world? How do we turn away from the arsenal of scientific equipment provided by a large urban hospital or even what is available in a local community hospital? How can we take a patient home without worrying that we are shortening life? Is "natural" death today synonymous with not taking fullest advantage up to the last minute of all available technology? Is it another phrase for killing or suicide? You may hear people talking about "good" death on radio talk shows. Your neighbor may have a friend whose aunt died "peacefully" at home. But what does this mean to you, now? When it comes right down to the present and someone you love is dying, how do you make the right decision?

The simple answer is that real physical limits exist to human life, reached through either age or the accumulated wear of disease. At some point technological intervention is futile, even absurd. Patients, family, and doctors in some combination say they usually know when that point has been reached.

As my grandmother's disease progressed, it became clear that her body had worn out. There wasn't any point in further treatment or hospital care. She wasn't sick, she was dying. She had lived in her home for forty-three years. She hated the hospital and there was nothing the hospital could offer her. Further radiation or another operation was useless, the doctor said. She knew it herself. Of course, there was no question but that she would stay in her own bed.

Home care can be the obvious conclusion after determining what care is really appropriate for someone who is dying. When a person's disease is judged to be no longer affected by active treatment and he can be expected to live only several weeks or months, what remains important is attention to the quality of life each day. Highest priority is given to physical and emotional comfort. This is called palliative care—care of symptoms. It is best pursued in an environment which supports privacy, relationship, intimacy, and continuity.

> The point is that the fight with the disease is over. It is time to nurse the patient. Prevent or nurse whatever hurts or distresses him. Encourage everything that produces comfort or cheer. If he wants to smoke, let him smoke. If he has a sore ankle, care for it. Treating the aches and pains can create more relief for everyone than any discussion or attention to the fatal disease.

This statement is from a doctor, who after experiencing his own near-death has devoted his life to teaching doctors and nurses what he learned about being terminally ill. To a life measured in days, a sore ankle matters: caring for the ankle not only brings the person relief from pain but provides a proper focus of concern for him and those who love him.

Understanding terminal care to be care of symptoms makes the option of home care clear. While we might want to imagine that the patient would somehow be "saved" through hospitalization, we know he is dying. Staying in the hospital now probably means he will receive inappropriate treatments. What he really needs is peace and simple attention to symptoms. He stands a far greater chance of receiving the emotional support he needs, as well as the best physical care—relief from pain, proper nutrition, bowel hygiene, skin care—at home.

PRACTICAL CONSIDERATIONS

Several practical considerations also make home care a good choice. Hospital care is likely to be terminated at the point where everyone agrees the patient is dying. Hospitals provide what is called "acute care." Most patients who are dying do not need, and are best free of, the routine procedures and aggressive treatment of this level of care. On the assumption that the patient and his family prefer hospitalization, many well-intentioned physicians will continue unnecessary treatments in order to satisfy the hospital and the insurer that the patient needs this level of care. When a patient is judged by hospital officials no longer to need aggressive treatment, insurance coverage for the hospital is terminated. Even if the patient can and wants to pay, the hospital may demand that the bed be freed for someone needing more active care. At the very moment families and patients are struggling with the news that the patient will die, they must either pack up and move home (with the sense that home is second best) or to another institution. Or, if the hospital will allow, face the burden of a lifetime of hospital bills. The patient who has not thought of being at home is now forced to consider it. This nightmare scenario can be avoided by planning ahead.

If you are now undertaking home care out of necessity, without prior consideration, you may be feeling some anger and disappointment. Adopt the attitude that you are grateful to be given the opportunity to care for the person. It isn't a decision you could have made yourself because of your own fears and doubts, but here you are and it's going to work out fine. Chances are very good that it will.

HOME IS WHERE I BELONG

The poet Robert Frost says in "The Death of the Hired Man," home is "Something you somehow haven't to deserve," and "The place where, when you have to go there, They have to take you in." Most people have a place where they go for cover. It may be their own room, a family home, a person, or a town. Home is found somewhere in each person's psychic fabric. In the chaos of our lives, we all consciously or unconsciously build block by block, memory by memory, a place where we feel safe. Whether or not we can go to that exact place to die, we have the right to make the choice where we—considering everything—will feel most comfortable.

This is where I belong. People told me, "You live alone, you're having a lot of pain. Shouldn't you be in a hospital?" No, this is where I should be. I have my window, my tree, my squirrels, my friends who come by. This is my home. It's impossible to think of being anywhere else.

With the help of family and friends, the patient can decide where she belongs now. Home will be a location, as well as a selection of people to be close by. Some make the move when they do to prove to themselves or friends that they are "well enough" to leave the hospital. One grandmother admitted she needed to know her family loved her enough to care for her. Others simply want their lives to continue without intrusions from strangers.

I was convinced that I could be just as comfortable at home as in the hospital. My daughter could care for me just as well as any medical professional. I felt peaceful knowing she would be caring for me. We had always been close and I wanted this chance to be together. I wanted to be among familiar people, family, friends, and surroundings.

At home, the patient lives in the continuum of her own life. It is reassuring to see that life goes on and to be able to watch and participate. As the patient's illness gradually prevents her from caring for herself, people who know her wishes can take over gracefully. Hospital patients are afraid of being hurt, mishandled, forgotten, of calling out and not being heard, of not getting what they need, of being alone. No one wants to approach death without someone there, or with strangers.

At home, care—even medical care—takes place within the context of a familiar setting and when it is needed, rather than on the hospital schedule. The patient's caretakers are constant and know what she likes. When she expresses a need or is in pain, help can be given immediately, not at the appointed hour by the appointed staff member. She can wear her own clothes rather than the antiseptic robes of a hospital. Her own bed, or even a hospital bed with her own sheets, can make all the difference. She can eat her own food, prepared the way she likes it, from her own dishes. Institutions cannot afford to pay attention to the little things that are so important for someone dying, such as being served a scrambled egg when a boiled one has been requested. What may seem like insignificant mistakes or changes can be painful reminders to a dying person that he is not in control and perhaps is no longer loved.

Home is the only place where the infinite variety of emotions and actions that naturally take place in a person's life—and that most of us take for granted—can occur as they will. Little events so important to relationships are awkward in a hospital room, yet can happen naturally at home.

"You're all here. Why are you all staring at me?" John reached over and put a touch of her perfume under her chin. She asked Bill, her oldest son, to hold in front of her a sculpture which had been placed on her bureau. As he turned it, we all watched, and she smiled. "That's all of us, it's the dance." She frowned, then a look of sadness, then fear. I took her hand and she smiled again. John was sitting in the corner of the room reading the Sunday paper. She asked me for her glasses. "Look at John," she said, "he's beautiful." His profile in the afternoon sun was exactly hers. Her youngest, Tom, came into the room with a small mug of veal stew he had made for her. He'd been cooking all morning.

Someone dying wants to be satisfied that everything is in order. Being at home enables him to review his life from a comfortable and secure vantage point. He may wish to balance his checkbook, sit in a favorite chair, or reminisce over old photographs. Satisfying these desires when they are expressed, and not tomorrow—who knows what will be possible tomorrow?—is one of the most rewarding benefits of home care.

My father got cancer in the midst of his career, and he worked until he died. We all lived prepared to respond to whatever he felt was important. He spent his last days in his study on a hospital bed. We all ran errands for him. It was the way it had always been and we certainly didn't want to change now that he was dying.

LESSONS OF HOME CARE

For family and friends, helping someone stay at home is a real lesson in receiving through giving. An important benefit too is that most people say they are relieved to be free of the guilt they anticipated if they hadn't brought the person home. Giving physical care and the unscheduled opportunities to talk and be together liberates people from the anguish of not having said or done enough.

Acting in a close relationship to someone who is dying makes sickness and death very real and works to change personal attitudes toward physical mortality. Many caregivers say they become less frightened of death.

Living with the presence of death can even be a stimulant. "To be a little bit afraid of dying can do wonders for your life," wrote Betty Rollin, author of *First, You Cry,* a book about her own experience of living with cancer. She refers to death as "a lively presence in my gut" and explains what this presence has done for her life:

> I am less afraid of other things, like bosses, spouses, failure, aging, housework. I am less worried about what people think of me, where my career is going. I think about where I am today, and how I feel about it. I stopped being "sensible."

Dying at home makes caregiving a way of life for the individuals involved. As part of daily life, people accept difficult tasks and learn to be flexible and attentive to what is important in relationships. When living with dying as a day-to-day reality, one caregiver said, "There's not time to develop or put up with a lot of drama."

> Having Grampa spend his last months in our home has opened our whole family to death in good ways. If his cancer seems useless and cruel, it was nonetheless a communicative last illness and a good death. We pray it be given to us to die among those who love us, to go as good soldiers, without sniveling or recriminations. But it was not only being a God-believer that enabled him to die as he did. It was also common sense, good humor, and playing down drama. When we embrace real events, we don't need soap opera to heighten our awareness, and there are practical, concrete ways to help when someone dies at home.

Home care may not work for everyone, but it is worth consideration. If you are in the midst of caregiving, this book is a practical guide for how to provide care. If you do not currently know a person who is dying, this book can help you understand some of the practical concerns. Now is a good time to think about home care and what it can mean for you or someone you care about.

Who can provide care? How would the family survive? What would it mean for how you live today? What do we do when the person dies?

It's all worth it, just for that tenth of a second when she was dying and knew she was safe. I wasn't around when my father died and I know he must have wondered whether or not I cared to be. He slipped through my hands, my life was too busy. But for Mother, she knew. She cried. I wiped her tears away from her eyes. She never turned her back on anyone in her whole life . . . we couldn't think of doing that to her.

2
WILL HOME CARE WORK?

Home care sounds right, and you can't argue with its basic logic or sentiment. It worked just fine for your neighbor. But you have also heard of cases in which the whole experience was a series of problems: someone a coworker knows took care of her mother and said it was a nightmare. How do you decide if it will be feasible for you? Your life and circumstances are unique, and you ultimately have to decide and then take action best suited to you.

Some general questions can be considered to evaluate the possibility of home care. Essentially what is required is a careful appraisal of the resources available to caregivers. While a decision may be clear in the abstract—"Why of course I'll take care of Father *if* he gets sick" or "It wouldn't possibly work in our busy household"—the final choice is a very personal and difficult one, a choice that must be made in view of all the circumstances—emotional, physical, and financial—at the time.

My mother-in-law wanted to go home. She had been told she could expect to live for a month and a half to three months. Her great fear of hospitals and doctors meant she had never been in a hospital except for the delivery of her children, forty-eight years ago. She and her husband both wanted her to be at home, and no other choice seemed appropriate. It also seemed natural for them to live with us. Our home supports were realistic and manpower appeared adequate.

Facing a decision about home care, the couple in the case above began by objectively assessing their situation. Was financial and family support available? Could the patient be comfortable at home? Was there adequate medical assistance? Questions like these are a good basis for judging the feasibility of home care.

The following questions have been assembled with help from hospice and hospital workers responsible for helping families decide about home care. They offer general guidelines for you to consider. Each issue raised is treated in greater detail later in the book. Even if something seems beyond your ability now, your willingness to try and to learn will probably see you through all potential troubles.

DOES THE PATIENT WANT TO DIE AT HOME?

If there has been no discussion with the patient about dying at home, carefully broach the subject. Here is the advice of a daughter whose mother died in her home:

> If anyone is seriously considering home care, I urge him to speak to the person who is ill and lovingly talk about how he would like to spend his final days. If the sick person would like to be cared for at home, I would encourage them to work together to develop the resources needed. When I told my mother—several months before she became bedridden—that I would take care of her if she could not take care of herself, the smile on her face and the relief in her eyes were indescribable.

By simply stating that there are options to be considered in how the next days may be spent and that you feel a need to talk about these options, you may help the patient to unburden himself. He will probably talk about what kind of care he wants to receive and whether he prefers to be in a hospital or other facility, at home, or with a relative. Be careful to let the patient take the lead, and remember that it is his feelings and his decisions that are important.

Try to avoid telling him what you think he wants. Be frank about the extent of your own commitment to his comforts and desires, and express your support. If you will be providing care, share your thoughts about what being at home could mean for both of you. Acknowledge your own fears as well as your confidence in being able to set up a workable home care team.

Try to help the patient work out any difficulties so that she has a choice, even if the circumstances are less than ideal. If the patient lives alone, for example, staying at home may require special assistance and cooperation among family and friends. Remember she is used to being on her own; try to avoid the assumption that she may be "too lonely" to stay in her own house. Try not to make other assumptions—her house is too sparsely equipped or too isolated—which lead to the conclusion that her house is somehow not the right place to die. Be objective by separating what she wants to do from how it can be achieved. If her will is to be at home, chances are very good that combined forces of family, friends, and members of the community can make it possible.

While it is your responsibility to help the patient assimilate the necessary information to make an informed decision, you must avoid making that decision for him or her. You simply cannot take on that responsibility, because it is bound to backfire, causing resentment for everyone involved. Even if the patient has deferred decisions all her life to others, or is now feeling incapable of having any opinions, the choice must be hers. Keep the discussion open by saying, "I know you don't want to talk about this and neither do I, but you have to decide what you would like to do." Remind her that this is her life, not yours.

WHAT IS THE PATIENT'S CONDITION?

Usually home care is first seriously discussed when the patient, caregivers, and physician have agreed—or are at the point of agreeing—that nothing more can or will be done to reverse or arrest the illness. The doctor will have simply said nothing more can be done. However, this prognosis is very hard—often impossible—for doctors to give. A member of the family, or the patient, may have to ask directly, "Is there anything more to be done? Is she dying?"

Press for a detailed response. Although they may hesitate to admit it to anyone, even to themselves, doctors usually know when further surgery, radiation, or drug treatment will not halt the process of dying.

> Our family doctor said that any further treatment was "contraindicated," medical jargon for useless. He said radiation would only increase the pain and surgery would not alter the disease, would only create great pain and disfigurement. He agreed to attend to her at home and assured us that she would be comfortable, but nothing would be done to prolong her life. We would treat only the pain. We were assured that her death would be peaceful.

Depending on the patient, the doctor, and the disease, acknowledgment that the illness is terminal may be gradual, even avoidable. The shift from aggressive care to care of symptoms—palliative care —may be subtle; it may not be the result of a dramatic moment or single decision. It may occur as a series of small decisions to discontinue medical procedures that have been prolonging life. Caregivers and patient need to maintain full communication with the physician throughout the course of the disease and be prepared to question and challenge procedures. Talk honestly and directly about the advantages and disadvantages of each treatment and medication as it is suggested. Bring up the possibility of choices when you sense an assumption is being made about the patient's life-span, or if you think the doctor is ignoring the obvious truth. Be open about your concern. You have the right to receive as much information as you want and to participate in all decisions.

You may worry that your willingness to dispense with aggressive medical care will result in the physician's no longer being concerned with the patient or not providing symptom care or emergency support. Discuss these fears openly and specifically. Gather all the information you can about the patient's condition, what may be expected, and what help the physician will give. Most important, is the doctor unreservedly committed to the patient's comfort? (Skills for talking with your physician are described in Chapter 5, "You and Your Doctor.")

Next, find out what the patient views as his condition. If you are a spouse or friend in the position of assisting a dying person to understand his or her situation, remember you are there to help, not to control. Some patients never fully acknowledge—to others or to themselves—that they are dying, and this is their right. Discuss the patient's symptoms with her and tell her what care the physician thinks is necessary, and what does not need to be continued.

If the patient is able, let her lead the conversation. As long as she can plan realistically for herself, participating to some degree in her life, it is most humane to allow her control over what she will and will not think or say. Be honest and direct to the extent of her desire for information, remembering that it belongs to her and she needs all available facts to make her own decisions.

The patient may express her wish to discontinue aggressive treatment by saying she wants to die naturally. She may say she is afraid of pain. She may say she wants to go to a hospital where she feels safe, or that she doesn't want procedures that prolong life. As she talks, acknowledge her concerns and wishes, express your own as clearly as you know them.

These exploratory conversations between and among the patient, her family, and the doctor enable a general consensus to be reached about the patient's condition and the shift to palliative care.

IS THERE MEDICAL SUPPORT?

You will probably not need regular medical services. Usually the decision to have someone be at home follows the realization that medical care—as we usually think of it—is no longer needed or desired. Still, knowing a physician is accessible twenty-four hours a day provides much-needed security.

My mother's doctor completely supported our decision for her to come home with me. She advised us on equipment and pain medication and said she would be available for consultation. Since I live a hundred miles away, she suggested, and I agreed, that we find a doctor in my town in case we needed home visits. Both doctors remained cooperative, urging me to call them at any time, day or night, and this made all the difference.

Before you attempt home care for the patient you need to secure a physician who either personally or with associates will make home visits, provide twenty-four-hour consultations, and come to the house when the patient dies. Many people experience difficulty in finding a doctor who will make house calls, especially on a weekend or in the middle of the night. It is important to get a commitment in advance.

If your own physician cannot or will not provide home care, ask for a referral. Your hospital, visiting nurse association, and medical association are all resources for the names of doctors who make home visits.

CAN THE PATIENT BE COMFORTABLE?

Management of pain and attention to symptoms are essential to terminal care. Understanding the disease and its effects on the patient's physical and emotional state is crucial to evaluating the potential success of home care. Even a minor symptom, such as a dry mouth, which a well person can tolerate, can make the patient so miserable that he does not want to live. One important aspect of promoting comfort is to take each symptom seriously. The other is to provide an environment in which the person feels secure, cared for, and accompanied. If feelings are well cared for, the patient's physical pain will be easier to treat. With careful attention to all sources of pain, most patients can be quite comfortable at home.

Your physician may advise you that some equipment and medication will help keep the person comfortable. A catheter, oxygen, or humidifier, for example, is easily available, and your doctor or social worker will help you obtain what you need.

Foremost in your mind—and, no doubt, the patient's mind—is the question of whether you can cope and find solutions for pain at home. You have obtained a commitment from your physician. Also remember what one mother said about caring for her seven-year-old son: "If I had the least intuition that my care was insufficient, or that Tim was suffering at home, I would have sought hospital care." She kept in constant contact with the doctor, who continued to reassure her and provide what was needed at home. You can too.

WHO WILL PROVIDE PRIMARY CARE?

Continuity and consistency are very important to a dying person. The patient must be assured that all her physical needs, whatever they are, will be maintained. Although initially the patient may be able to organize her care, at some point another person (or several people working together) will need to coordinate it.

The primary caregiver may already be living with the patient as child, parent, spouse, or friend; someone may volunteer or be recruited from among family, friends, or neighbors; or a housekeeper or health care worker may be hired through an agency, hospice, or personal recommendation. He or she must above all be someone the dying person likes and trusts. No special training or professional skills are needed, only the ability to be reliable, caring, and attentive to the patient's comfort. Everyone has the potential to care for another person and to do it well. Despite initial fears, caregivers come to realize that most of what is required are everyday skills. Whatever specialized abilities are necessary can be acquired with a little practice. Giving injections, monitoring a catheter, feeding an immobile patient, and giving a bed bath are easily learned.

Although the mechanics of home care and the human skills needed to carry it out are well within most people's abilities, the daily reality of living in the presence of dying is a major physical and emotional strain. After assessing the patient's needs and wishes, the person who will assume the primary role in caregiving must decide whether he can do what is necessary. The caregiver's well-being is as important as the patient's. The qualities for someone who will provide care are discussed at length in the next chapter.

If you are not certain of your ability to make a commitment, specify a length of time as a test period, make the provision clear to all involved, and give it a try. If you find you cannot handle the responsibilities, step aside and permit others to take over, even if this means returning the patient to the hospital. This will not mean you have failed or that the situation is impossible, only that it is not feasible, in view of your circumstances, right now, for you. You may be at a time in your life when the emotional strain could be seriously harmful or when your life simply cannot be rearranged.

Taking responsibility for your decision either way permits others to help and mitigates blame and guilt.

DO OTHERS SUPPORT THE DECISION?

When you decide to undertake home care, wisdom suggests that consulting other related people will smooth the way.

Talk with members of the family and close friends. Advise them of the patient's wishes to be at home. Review considerations that went into making the decision and how you think it will work. Begin to involve others in planning, even assembling supplies. Ask what contributions of time and skills people would like to make.

The primary caregiver in a household will want to discuss his or her role, concerns, expectations, and needs with the other members. Be clear that you will need everyone's help, and that each will have responsibilities, and their way of life may be temporarily changed. In a household normally organized around the schedules and needs of preschool children, for example, the demands of the dying father or grandmother may mean changes in routine and even in the mother's ability to provide all the child care. Now is a good time to anticipate what may be necessary and let everyone talk about their concerns.

Since you can anticipate so much emotional and practical upheaval in the household, make it clear that members will need to make an extra effort to talk with and care for each other. Tell them too that other families have learned that the rewards of providing home care are as great as the effort it takes. Without exception, we are told that home care has taught adults and children invaluable lessons in living.

ARE NECESSARY RESOURCES AVAILABLE?

While home care does not require advanced knowledge, it does create demands, and you will need others to help you meet them. Personal and nursing care of the patient, housekeeping, transportation, procuring medical supplies, and relief for the caregiver must be planned carefully. You may also want occasional professional help, such as a physical therapist to teach you ways to move the patient without injuring yourself and how to give her a massage. Your doctor, hospital social worker, nurse, and friends will offer advice about what you need and what assistance is available. Many people who have provided home care say that they wish they had sought or accepted more help and that there were untapped resources among family, friends, and community agencies to meet home care requirements. What is crucial is that an inventory be taken early and a commitment made to ask for and accept help, beginning right away and not "later, when I need it."

WHAT ABOUT COST?

Most people do not opt for home care solely on the basis of cost, but it certainly is an important factor. Some must choose home care because insurance benefits paying for the institution the patient is in are being terminated, making the bill exorbitant for everyone concerned; others will base the decision solely on the wishes of the patient and family.

Dying at home can cost more or less than dying in an institution, depending on the patient's requirements for care, insurance coverage, level of income, community resources, and a variety of other factors. Medications, doctors' visits, and medical equipment are normally covered by medical insurance. Out-of-pocket costs will be partially determined by the extent of your reliance on paid services for housekeeping, transportation, or patient care. Personal items and clothing will probably not add much to the cost. A major expense may be the loss of pay for the primary caregiver, who may have to take a leave of absence or work half time in order to provide care.

Whatever your situation, review now what you will need in services and supplies, their approximate cost, and the amount you can expect to be reimbursed. Discuss the financial needs you now foresee with your company benefits advisor, insurance agent, or social worker at the hospital. You have paid for this financial protection; you are entitled to ask questions. Since many forms of coverage are under review and may be changed, it is wise to keep current on the amounts to which you are entitled. Keep notes during conversations with insurance representatives since you may want to refer to them or ask questions later. If the first person you reach is not helpful, seek another. Be sure to ask for the name of each person you talk to and note the date of your conversation so that you can develop a connection with a specific person.

If you are fortunate enough to be considering home care in advance of the need for it, plan now for the best coverage by talking to your employer's benefits adviser, insurance companies, health maintenance organizations and medical groups, and hospice programs.

If you are in current need of home care reimbursements, you may be disappointed; many of the services needed by someone dying are not yet covered. This situation is slowly changing. Many private insurance companies, Blue Cross and Blue Shield, and Medicare now cover various costs and services necessary for home care. Since the national trend is to reduce cost of medical care by developing alternatives to expensive hospital stays, we can expect that coverage for home care will continue to expand.

In addition to insurance, you may find other ways to fund aspects of home care. Family service agencies, a "meals on wheels" service, visiting nurse associations, and other community organizations can provide services at little or no cost. The American Cancer Society, the American Heart Association, and similar organizations frequently offer supplies and limited aid to purchase goods and services. In addition, your church, local clubs, place of employment, the Veterans Administration, Social Security, your local Office for the Aging, and other organizations in your community are prepared to give help when asked.

You have come to the difficult decision of home care because someone you know is dying. You cannot know where the decision, whatever it is, will lead. If you do decide to try home care, give it your best effort. As you consider alternatives now, try not to anticipate all the possible outcomes. You cannot foresee what course the illness will take, or anticipate all the possibilities for successes or failures.

A WORD ABOUT ALTERNATIVES

While staying at home is preferable for most people most of the time, do not agonize over seeking respite from home care for a few days or longer. The idea to seek help may even come from the patient. One young woman decided to move to a nearby nursing home that provided good hospice care because she wanted to relieve her household of intensive, twenty-four-hour care required to keep her comfortable. Family members and friends were able to care for her at the facility, as well as get good rest and relief from the constant strain.

Good alternatives exist in many communities and only need to be found. You can bring in a carefully selected helper to provide care for parts of days or even an extended period. Or, you can choose a facility offering hospice-type care. Care of the dying generally is becoming much improved, as more is known, written, and accepted about pain control, emotional needs, and appropriate physical care. Learn now what is offered in your area, in case you choose to seek an alternative.

Remember: the decision is always subject to review. Try to have home care work for as long as it honestly makes sense for everyone involved. You will do the best you can, and this will probably be more than sufficient. If necessary, you can find good respite care to back you up, either at home or in a nursing home or hospice. With the proper consideration and support, using what you can from others' experiences, home care can be very successful and rewarding.

3
CAN
I DO IT?

Staying at home cannot be accomplished by the patient alone; it depends heavily on the willingness and strength of someone or several people to coordinate and provide care. Fear of things "medical," of cost, of the radical change in day-to-day life, and of dying itself can lead even the most loving friend or relative to despair of being able to offer such care. Suspend these worries and open your mind to the idea that providing home care is well within your emotional and physical ability.

Why would someone want to provide home care? A doctor caring for his father, a scientist for his wife, a teacher for her mother, and a housewife for her husband have their own reasons, all of which reflect the basic need simply to be there and give comfort.

For me, I could not leave a father. Dad and I traveled many miles together. He would not walk his last mile alone. All else failing, I can hold his hand. To me dying is a lonely affair. Some people say that medication clouds the mind, that it makes little difference if you're present. I doubt it. My advice is not to forsake the patient as death approaches, for his sake and yours.

When my mother smiled at me, spoke to me, hugged me, or just squeezed my hand, I knew every one of my efforts was appreciated and cherished. For me it was a wonderful opportunity to do something special for a person who had spent a lifetime taking special care of her family.

I fell in love and knew I had some of the necessary qualities for caring for a dying person. We finally married when we thought Sarah had six months to live. She lived for two years, despite a colostomy, mastectomy, and quite severe complications. I found it exhausting and harrowing, although spiritually rewarding. If someone dear to me should fall ill, I would do my best for that person, but I am going to avoid full-time caregiving. I marvel at those who take on this job and provide loving care professionally. They are exceptional people and priceless in our society.

I would have undertaken my husband's care under any circumstances. Neither of us could have stood the loneliness of being separated. I had taken the Red Cross Nurses' Aid course many years before and worked as a volunteer in a hospital, which had helped me with valuable experience in terminal illness. But even if I hadn't had this training, with today's visiting nurse and medical assistance, I would do it.

The reasons given by these individuals who undertook home care indicate that we all respond to the needs of other people in our own natural and learned ways.

A PERSONAL INVENTORY

You are open to the idea of providing care. How do you know if you'll be any good at all? While being big-hearted and well-intentioned are necessary qualities, you know they won't suffice. Self-examination will show your strengths and weaknesses. As you take an inventory, look with some humor at the person you are and the person you want to be. Many caregivers say that the intensity and difficulty of being with someone who is dying caused complicated aspects of their behavior to surface, including some traits that they disliked in themselves. This is an opportunity to exercise new behavior and begin to exorcise habits you've been meaning to dump. You need not have a perfect score on your answers to these questions. They will focus your thinking about your own abilities and can also be used later when soliciting volunteers and paid helpers.

- Given the situation—someone you know (and love) is dying —what do you want to do? After the person has died, what will give you peace, what will you have wanted to do or offer?

- Are you able to welcome new ideas and suggestions from others? Do you enjoy learning new skills, asking questions, and learning how things work?

- Are you organized and able to set priorities?

- Are you able to make the necessary time commitment or to solicit others to cover for you now and later when twenty-four-hour coverage is necessary?

- Do you enjoy thinking of creative ways to solve problems? Do you take pleasure in applying "common sense" to a new challenge?

- Can you apply a sense of humor to awkward or embarrassing situations? Can you ease others' attitudes toward problems and stay with them when the going is rough?

- Do you enjoy being with people? Do you feel natural about offering help?

- Are you healthy and energetic?

- Are you flexible and able to adapt yourself to immediate needs?

Self-examination reveals the instincts you bring to caregiving. Discuss your inventory with someone close to you, and even with someone who has provided home care. Such people can advise you and also help you find others to supplement your own abilities.

If you are concerned about negative traits, take this time to see if they can just as easily become positive attitudes. While an aspect of home care may first appear to be a "burden," see if it can also be an "opportunity to serve." Be honest about your attitudes, and your willingness to work on them, since home care will not be easy if you feel enslaved. The patient is probably very sensitive to what this undertaking means to your life and the ability to be sympathetic, kindly, and even cheerful will make a great difference in her general well-being and yours.

ANTICIPATE SOME DIFFICULTIES

The question "Can I do it?" is an expression not only of concern about whether or not you have sufficient personal resources but also of very reasonable fear. It is completely natural to approach this decision warily. Home care will almost certainly present many of the difficulties you imagine and probably more. It is physically and emotionally exhausting, and many tasks are unrewarding and unpleasant. It creates demands you never would have chosen—on yourself, your finances, others you love, your work. From now until the patient dies, your life will not be the same. At times you will resent everyone around you who is freer than you are, even the patient who has trapped you in this impossible situation.

> I had a job as well as looking after my wife. I got tired, became impatient with her needs, felt neglected and sexually starved, became jealous of her other friends, and constantly felt guilty because I wanted more from our relationship. I felt I, too, lived under and with the sacrifice of death. Still, our love made it work, as hard as it was.

General doubts which many people have expressed as they try to decide about caregiving fall into three broad categories:

- Fear of things "medical" and of the inability to provide sufficient medical care for the patient.

- Fear of the inability to hold up under the daily pressure of living with and caring for a dying person, including fear of being present at the time of death.

- Fear that the relationship with the dying person will not stand up to the expected strain.

Let us look at these fears.

I AM NOT A NURSE

The fear of anything medical—drugs, equipment, procedures—and of a possible inability to care for a seriously ill person makes us feel both uncomfortable and inadequate. Even though most people are familiar with equipment and treatments because of experience with one illness or another, nonetheless a particular mystique exists about things medical that makes us consider them the guarded province of health care professionals. For this reason, it may be difficult for you to see yourself or your home as offering adequate support.

The truth is, there will probably not be anything very difficult about medical care. Most people and most homes are able to support terminal care. People who are dying usually do not require complicated equipment, and much of the nursing that will be necessary is similar to what you may have previously provided for yourself, your children, or sick friends. Mouth care, turning a patient in bed, bathing, feeding, and other tasks to promote the patient's comfort are common to nearly everyone's experience or can at least be learned. Remember that professionals and hospitals can be called upon whenever advice or help is needed.

Certain tasks or conditions may not be manageable. The most common problem is simple physical capability: the caregiver may not be very strong or the dying person may be too heavy, making the matter of lifting and turning a major difficulty. You can learn in Chapter 9, "Physical Care," how to move the patient; if in fact outside help is required, Chapter 6, "Creating a Team," describes ways to seek and organize help. Anticipating needs and careful planning will head off most routine problems of home care.

You may experience fear of doing something that will harm or even kill the patient, a fear similar to that experienced by new mothers in caring for infants. To ease this anxiety, discuss your specific worries with the visiting nurse or doctor. Learn the patient's physical weaknesses and what dangers to expect. If you are concerned about a procedure such as giving injections, get help and practice. Dying people seem to be and are vulnerable, but the danger of potential harm is far outweighed by the value of being cared for by familiar people. While mistakes will happen, we can try our best to avoid them. A psychiatrist who works with terminally ill patients has found that interactions between patients and caregivers over small errors are very productive: each has an opportunity to cry or laugh over the limitations of being human.

CAN I TAKE IT?

While potential caregivers may be concerned about physical care of the patient, they also need to consider their own stamina. Concern for the caregiver is quite genuine among most professionals involved in terminal care. A nurse explains what the caregiver can expect:

> The dying takes care of itself. What I watch for is the caregiver. He or she shouldn't do it alone. She needs to keep on with her life, keep in touch with friends, and allow people to spell her. She needs to know it's okay to talk to people about it. She needs to know what to expect in symptoms, acknowledging as best she can that the patient is going to die. I tell her it will be as peaceful as we can make it, but I also tell her what the grim possibilities might be, depending upon the patient. I tell her it's fine to bring the patient back to the hospital if it gets too hard or too scary, or if she doesn't want to handle the death itself at home. I warn her that the nights are the biggest problem emotionally and physically and that nights are also the hardest time to get any help.

The patient may be someone for whom you care deeply. You may be suffering the greatest loss of your life. How can you add to this pain a role full of responsibilities and hard work? As caregiver, you must be many things to many people. You will have to rearrange your own life, help the dying person organize her life, be the main support and information center for the family, friends, and a network of caregivers—all when you just want to curl up and cry.

Even at the level of day-to-day nursing, it is physically and emotionally difficult to be the primary caregiver for a dying person. You will have to accept responsibility for things you may always have thought someone else would do. You will be told that giving injections, emptying bedpans, changing dressings, and other procedures are simple, but, you may think, they are not for you. Remember that while disease is undesirable, unpleasant, even dirty, the person suffering from it is not. Try to focus on your relationship and what you share with the patient, and see if this perspective overcomes the obstacles.

At times, you will find yourself tired and feeling alone, isolated, resentful. While you will truly be alone in some ways, there are very real ways in which you will have support. First, you will share this experience with the patient, and the companionship you develop will be very important and nurturing for both of you. Second, you can create a team of companions, professionals, and helpers who will run errands, visit, and advise you. Third, you will develop a new relationship with yourself. Providing home care is a rite-of-passage experience like boot camp or childbirth; each moment is full of new understanding and self-awareness, with opportunities to learn to care for yourself. New habits will become lifetime resources: living each day fully, meditating, keeping a journal, exercising, asking for help. Each caregiver cites these experiences as pivotal for personal growth. Said one, "I never would have asked for it, but the three months I spent caring for my mother was the most significant period in my life."

IS OUR RELATIONSHIP STRONG ENOUGH?

You can anticipate that a major challenge in home care is the stress it may place on your relationship with the patient. Chances are good that you will be more intimate than you have been previously, and that this will cause some anxiety. You may wonder whether or not your bond will be strong enough. If you are a close friend or family member moving into a home to provide care, also examine your relationships with others in the household. Reassure yourself by examining carefully how your relationship with the patient and with others, works.

Think about these questions:

- What connects you?

- Do you feel secure about your bond?

- What do you like about each other?

- What is unique about your relationship?

- Have you shared crises before? How? What was good about your relationship during these occasions? What caused pressure?

With this foundation of understanding, you can begin to develop strength and tools for maintaining and expanding the bonds. You will learn more about what connects you as the days go by. No bond is without its complications. Emotional injuries inflicted during the lifetime of each person will surface in surprising ways, whether or not they occurred in shared experiences. Because of a personal conflict that took place long before you knew each other, the patient may say, "I don't need any help" at precisely the moment she wants help the most. Similarly, it may take only a chance comment to trigger an old unresolved anger between you and the patient. Remember that incidents like these are temporary and do not diminish the strength of your relationship. Our ability to understand and express ourselves at such times reinforces our connections to ourselves, the patient, and others.

In general, to combat the fears you have about home care, understand as much and as early as possible what to expect from the experience. Often the anticipation of difficulty will be more difficult than the reality. Many specific fears can be eased with real information. If you learn, for example, by reading Chapter 22, "Dying," and by talking with your physician and friends what happens at the moment of death, the anticipation will not be as frightening. List for yourself specific worries you have about caregiving, being with a dying person, and dying itself. Then seek out a doctor, a counselor, or an experienced friend who can give you answers and details.

Most caregivers say they had some anxieties about providing home care but they did it anyway and it was the right choice. Their fears and doubts were replaced with facts and experience. While you cannot anticipate all the problems, you can be assured that you'll have lots of help understanding and dealing with them.

UNDERSTAND YOUR OWN DYING

As you appraised your abilities and acknowledged your own fears, you may have experienced some fear of your own death. Examining this fear now will probably help you understand the patient and reduce the trouble it may cause you later.

Think about your own dying and consider these questions: Whom would I say goodbye to? Where would I want to die? Whom would I like to have with me? What are my regrets? What do I want to do before I die? Who should know I am dying? How should they be told? How do I want to be buried? By what do I want to be remembered?

By imagining your own death and really looking hard at what frightens you, you will grow stronger. By asking and answering for yourself these important questions you will be able to help and develop sensitivity to the patient. While her answers to similar questions may be different, her motivation and needs will be much the same. Understanding what dying might mean is another preventive step to survive the days, weeks, or months ahead.

WHAT ROLES DO YOU PLAY?

As primary caregiver you will be at the eye of the storm, playing a number of roles which can be sources of strength as well as stress, for yourself and for all concerned. An honest evaluation of what roles are necessary and comfortable for you, what is essential about them, and what can be let go will strengthen your position when other demands hover about. Here are some of the hats caregivers wear.

Standard Bearer: Early in caregiving you, the patient, and others will set standards for care. Everyone will discuss what will and will not be done to give comfort and support the patient's life. While you can be reassured by this discussion and agreement, daily contact with a discouraged or uncomfortable dying person can make specifics of agreed-upon care a huge burden. Your responsibilities may weigh heavily, and you will need to ask often for respite and support.

Patient Advocate: Maintaining the rights and wishes of the patient, as well as providing good care and control of symptoms, often takes aggressive patient advocacy. You may need to be critical, or at least questioning, of the professionals who are there to help you ensure the patient's comfort. You may need to press the doctor for stronger medication, push the insurance company to cover claims, demand that a family member participate more fully, and undertake emotional, organizational, or medical "errands" the patient cannot run himself.

Team Captain: Everyone who has been involved in home care speaks of the need for some person to be identified by the patient and doctors and other team members as the leader. As anyone who has supervised coworkers, volunteers, or even a scout troop knows, being captain requires patience and assurance. While the patient may be captain at first, someone needs to be in line to take over the coordinating role when she is unable. The position may involve finding a replacement for a specific duty or filling in when someone doesn't show up. It usually means being the one everyone turns to for advice. Be aware that this is a seductive role and can easily lead to thinking you should fill in for everyone else's shortcomings and cancellations.

Information Please: Someone on the scene has to be a resource for information. You will be the one who knows where family and friends can be found and other routine household whereabouts. In addition, you will know where the linens are, what medications need to be given and when, what is the patient's state of mind, which sores need what ointment, what are the preferred foods and meal schedule, when she last used the bedpan, and where the doctor can be reached. You can ease the burden of this role by appointing a trusted "second mate" and by keeping records current in a notebook (see Chapter 8, "Keeping Records"), but the demands for information—especially in a large household—will be constant.

Soothsayer: You may be the one to tell the patient about his disease, what is to be expected, what the most recent symptom means, and what can or cannot be done. Others in the family may also come to you as the one they trust to share honest information and feelings. You will learn to be both truthful and gentle, but it's hard.

Bereavement Counselor: People around the patient will be in various stages of grieving, all reacting differently. As you will learn in Chapter 23, "Grieving," the best you can do is to give everyone the room to be him or herself and encourage everyone to talk, cry, ask questions—including you. The biggest problem for caregivers is that they may not get the attention they need for their own grieving.

As you consider whether or not caregiving is for you, try on these various hats and see where they fit and where they are uncomfortable. If you need help getting used to one or more, now is a good time to ask.

ADVICE FOR "OUTSIDERS"

If you are a caregiver who is not in the immediate family, has not been in recent daily contact with the patient, or does not have a long association with him, you probably have more than the usual misgivings. How do you know if you even like each other?

In the very beginning, make a special effort to establish sound contact with the patient by learning about him. You need to find out about his life, his illness, feelings, likes, and dislikes. Ask him to tell you about himself, picking up on his leads and hints. There are any number of ways to inquire about a person. A simple question such as, "Where were you born?" or "How long have you lived in this town?" will get the patient started. Ask about people and events he mentions in passing. More specific conversations can inquire about preferences and sensitivities to help you with planning the details of care.

Share little pieces of your own history to show that you are not just an observer. You may tell him, "I was divorced three years ago"; or "I never had any children but I am very close to my nephews"; or share the suggestion, "When I'm not feeling well I love a back rub." Don't ask for sympathy or tell your life story, but give facts that show you are human and have experiences which enable you to understand something of what he is like and experiencing.

A caregiver from outside the family needs to be particularly aware of "how things are done" in this family. Ask before you do anything—from boiling an egg for three minutes, the way you like it, to putting a towel under the bedpan the way you did for your father when he was sick. Ask and sense your way into knowing what the patient wants of you.

You need to be especially sensitive to the difficult issues that may be raised in care. What do the patient and family members know about the disease and its course? How are they reacting to what they know? Has the family discussed options of care? To what degree does the patient want to be medicated from pain? What about measures to keep him alive or revive him? What is to happen if the patient contracts pneumonia or when he stops breathing? Does the person want treatments that may prolong his life? If answers to these questions are not offered to you, try to seek some information. (See Chapter 19, "Some Hard Choices," for help in understanding these issues.) Talk with other members of the family or friends, or the social worker if there is one, to gather information about the household, the family history, and the patient.

As an "outsider," you should not try to be the one who is closest to the person, or to be the one who "really understands" what she needs or is going through. While your close contact with the patient will offer a continual temptation, be aware that exploiting this contact will upset the lifetime relationships among family and friends, which, no matter how "good" or "bad," must be the focus. Act as a facilitator to allow time and comfort, to make it easy for the family to be together. Similarly, if there are children in the family, do not compete with their parents for affection or discipline.

Joining a patient and household involved with terminal care is difficult work. Since it is unlikely that your stresses will be noticed or of concern to those you are caring for, go easy on yourself. Acknowledge your limits and make them clear to others. At times, you will feel like an outsider, particularly when important decisions are being made, and then later, when the patient dies. It's easy to feel resentful toward the people who seem interested in you only when you are doing something for them. Talk to a friend about these natural feelings so you don't suffer from them. The truth is that providing support for terminal care when you don't "have to" is a particularly compassionate vocation and worthy of great admiration.

A WARNING

Caring for someone dying may be the most difficult project you ever undertake. This chapter has discussed some of the emotional, physical, and spiritual stresses likely to be encountered, but the health of the primary caregiver is so important that we cannot end with simply reiterating the problems. The fact is, you may not be able to sustain yourself or the patient over the weeks and months ahead. You may need more relief than you are getting and may have to call in help or admit the patient to a hospital for a few days. You may even feel you cannot continue. Count as a real accomplishment the days you were able to provide care at home, and if it is necessary to move to a hospital, set your mind on continuing there whatever elements of home care are possible. To ease your conscience in advance and understand how to manage good care in an institution should you need one, read Chapter 13, "Hospitalization."

4

HOME CARE BEGINS: PREPARE THE WAY

When a patient and family have decided on home care, they begin to talk and think differently about the disease and make changes in care. Having acknowledged that the illness is terminal, a transition period begins usually on several fronts: geographical (from one location to another), medical (from active to palliative care), and mental/emotional (from hope to acceptance).

Understanding what needs to be done requires thought and work. One caregiver spoke of the first steps she took in making the transition:

When we decided to take Bill home from the hospital, we first contacted the visiting nurse association, arranged through our local hospital appliance store for a bed, air mattress, oxygen, side rails, and a commode. We had a family meeting with his physician so we could all ask questions. We were encouraged by our local doctor, who agreed to provide round the clock backup if we needed it.

Whole chapters in this book are devoted to necessary and helpful preparations. You will need to find a doctor who will support you in your commitment to the patient's comfort and be available twenty-four hours a day. You may need some "hospital"-type equipment, such as oxygen or a mechanical bed. You may need a visiting nurse, friends, and community services. Much help is provided here as you go about assembling these resources.

At the start, everyone involved may have misgivings, even fears, about whether home care will work. The patient may be frightened about whether his pain will be manageable at home; the family may wonder if they will be able to cope. Whatever the real or imagined difficulties, be assured that they can probably be solved. Use your fears as fuel for developing a transition plan, using the guidelines laid out in subsequent chapters. Planning means that if you need a doctor, an oxygen tank, or a medication, you will be prepared, and need not live in constant fear of "what if?"

HOME IS THE PLACE FOR CARE

The first indication that a transitional state has been reached is often the patient's recognition of the futility of further treatments. He may simply decide there won't be any more trips to the hospital.

Mom went in and out of the hospital for several months to treat a chronic infection, receive radiation for pain, and be treated for the buildup of fluid in her abdomen. She was aware that the adjustments were not lasting and that the disease had taken over. She announced she was going home, without oxygen, and would not come back again. There were three of us sons, a niece, a college friend, and a woman who had become a friend during her illness. She told us what she had decided and that she wanted us to "be around." We all knew it meant we were to care for her.

The patient often recognizes that whatever curative medications she has been taking are not succeeding. Intervals of well-being may have become quite short and are only prolonging her uncomfortable life. "This isn't the way I want to live," concluded one woman as she explained to her family the decision to remain at home.

I've been in the hospital three times now because of pain and nausea. I come home as soon as I am stable and my medication is adjusted. I've spent the last Christmas of my life in the hospital. I just won't leave home again. I've decided not to have any further medication except for pain.

Another frequent scenario takes place in the hospital where the patient was admitted for an operation or extended treatment. He and his family are accustomed to the hospital routine. They feel secure being cared for by professionals. Now, because the patient wants to stop treatment or no longer needs aggressive care, the hospital determines that his needs do not require hospitalization. He has been told he will be discharged. If leaving the hospital is not his first choice, or is not welcome by his family and friends, everyone may be very frightened and uncertain of what going home will mean. Beginning to make preparations will ease everyone's anguish.

PLANNING THE MOVE

Whatever the circumstances, once the decision has been made that the patient will return home, several days should be allowed to prepare for the move, especially if he has been in the hospital for a while. The key to an easy transition is careful planning while the patient is still in the hospital. Although you may be allowed only a short extension, ask the social worker, discharge supervisor, or your physician for the time you need. Here are several matters you must attend to:

- If the patient would be most comfortable in an ambulance, or you need help, arrange for transportation from the hospital to home.

- Ask about the hospital's checkout time, so that you won't be charged for an extra day for only a few hours' stay.

- Check with the cashier to verify any discharge requirements; arrange for payment and fill out the necessary forms.

- Take everything that has been accumulated in the hospital—gifts, flowers, cards, and other paraphernalia—home in the

days before departure, so that the patient has your full attention for the homecoming.

Your most important task will be to meet with the doctor, social
worker, discharge professional, and nurses on the floor to learn
what care has been provided in the hospital and what must be
continued. The easiest way is to watch what the nurse and aides do
and be present in meetings when the patient's care is discussed.

This transition period is also the time for the patient and
caregivers to remind medical professionals that you want all possible ongoing support for the patient's comfort. As you shift from
seeking a cure for the illness to an all-out attack on symptoms—
palliative care—everyone must share the same goal: comfort. Frequently, several doctors are involved, each with his or her own
specialty, program, and relationship to the patient.

Our medical team evolved during the course of my husband's illness.
First there was the oncologist, then the radiologist, then the chemo-
therapist. My husband received several experimental treatments and
he was shuttled from one to the next. The problem was, the specialists
did not communicate very well among themselves. When it came time
to stop treatments, there was some confusion. I realized I had to become more involved in order for my husband to be as comfortable
and peaceful as he deserved to be.

Caregivers and the patient need to be quite specific about what
they want. Once care guidelines are established, everyone involved
—including homemakers and visiting nurses—must be informed
and have the opportunity to ask questions. Ask the home care
nurse, or representative of the visiting nurse association or home
health agency supporting your care, to be present in any sessions in
which the care plan is discussed.

As you assemble information about care, collect instructions in a
notebook. Write in detail what to do about rest, bathing, meals,
equipment, schedule for medications, and suggestions and limits for
activities and exercise. Remember, because most people do not
"hear" instructions in the same way, it is important, especially if
there are several caregivers, that discussions take place among all
who need to understand what to do. If anything seems complicated,

ask for help. Ask a nutritionist, physical therapist, nurse, or other specialist to make a home visit to show you how to make a bed, give an injection, or tend to other aspects of care.

PREPARING THE HOME

Whether the patient is coming to her own home or to someone else's, she needs to be greeted with an atmosphere of hospitality, and also with whatever personal items, including clothing and linens, that will help her sense of security. Good food, a clean room, warmth, and constancy are very precious. Her room or rooms should be filled with the things she treasures. Within the range of her vision, place simple things she loves. Find out what they are by asking her; be willing to rearrange things until she is pleased.

Acquire the proper equipment, help, and skills for caregiving: have all the necessary equipment in place before the patient arrives. Hospital bed, bedpans, commode or raised toilet seat, and tub and toilet rails may make care much more manageable. All prescribed dressings and ointments should be on hand, and the caregivers should know how to use them. Specialized equipment for a catheter, intravenous treatments, or stomach care may be advised by the attending physician. Instructions for use of any prosthetic devices should be obtained beforehand.

Take the time to practice making a bed with a person in it, bathing someone, and using equipment. Something unforeseen may require attention that you cannot plan for now, so use any available time to learn what you can anticipate. If the patient is going home alone or to a home without an extended family, arrange for special care in the areas of nursing, homemaking, shopping, and transportation. If the patient needs to get to appointments outside the home and no one in the family can drive, these arrangements must be made.

Safety in the home is important, especially if the patient is walking about. Remove or rearrange furniture and hazards in rooms and hallways, and check that floors and rugs are safe for walking or passable in a wheelchair. If the patient is using the bathroom, make sure the pathway is clear and install simple safety appliances. You may also need to take precautions that are specific to the patient's illness or recent surgery. Visiting nurses can help assess what should be done.

> I realized that for my husband to be comfortable at home, we had to eliminate stairs in our lives. I found a first-floor apartment in a nearby neighborhood. We could take short walks within range of the house, sit on chairs outdoors, and we enjoyed this for a few months before winter and invalidism set in.

Have an ample supply of all medications the patient needs now and what you can anticipate needing. Medications that have been administered in the hospital, particularly special mixtures for pain and nausea, may not be available in the local pharmacy or may be restricted from being filled by telephone or from home delivery. Whoever is responsible for medications—caregivers and/or home health nurses—should know how to prepare them and know their frequency and dosages. If this is at all confusing to the persons responsible, ask the hospital or home care nurse to prepackage them according to the correct time schedule for several days in advance. If there are to be injections, ensure that whoever will give them is informed of the site of administration. If side effects of medications or bad reactions to certain foods are expected, they should be made known, and procedures to counteract them should be explained.

If the patient requires treatment given by specialists or therapists, nutrition counseling, or physical therapy, make certain that you know what services are needed and that appropriate people are assigned and understand their responsibilities.

Plan also for ongoing supervision from those who have been involved in recent care of the patient. The person primarily responsible for care and a representative of the home health agency or visiting nurse association should keep in contact with the discharge nurse, doctor, and/or social worker at the hospital, so that assessment will continue of the patient and the family's ability to manage and comfort the patient, and of the general quality of life in the household. The patient's condition and needs will change frequently, and a caregiver who is working closely with her may not see the changes as clearly as an outsider.

Other preparations include arranging for a doctor or nurse who will be available to come at any time of day. You will need a doctor to come when the patient dies, to pronounce the death and sign a death certificate. While it may seem too soon to think about this, some families have suffered an uncomfortably long wait for a doctor to arrive. The body cannot be removed from the house until there is an official pronouncement of death.

MAKING THE MOVE

While the patient is probably looking forward to the move, be aware that it will be strenuous. Moving is a real jolt under the best circumstances. Especially when the patient has been in the hospital for some time, becoming accustomed to another room, people one hasn't seen in a while, a change of food, and different toilet arrangements is disorienting. Someone who is dying is extremely sensitive to the dislocation. Here is a typical case:

> John enjoyed the ambulance ride to his home and even requested the driver to use the siren, joking about wanting the fanfare. His spirits were high as he was carried to his bedroom. That night, however, he was weaker than he'd ever been and vomited his dinner. It took several days for him to regain the energy he'd had in the hospital, although he was so cute and reassuring to all of us caring for him. He was delighted to be home.

You may want to ask the physician to provide a sedative drug to ease the change, in case the patient becomes fitful or anxious. In addition to medication, use your own intuition about how to minimize the move. If you have a choice, ask the patient whether he would prefer the family car or an ambulance. Depending on the patient, certain foods, bed clothing, a favorite plant from the hospital, placement of personal items as they were in the hospital, and many other thoughtful provisions can make the day easier.

The same care and planning should be taken when moving the patient from her home to another, as described in the following not unusual example. A daughter had been commuting a hundred miles in each direction to spend nights and weekends with her mother. It became clear that the patient was not getting better, and she decided not to continue her treatments. The two women agreed that they could share more time with less stress if they lived together. Joan was a teacher and needed to keep up her profession, so they agreed her mother would move to her home.

> I brought Mother to my home. It was a long journey, and many friends helped. She kept thanking people and telling them not to worry ("I'm going home with Joan, we'll be just fine"). I brought household items and equipment from the American Cancer Society with me. I had prepared my house in advance so it would be ready. I arranged with Mom's neighbors to take care of her house, shovel the snow, and take in mail. I had arranged for first-class mail to be forwarded. I had also taken care of banking and business details. Before we left Mother's house, I emptied it of perishable food and cleaned. I realized that probably the next time I would be there would be for the funeral.

When a patient is leaving her own home, the departure can be wrenching, as it marks a terrible realization that her life has permanently changed. Every effort should be made to help the patient feel welcome and have her own surroundings in her new home. Help her select favorite things to anchor her in the new environment.

During this transition to home care, gaps or overlaps in care are likely to occur, even with the best planning. Most likely, none will be critical and humor will be the best antidote. If something occurs that is judged to be serious, try to respond quickly and with assurance, remembering that tomorrow is another day and most "mistakes" are soon forgotten, properly replaced by the overriding warmth and attention inherent in home care.

So, care begins. The patient is home, or on her way. Her room is cheerful and well equipped. You are assembling the people and medical supplies that may be needed. Read on. Subsequent chapters cover every aspect of the care of someone dying, with many more specifics about subjects raised here.

5
YOU AND
YOUR DOCTOR

Organizing good home medicine for someone dying need not be difficult, although it takes some planning and probably persistence until you get what feels right and ensures quality care.

A good working relationship with the physician is so important that those close to the patient must consciously monitor not only the results of medical care but the process. Is the doctor available and listening? Does the patient express her needs? Is she being heard? Is she comfortable? Do caregivers have the medical information they need?

While well-informed nonprofessionals can provide most if not all necessary medical care for a patient, support from a physician may be important for symptom control, objectivity, information, and reassurance. Finding a good doctor should be one of the first tasks you undertake.

I first spoke to my mother's doctor about the decision and he supported us and advised me regarding specific care. Since we lived fifty miles apart I had to contact a doctor in my town. He was completely cooperative and supportive, urged me to invite my mother to stay with me, and told me to call him any time, day or night, whenever I needed advice or direction.

Perhaps the most frequent obstacle to developing and sustaining a working relationship with a doctor is that physicians often prefer to treat patients in their offices or hospitals. A doctor who has been caring for the person throughout the illness may hesitate or be unwilling to come to the home. It takes more time, and the physician may want equipment that isn't fully portable or may prefer to work with an assistant. Doctors give many reasons for asking patients to come to them.

The hardest part about the whole two months was the fact that we always had to go *to* the doctor; he insisted that we go to his office in the hospital where my wife had all her surgery. Getting there and back was a nightmare, and the place was full of horrible memories and symbolized for us the failure of many of our efforts.

Another problem caregivers face is that physicians are not necessarily comfortable with terminally ill patients and their families. Many have little or no experience with dying or with home care, and few understand the concept of palliative care. You may find a doctor willing to support you at home, but she may not communicate well or keep current with your situation. A distracted physician not aware of the acute sensitivity of the patient and family may neglect to pass on a piece of information that would provide peace of mind.

Making matters even more complicated are our own extremely confusing and conflicting feelings about doctors. We tend to feel angry, frightened, powerless, or childlike. We want to be on our best behavior, or protect ourselves, or totally surrender. We want to know more, yet are afraid to ask questions.

What we need to remember is that physicians are people, with strengths and weaknesses as technicians and as human beings. Some doctors do treat patients like children; instinct tells them people are easier to manage when they are submissive. The patient wants to be taken care of, and so the doctor naturally responds by making decisions for him, telling him what to do, how he is feeling, and trying to cheer him up.

But some physicians say they feel isolated by this role of decision maker. They prefer the involvement of the patient and family and are relieved when they are not having to manage all the options alone.

> Meg was an easy patient because she asked so many questions and helped with each decision. As her physician, I was grateful to her for making it easy for me to know what would work for her. She always wanted to know what was going on. I much prefer a partnership with my patients.

Samuel Putnam, M.D., who is engaged in research about patient-and-doctor relationships, concurs that many doctors find they enjoy active patients.

> A dying patient who is in charge of his terminal illness is almost like a magnet. Physicians usually *like* to take care of these patients because they feel they are doing something and they feel less hopeless. Although I can't document this, I know that this kind of patient gets more visits and better medical attention.

Putnam adds that if the patient can find a good listener in his family or a friend, and therefore can "dump all the stuff his physician doesn't want to hear," then he is much more apt to take charge and even be cheerful with his doctor, receiving more and better attention. Active participation with the doctor also seems to create a healthy spirit in patients. Six weeks before she died at home, a young mother talked about how she managed her doctors:

> Once this surgery is over, I'm coming back home to live with my family for the summer. I have made all the decisions about what treatments I will have. A lot of people create their own problems by not asking questions of doctors, or by not listening or not accepting the news. We've had a good attitude toward doctors. If we didn't like them, we got rid of them. I've called all the shots.

The patient and caregivers must select a physician who is committed to the patient and family, willing to make house calls, provide information, attend to the patient's symptoms. This chapter will help you learn what you need to support terminal care at home, select the right physician for you, and understand doctors and how to be understood by them.

WHAT DO YOU NEED FROM A DOCTOR?

Terminal care, as we have seen, is fully directed to the comfort of
the person and the well-being of family members and others involved. Because you are taking care into your own home, out of its
usual setting, you have to determine what support you will need
from a doctor.

The extent of care depends on the needs of the patient, the illness and its symptoms, the family, and the caregiver(s). No matter
what the circumstances, some physician contact will be necessary.
You may not need more than one visit, but if it means the difference between pain and comfort, the visit can be the most crucial
single event of caregiving. In addition, knowing that support exists
—just in case—will head off much anxiety.

> My mother became very frightened of her pain, and I was too. I had to
> make sure that our family physician would make house calls and that I
> could reach him in the middle of the night. Otherwise, I knew home
> care wouldn't work, that she would feel more secure in a hospital,
> though she hated them.

First, secure a commitment from a physician familiar with your
case. If the regular physician is not available around the clock, make
sure that informed physicians will cover. In an emergency—which
is *whenever* fear or pain arises—time must not be wasted either finding a doctor or giving medical history. The covering physician(s)
should be sympathetic and understand that you are looking for
comfort above any other consideration.

Information is another requirement. The patient (if she wishes)
and the caregivers need to know what the symptoms and stages of
illness will be. Doctors may be protective, thinking the less known
the easier the burden. Most people find this is simply not true. Tell
your doctor you want to know the patient's condition at every stage
of the illness, since having facts and foresight takes much of the fear
out of the real events.

The doctor is the highest-ranking medical professional on your
team. Make sure he will help with establishing a hospital or hospice
affiliation so that if you or the patient need respite—from each

other, from pain, general weariness, or anxiety—it will be easy to find a temporary second "home." Support services, procedures for emergencies, and suggestions for supplies all should be part of the assistance you can expect from the doctor.

What you need most, is an absolute commitment to the patient's comfort. The physician has to be willing continually to review results of medications and treatments; if the patient is not comfortable, changes must be made until she is. Is the physician skilled in and fully sympathetic to pain control? A doctor may be so dedicated to lifesaving that he may dwell unnecessarily on the theoretical risks of addiction, excessive sedation, and interference with natural breathing. Will the doctor give complete instructions to the nurse in charge of dispensing? Some doctors may agree the therapeutic goal is comfort but leave the critical task of administering medications to nurses, who in turn hesitate to give adequate doses for fear of harming the patient, shortening the patient's life, or prosecution for giving an overdose. Comfort may get sacrificed to many understandable fears, unless full communication occurs.

Finally, both patient and caregiver need to be assured of continuity of care. A physician dying of cancer wrote about what he learned he needed from his own doctor. Simply stated, it was: do not leave me.

> I needed to know that no matter how far my cancer progressed . . . I would not be abandoned. I wanted to know he would not make my dying more difficult by prolonging my life or resuscitating me. If I needed something to ease the last hours, I wanted to know he would help.

The patient has the right to an accessible physician throughout care.

SELECTING A PHYSICIAN

The obvious place to begin the search is with the family doctor, or with the doctor who originally diagnosed or treated the disease. Do not be surprised, though, if the family doctor does not accept your case or your requirement that you remain at home. Close association with the patient and family, such as delivering family babies, does not necessarily dispose a doctor to terminal care. He may not even be the best choice. Familiarity with the patient can mean the well-loved family doctor is more likely to make assumptions, not listen very well, or discount symptoms. He may have difficulty caring for an old friend dying.

Similarly, if the physician currently attending the patient hedges or says he can't make home visits or gives another indication of not being able or willing to stay with you, begin now to find someone who will support home care.

Since finding a doctor who meets your specifications may be difficult, begin as early as you can. You will feel a tremendous relief once you have a doctor everyone likes. Start the search by letting people know you are looking: friends, someone who has done home care, the discharge nurse or the social worker at the hospital. Contact the local visiting nurse association, hospice group, and homemaker–health aide service to ask for names of doctors who make home visits.

In selecting a physician, many people have described particular qualifications that they have found beneficial:

- Choose a primary care physician as opposed to a specialist. While specialists have their place, now you need someone who sees you as a total person, not as a particular organ or joint, or as a disease. The home care physician should be either a family practitioner or an internist who can keep track of all aspects of comfort and even seek help from a specialist if required.

- Check the doctor's training, credentials, and hospital affiliations. Choose a doctor who is either certified in internal medicine or family practice or is board-qualified (completed specialty training but has not yet passed the examination). This information is available from a doctor's office, the local medical society, or the public library's *Directory of Medical Specialists* or *American Medical Directory*. The doctor should have admitting privileges at a nearby, fully accredited hospital, preferably one affiliated with a medical school. This means your doctor will have access to the latest medical techniques for pain control and to qualified specialists. If a hospice facility or support program is available in your area, ask if the doctor is affiliated with it or qualifies for hospice reimbursement.

• Be clear about your biases. Decide whether you and the dying person have any preference in regard to the doctor's sex, religion, age, bedside manner, etc. Weigh the possible benefits of a younger doctor's knowledge of the newest medical treatments against an older doctor's experience and understanding.

• Listen to your intuition. Even when a doctor meets all the objective criteria, you need to like him. Is this someone you trust? Is the doctor accessible if you become concerned about the emotional or physical health of another family member? Is this someone who makes everyone in the household feel cared for? Is it someone who will comfort you in an emergency? Are office personnel courteous and do they answer questions fully? Observe the patient's feelings toward and communication with the physician.

• Before you make any commitment, determine the physician's willingness to consult with those doctors who have been involved in recent treatment. The physician should perform a thorough physical examination, and share his or her assessment and recommendations for care. Make sure the doctor has reviewed the medical history and that necessary information from it (an allergy, a prior illness) is assimilated into the care plan.

• Some doctors do not offer alternatives, never question a diagnosis, and insist that the medication is appropriate even when the person is uncomfortable. Is the doctor willing to participate in informal discussions and decisions about the person's condition or course of care? Will the doctor accept another opinion? Assess the physician's ability to observe signs and symptoms and to listen and respond to the patient and others involved.

• Determine fees in advance and talk about them openly. Find out what the insurance covers. After learning the fees, if you feel you might avoid summoning the doctor because of the expense, talk to him about what can be arranged or negotiated. Your visiting nurse association may be able to advise you about other sources of funds.

Many doctors use nurses, or nurse practitioners, or physician's assistants in their practices. While your immediate instinct may be to want all care provided by the physician, in most cases paraprofessionals are a real asset. Nurse practitioners, particularly, are trained to handle psychological aspects of people's well-being, as well as basic medicine. A physician who has such an aide on his staff probably acknowledges the importance of the emotional and social aspects of medicine, works well in a team setting, and is able to give more time to the patient through the nurse practitioner.

When you first meet with a new physician, or with your current one who will remain with you, ask whatever of these questions remain for you. You should feel satisfied with the answers you receive. (You will be especially lucky to find a doctor who is willing to say she doesn't know the answer to something but will find out for you, and then does.)

- What is the disease?

- What is the diagnosis?

- How certain are you that it is correct?

- What are the costs/benefits of additional diagnostic tests?

- What is the treatment now/later?

- What are choices for treatments? What effects or risks do they have? What is the likelihood that those effects will occur? What are their costs?

- What will happen if nothing is done?

- Should we consult anyone else? Whom?

- Could we review the patient's records and will you explain them?

- Will you tell us about what we don't know enough to ask?

- What will the dying be like?

- What will cause death?

- How much pain will there be?

- What can be done to anticipate and treat the discomfort?

- How frequently will you make home visits?

- Are you available by telephone with twenty-four-hour access; what backup do you have?

- What emergency arrangements are there?

- What equipment should be on hand?

- What are your fees; what can we expect the total cost to be?

- Will you be alert to the physical and emotional health of others in the household?

- Will you come at the time of death?

If you do not feel satisfied by the answers to these questions, don't rewrite them or sweep your concerns under the rug. First, ask again. If you are still dissatisfied, seek another doctor.

THE PHYSICIAN'S VIEWPOINT

No matter how well chosen your physician is, be aware that both home care and terminal care are probably a departure from his standard practice. Keep in mind that what you are asking him to do is different from how he usually operates.

Since we are asking the doctor to understand what it's like to be the patient, and to listen and respond to the family according to the patient's view of his illness, then it is appropriate that we have some understanding of what it's like to be in the doctor's position.

During this century as medical care has become more scientific and specialized, the training and perspective of a physician have necessarily become increasingly oriented to science and technology. Although medical education has recently begun to devote more attention to the emotional needs of the patient, these needs nevertheless remain secondary for most physicians, who are more interested in technical mastery aimed at diagnosis and treatment.

A doctor learns how to keep patients alive, and with today's sophisticated medicine and machinery, "miracles" have become near to the norm. Dying and death are less inevitable and less specific. For example, a patient can be kept breathing and seemingly alive even though his heart and/or brain has ceased to function. Since sustaining life is the goal of medical practice, we can understand how difficult it may be for your physician either to "give in" to dying or to focus not on cure but on *comfort*. One physician came to realize the importance of this shift in attention during a personal experience with serious illness.

As a young intern, I discovered that the first rule was never to have a patient die under my care. For years I'd been rushing about, curing and prolonging life. When my father was dying, his very personal crisis brought me to a sudden halt. In his room I watched the medical world from a new vantage point. I realized we would never be able to treat the dying with efficiency experts. Love and compassion are what the acute patient needs.

Competing theories of treatment and new drugs and machines further complicate the physician's task, especially when a number of doctors are involved in a single case. Depending on their specialties, each will tend to approach a problem in a different way. Although such competition may sharpen the physicians' skills, it is more likely to confuse or frustrate the patient.

I remember that my husband and I decided there should be one doctor who would take charge of the other doctors and make sure they were communicating with each other. We asked the doctor who had first diagnosed the disease, and it was a disaster. He didn't seem to have any interest in having things run more smoothly for us or in sharing and connecting treatment plans with the other doctors. It became clear that each was on a specific track and wanted Bill all to himself. I decided that I had to be the monitor.

While territoriality may be one problem, the physician's sense of duty may create another, leading to his being meddlesome or overprotective. Especially if the doctor is a friend of the family, he may well try to be more of a presence than is comfortable. One young physician told her own story:

I was in my first year of residency when my mother began dying of cancer. I could feel in myself—and I think it's true generally—an instinct to take over the situation as completely as possible. I wanted to do everything for my mother; in fact, nothing was good enough. I tended to dismiss suggestions about care that didn't produce perfect results. I drove myself crazy, and I don't think I did my mother much good either.

Because of a training based on efficiency, professionalism, and objectivity, the physician may not be prepared to place a value on or be attuned to the patient's feelings, or even to her own. It is not uncommon for a doctor to become angry—without being aware of that anger—with her patient for not getting well. When a doctor greets a dying patient by saying, "Well, that arm is healing nicely," or, "You're looking better today," she is probably confused about her own emotions. In reality, the patient probably feels weaker, may be suffering from a new symptom, and is struggling to accept his increasing and irreversible limitations. We should also be aware that doctors are as prone to unfounded optimism as any of us.

When my eighty-eight-year-old grandfather became seriously ill, we all went crazy. We dragged him to the hospital and ordered the doctor to do everything he could to save him. The doctor wired him up to a lot of machines, but my grandfather died late the following night, alone. I don't know what we were thinking. We never stopped to consider that it was natural to die at that age. If the doctor questioned the appropriateness of all that medical care, he never raised a question with us.

Being alert to the physician's training and humanity, we can learn to press for the care we need.

THE PHYSICIAN AND FAMILY

From the physician's point of view, probably a major difference in home care is that the patient-physician relationship has become public. What has been shaped in the private and somewhat anonymous environment of an office or hospital room is now surrounded by the personalities, culture, curiosity, and concern of many related people. Other doctors may be involved as well as the family and many friends, some of them overwrought, others bereaved, many distressed. This situation can make the doctor very uncomfortable. With so many people actively involved, communication becomes both extremely important and more complicated. He needs to listen and communicate with all concerned, and spell out the patient's condition clearly and simply to a number of audiences.

Another difficulty is that there are often multiple physical problems and many approaches to them. Nagging problems of terminal illness such as a sore mouth, constipation, and body aches often mean that the doctor must be constantly adjusting medications to create comfort. Disagreement may arise among or with the family about courses of action. Everyone involved is extremely sensitive, and doctors want to offer something hopeful or to ease the situation. Solutions some choose may be immediately or superficially comforting, but subsequently require further care or discussion. The process of explanation and negotiation can be very frustrating. Other problems for the physician may be that the patient is very frail and major changes can occur rapidly; the physician may want to treat a symptom, but the patient says no; or when some time may be needed to do a proper diagnosis, the family may urge him to make the visit brief. Whatever the case, the home is not often the easiest environment for a physician.

PATIENT ADVOCACY

While you may make it clear to your physician that the medical plan is to care for symptoms, this general guideline may not solve all problems. While many pain medications can provide comfort, they may affect the level of the patient's alertness, or weaken vital functions. Procedures such as suctioning to clear the lungs can promote comfort, but they are temporarily uncomfortable and can prolong dying.

The physician in a family environment must explain options and their benefits when body changes are not reversible. This kind of thinking may not be very easy for anyone, and doctors, being quite human, may want to avoid it.

As the patient becomes less competent and her tired and overwhelmed family less objective, the doctor may be tempted to become more paternalistic and to assume more and more of the decision-making responsibility.

Since terminal care is ultimately self-care and self-management, the patient and caregivers must feel, during all stages of the illness, that they have an equal voice with the doctor. Large and small decisions about care and treatment need to be made in open communication among all participants. The patient and caregivers should feel free to speak up when they feel the physician is not providing what they need. Feelings of helplessness, dissatisfaction, and anger are indications that something is wrong.

> My grandmother's doctor made me feel guilty for asking for stronger pain medication, saying that it would probably kill her. He never presented any alternatives to the medicines we were using; he talked about patience and acceptance of the way things were, indicating that there were many things I, as a layman, could never understand. He kept saying she was more comfortable than she said she was. She kept saying, "I don't think he understands that I mean what I tell him." The doctor didn't feel the pain, so how did he know? My grandmother knew.

The conflicts that arise out of poor communication and loss of control can seriously erode the quality of care. The patient feels the doctor is unsympathetic; the physician believes the caregivers are uncooperative.

To maintain the quality of care, one or several people who are usually present and are willing and constituted to go to any lengths to obtain satisfaction should act as advocates. If you are unsure about your own ability to be tough, ask for assistance from a close relative or friend who is a health care professional, someone comfortable with the language, equipment, and manner of medicine. The patient may serve well in her own behalf but simply cannot be her only advocate. In the last weeks of her life, when attention to details of well-being and to choices about treatments is most crucial, she will probably be too weary to appeal effectively to anyone. For the same reason, the person providing primary care is frequently too engaged with a variety of demands to offer effective advocacy.

> Negotiating the terms of care for my mother was much more difficult than I bargained for. Her physician simply did not understand that

comfort was all we wanted. I was worn out and I kept thinking he would come the next day and attend to her pain. I kept calling his office, then would get distracted by the immediate problems of care. I didn't really even keep track of days. It was so easy to let time go by.

What is proper advocacy? Step one is to understand and support the patient's assessment of how he feels. This sounds easy, but it is not unusual for well-meaning people to debate the patient's ability to view himself. Trust him. Adopt the dying person's perspective by trying to imagine yourself in his position, and how you would want to be treated. Step two is to express the patient's needs until they are met. Again, depending on the personalities involved, this may not be easy. Strengthen your resolve to accomplish necessary results by recalling that you are not asking for yourself, but serving as a mouthpiece for someone no longer able to speak for himself. Whether that pain is physical or emotional, it must be addressed, beginning with the doctor and whatever help he can give.

In playing the role of advocate, be humble. Remember that communication is power. It is easy to slip into manipulation by use and abuse of information. Arguments about what the person really wants or what is best for him are all too natural in this circumstance. Try to stay aware of the pitfalls, to keep all information out in the open. You are a steward of someone's life and this means exercising your and his right to good care. The physician wants to be helpful. In order that everyone's needs are met, you have simply offered to keep actively involved.

WHAT DID THE DOCTOR REALLY SAY?

Even under the best circumstances, it is hard to listen to and digest information that is new and technical. This is especially true when the information is about you and your terminal illness or about someone very close to you. In such situations, we tend to hear what we want to hear. Caregivers need to have the doctor explain or repeat any information which is not understood or which seems vague or impractical.

Studies show that a wide disparity exists between what physicians think they say and what patients think they hear. Patients and doctors tend to place different meanings on the same words. Like all human beings, they may also use language to mask and not clarify meaning. Simple phrases such as "Take this medicine as needed" or "If you feel discomfort, call me" or "It may hurt a little" are open to a variety of interpretations. Not knowing how much is a little, or whether the discomfort is enough to call the doctor or to take the pill, causes patients and caregivers to delay in making the call and thereby suffer from anxiety, indecision, and unrelieved pain.

In order to understand fully the doctor's instructions, you must learn how to talk and listen. It is sometimes a difficult business, but well worth the effort. You cannot assume that your doctor knows instinctively when he is misunderstood, what frightens you, or what hurts, and he will probably be pleased to be told. Even if you feel the doctor will be displeased by something you say, remember: this is your life, not the doctor's. He is there to help.

Studies of the interactions between physicians and patients show that the greatest patient satisfaction is achieved when patients receive facts, not interpretations, about their illness and its treatment, and when patients feel they have explained their history fully. Make the effort to tell the doctor everything you think is important about yourself, and ask all the questions that occur to you. Try not to edit these interviews before they occur, for fear of taking too much of the doctor's time or of hurting his or her feelings.

Achieving a satisfactory session with your doctor can be accomplished in a variety of ways. If you find it difficult to talk to physicians or have trouble remembering questions, make a list of items you want to talk about. Often if you first share your fears with a friend, you may later be able to discuss them more easily with a doctor. Holding a piece of paper and pencil to write down the doctor's answers can also give you courage during a session. A tape recorder allows you to review the entire meeting later. One physician said she encouraged her patients to have someone with them during important sessions, to provide another pair of ears.

A caregiver can assist the patient in a session with the physician merely by his presence and by asking his own questions (although the patient may only hear what interests him). If the patient does not want to know details the caregiver needs, then ask the physician to step out of the room with you. Caregivers and physicians say most patients slowly want to learn more about their illnesses. As this occurs, be ready to help.

If your doctor seems rushed or unwilling to "just talk," schedule another appointment so you can have ample time to get the information you need in order to fully understand what is being recommended.

INFORMED CONSENT

Understanding what the doctor says, in fact, is your legal right. Doctors must obtain the patient's informed consent for any proposed treatment, drug, test, or experiment, except those considered common procedures, remote risks, or emergency procedures. Consent is also waived in cases of "therapeutic privilege," in which the physician judges that disclosure would put the patient in such jeopardy that it could be considered bad medical practice. The physician must provide information in terms that can be understood and must answer questions and present alternatives. The patient has the right either to terminate the discussion (either to reject or accept the procedure before the doctor has finished explaining) or to continue asking questions until fully satisfied.

Although intended to protect a patient's rights, the legal doctrine of informed consent doesn't solve all problems. Many people prefer not to hear about their disease or treatment. "Doctor knows best" is all too often an attitude shared by both doctors and patients. Another common breakdown is that doctors can intentionally or unintentionally exercise a subtle form of coercion in presenting information. As in all communication, the tone of voice or choice of adjectives will encourage the patient to choose one form of treatment over another. What is more discouraging is the fact that, on the whole, patients tend not to take advantage of the information to which the informed-consent ruling entitles them. In a study reported in the April 16, 1980 *New England Journal of Medicine,* two hundred patients were questioned within a day of signing consent forms for treatment. Among those surveyed, only 60 percent could correctly describe the treatment, 59 percent could describe the purpose of the treatment, 55 percent were able to list a single major risk or complication, and only 27 percent could name an alternative treatment.

Remember, you and your doctor are a team. Your consent

should not be simple submission to whatever the doctor suggests. Especially in terminal care, the patient if he is able, or caregivers if not, must ask questions, discuss alternatives, and make informed choices.

ADVICE TO PHYSICIANS

Dr. Robinson would stop by on his way home around 6 P.M. and just say hello. Mother expected his company and would always have a question for him, frequently not a medical question, but something related to things they shared about each other's lives. His visits gave everyone the assurance that nothing could go too far afield, that a professional was coming who could help measure the patient's condition, answer questions, offer suggestions. In this way medical care was slowly let go. He believed that what Mother needed of medicine now was friendship, and he was wonderfully right.

As the disease progresses, what is required of the doctor becomes less "medical" and more "emotional" care. When symptoms are controlled, patients often reach a point where they are less conscious of the illness; their relationships become important to them, and they seek to connect with those close by, often with their doctors, who may not be accustomed to providing such care. Some doctors may be willing to give a brief backrub, considering this to be physical care. But if the patient should ask for a reading from the Bible, or advice on a child's career, or to share thoughts on immortality, the doctor may be embarrassed or feel that he is wasting his time, even though fulfilling these requests could provide greater relief at that moment than any medication. To the patient, responsiveness to "nonmedical" needs means the physician cares for and respects not just the illness but the living person as well. The person wants to be listened to, accepted by, and—most often, although some sensitivity is required—touched by his doctor. A patient remembers a physician's visit as longer and more satisfying when the doctor has sat at the bedside at eye level. Offering the smallest gesture or stopping for just one extra moment may be the most powerful medicine the doctor will provide.

A dying person will often be afraid to ask questions for fear of bothering the doctor or of getting answers he doesn't want. The physician can be aware that the patient may feel panicky when he asks a question about his illness. The patient may need a few moments of silence or gentle chatter before he is able to ask a hard question. The physician can ease the tension by talking generally about care he is being given or how medication works. Most often, the more knowledge a patient has, the more control he feels.

The physician need not always have the answer at hand. If he says, "I don't know, I'll check," it's fine. The doctor should be honest and direct but refrain from deferring questions to a higher, unknown, or remote authority ("God," "they," "medical science") which creates a vague, unsettling fear in the patient.

The person dying may have a stage of blaming his disease on his doctor, feeling angry that medicine, which seems to promise so much, cannot cure him. Some of his anger is closer to fear: "If you can't cure me, Doctor, are you going to desert me?" A physician can respond to this natural reaction and ease these concerns by talking and acting out a close connection with the patient: establish a common interest, express willingness to be called, describe a specific treatment for a symptom.

Other simple rules for physicians caring for dying people have been offered by Allan Hartfield, M.D., a doctor whose practice is primarily with cancer patients.

1. Never leave the patient with the feeling that all hope is lost. Give the patient some realistic sense of the future.

2. Be truthful and gentle with all parties. Tell the patient the same things you tell the family, and don't give out new information to third parties.

3. Take solace in the small rewards and remissions you can offer with treatment. A few days or a weekend of relief so the patient can have a good visit with someone important to him means a great deal and you can take pride in accomplishing it.

4. Be able to engage in small talk; to get to know the patient, offer something of yourself.

5. Try to express grief and other emotions over this patient privately so you will be free to help the family and patient. Let them know you are sad, but take care of it on your own.

6. Remember the high honor of caring for someone in an intimate relationship, and accept the satisfaction and joy of this trust.

Much of the security and success of home care rides on the relationship between the doctor and the patient and family. Armed with this knowledge of what issues and difficulties others have experienced and the determination to have this relationship succeed, you can be certain to get what you need. Not only will caregiving go smoothly, but the experience of working closely with a compassionate doctor will have a long-term benefit for everyone in the household.

6
CREATING
A TEAM

Caregivers often learn that they need help the hard way by running out of steam or becoming overstressed. Even though you may be tempted to assume the responsibilities of home care alone, don't do it. Don't minimize the size of the task or its demands on your time and your emotions. In fact, one of your greatest challenges will be one of the subtlest and most easily overlooked: taking care of yourself. No matter how strong you feel or what age you are, recognize now that undertaking the care of someone dying requires more skill, patience, and endurance than one person alone can safely handle.

Your desire to help the dying person may very naturally lead you to believe that caregiving is your sole responsibility. You may think, "I prefer to do it myself so it gets done right. . . . The two of us have always managed. . . . I don't want to bother my neighbors or friends. . . . I don't want the rest of the family to worry." People who step into the role of caregiver tend to be good organizers and are used to some amount of reorientation around others' needs. While you are well-intended and your abilities are unquestioned, this task is enormous. It has been well documented that people who work helping others, especially people providing one-on-one services, easily become physically and emotionally worn out. With its unceasing demands, home care can have especially severe long-term effects. Depression, serious gastrointestinal disorders, and insomnia are among frequent troubles. Realize that for the good of the patient and yourself, taking on so large a burden alone will ultimately be harmful. Don't try to go it alone; create a team.

Getting support does not mean acquiring a large cadre of highly trained professionals. When we are in trouble, we tend to turn—at whatever cost—to specialists. One curse of today's specialization is that if we don't hire the best (which invariably means the most prestigious and most expensive practitioner we can afford) we feel guilty. Our remorse can be especially acute when someone is dying; the pressure to give the very best can be great. While specialists may have a place in home care, committed lay people are often best at providing what the terminally ill person needs most: comfort, time, sympathy, attention, love.

Early in your thinking about home care, begin to identify people whom you can rely on for specific skills, or availability, or willingness to do certain tasks. Planning should reflect not only your present needs but also possible future ones. People can do the specific chores, and they can also just be around, relieving you for a few hours or more, bringing into the home a fresh point of view. Just the presence of the right people can lighten the load.

My sister's husband had died a few years before my husband's cancer was diagnosed. I asked her what she would do differently if she were caring for him today. She said, "I would talk about it more with friends, and I would ask for help." Bill and I decided then to offer the people in our lives the opportunity to be with us and to help. Some people did shopping, some answered the phone, some took our son to school, others cooked meals. I made lists of people available during the day for errands, and of others who said they could be called in the middle of the night. Some offered skills, like haircutting, and others equipment. In this way we built a small army, and it made all the difference.

While your own situation may not require or provide for such a full-scale mobilization, the model is important to keep in mind. The alternative to a small army of helpers may be "burnout."

Some first-person accounts of teamwork in home care suggest how important a broad-based network can be:

People overwhelmed me with their generosity. Some helped by carrying Mom up and down stairs. Some shopped for special things—like cotton nightgowns—they thought would make her more comfortable. One friend raises sheep and butchered one to make a sheepskin for her to lie on. Some brought other friends to visit, took me out to dinner, stayed with Mom while I went to mass, helped to prepare meals; one regularly spent the night so I could sleep through.

I always felt that help was at hand if I needed it. Friends regularly telephoned or called on us to ask what errands or services they could perform. My daughter, who lived an hour away, telephoned every day and visited frequently. We loved her visits and knew that she would drop everything and come if we needed her. We were very blessed in these respects.

During the last week of Mom's life, a semiretired nun with bedside nursing experience lived with us, and together we cared for her. During that week a visiting nurse came in every other day to help and check on Mother.

My husband's team was his family and a dear young priest he'd met at the hospital. The children arranged their working hours so each would give at least two to three hours with their dad; we are a large family and this meant each had a chance to spend some time with him alone.

Security derived from a fund of people cannot be overestimated. Even when you have the perfect strategy for getting through a problem, or a day, an extra hand will always make it easier.

PROFESSIONALS

As you begin to organize home care, you will want to solicit the help of various professionals—a physician, visiting nurse, and pharmacist for basic medical services. You will find these people through the hospital, the patient's doctor(s), your community health agency, and other resources. You will probably also need—if only for one consultation—a social worker or discharge planner, nutritionist, homemaker, physical therapist, hospice worker, and member of the clergy. Inform each person that you plan to keep the patient at home and that you are counting on his or her help and commitment to make home care work.

These professionals can either simply act as consultants to you or fulfill specific, necessary functions to supplement your own program of care. For example, a young mother caring for her husband said she was immediately relieved once she got a social worker involved. "What she couldn't supply, she helped me to find. I wouldn't have known where to begin," she said. Others find relief by having a health aide on call to provide backup when the caregiver needs a day off, or when the patient is uncomfortable.

The VNA sent a nurse once a week for an hour to assess Gramma's care clinically and a nurse's aide twice a week to bathe and change linen. A health aide came during the day primarily to give Grampa support and company. He called the doctor's office every Monday to report on her medications and her condition. The call reassured him that he had medical assistance if he needed it.

Many people have found—and doctors admit—that visiting nurses and home health aides with experience in terminal care are often much better at caring for the symptoms and general anguish of dying than physicians. While you need a doctor on your team, much of the day-to-day care and advice is well sought and provided by others. Nursing—and this is no doubt somewhat because of sexual stereotypes—tends to be the more nurturing, patient, comforting role.

Investigate institutions in your area that may provide temporary support. Increasingly hospitals are setting aside a number of beds for terminal care. While you will probably not have to use these facilities, it's good to know what exists, especially since many of these units also operate a twenty-four-hour telephone consultation service. Hospices or nursing care facilities in many communities sponsor special programs with staff trained for terminal care. In addition, a number of hospitals are developing outpatient home care teams and support for patients who prefer to remain at home.

Your peace of mind is at stake as you assemble a list of professionals for emergencies—a physician, hospital, pharmacy, and other health care providers. Having their names and telephone numbers will make the rough times easier and lessen fear of what might happen.

In Chapter 5, "You and Your Doctor," we describe how to select a physician. For other paid helpers, look for self-assurance, willingness to accept criticism, personal warmth, flexibility, tolerance, and a sense of humor. Study the references and, if feasible, ask for a demonstration of competence. Does the person feel at ease using his or her skills for terminal care? Does he or she have any trouble accepting the idea that the dying person's needs will come first?

If the candidate seems well qualified and willing and your instincts tell you this is someone you can trust, agree to give it a try for a few days or a few visits. Then talk again. Make sure you establish early on a commitment to periodic reviews, even if everything seems to be going well. Be discriminating about people you choose, then rest easy and trust the footwork you've done.

ASKING FOR HELP

While it is reassuring to line up professionals you can call, or who will come to the house at all hours of the day and night, most of your strength will be derived from compassionate and willing friends and neighbors who want to help.

Seeking and finding good support is the key to survival. If the household is young and active, lots of help will be necessary to keep up the familiar pace. If the household is only the patient and caregiver, probably what is needed is companionship and someone on call for emergencies.

In some cultures the family—and all its branches, amounting to a huge network of relatives—is considered a basic unit of support. Everything from food to money to troubles is shared as communal property. In such a social system, an individual who doesn't turn to his family for help or doesn't accept help when it is offered is considered to be selfish and ungrateful. If this concept of family is true for you, a mutual assistance plan like home care is probably a natural and comfortable undertaking. If you're fortunate enough to belong to a supportive family, you're not likely to have any hesitations about asking for help, and you ought to begin doing so now.

Most of us, however, have been taught to maintain our independence at all costs. Needing or appearing to need help, owing anyone anything, or expressing our troubles is associated with weakness. We pride ourselves on knowing that no matter how tough life is, we can say we never burdened anyone by asking for assistance.

In the main, this ethic of independent individualism serves us well. But trying to remain self-sufficient while providing home care becomes counterproductive for everyone concerned. Under the strain of being at home alone with a dying person, a caregiver working independently can suffer feelings of isolation and separation. If you find yourself thinking, "I'm the only one who can do this," it may mean, "I'm afraid if I ask for help I'll look stupid or weak or lose control." Instead of sharing responsibilities, the caregiver keeps them to him or herself, and because the person dying is usually in no position to help, tasks become unwieldy and often unmanageable. Many people let day after day go by, becoming more and more exhausted, because they assume they won't be able to find help.

The truth is, help is all around us if we only learn to ask for it. We have whole communities of people we don't even know—yet. Most people love to be asked for help, love to be able to respond, and then appreciate being thanked for their efforts.

> I was very clear about what I needed. I asked for, I thought, more than people wanted to give. But people have told me since Bill died that they were glad I asked them for help because they got to be part of it. They said they wouldn't have offered because they thought they'd be in the way, or felt awkward.

By not asking for help, we deny others their chance.

FRIENDS AND FAMILY

Everyone is a resource: men, women, and children of all ages have something to offer. Not only members of the family but also close friends and neighbors are a good place to start. People who ask "Is there anything I can do?" usually mean it as more than a half-hearted gesture, even though they may not offer or think of anything specific. You probably have a mental or written list of what needs to be done, and you can respond by suggesting a specific task. Another good approach is to ask a volunteer what he or she would like to do, what amount of time she has to offer, what skills she enjoys using. Some people will not want to spend much time with the patient; others will feel cheated if they are always sent off on errands. Ask initially for small time commitments and be clear about tasks. As you discover what people are offering, make notes so you'll be able to call on them when those needs arise.

I made lists of people, and as I wrote down their names I made them promise to say no if they wanted to when I asked, so I would feel comfortable about asking. If people couldn't help they would tell me. Sometimes it was their schedules, other times they were uneasy about being around us. People would say they'd do an errand, and then not show up or show up four hours after they promised. This was hard at first, but I soon knew enough to have a backup. People are wonderful, and their feelings control them; they do the best they can.

Once you understand what to expect from family and friends, move out to resources in your community established to help families in times of trouble. United Fund agencies, family service centers, churches, and the American Red Cross are among the many services available. An even larger sphere of possible resources includes people to whom you and the dying person are related by work, religion, age, hobbies, or sports. Simply who you are in life —divorced parent, race car driver, senior citizen, feminist, carpenter—can be the basis for contact with a large network of interrelated people, often established in organizations existing largely to lend a hand to those in need.

When calling an agency or community service organization, explain that you are caring for someone and ask what resources they have for home care. The first call to a stranger is always the most difficult; asking for help gets easier once you hear the interest and concern in another person's voice. If you have some connection with the organization, mention it; if you have specific needs, ask about them; if you have a problem you can't figure out, describe it. If the organization has a particular focus, describe your need in such a way that the person you talk to understands right away that he or she can be helpful. Always ask the person you are talking to if he knows anyone else who might be of help. Always write down the name of the person you talked with and the information he gave you. Follow up on suggestions.

As you research possible resources in your community, ask as well for names of people who have provided home care or have been involved with someone who died at home. Try to establish communication with people who are providing terminal care. In any difficult situation, we gain great strength from connecting with others who know exactly what we are going through. As one caregiver said, "I really found it valuable to make contact with other people who had provided home care, people who were willing to talk about it and tell me what they learned."

Once you begin to turn outward for ideas and help, the effect will be like rolling a snowball down a mountain. Each new recommendation will lead to others. This process is the basis of creating a team. Everywhere you turn, pick up new information, new leads, new resources, and new friends, all willing to help, offer advice, and lead you to more assistance, advice, and information.

WHAT HELP WILL I NEED?

As you read this book, you will learn specific requirements of caregiving and how to prepare to face and fulfill them. Here are some general categories, which can be used as a checklist of jobs that need to be filled. Make sure your assessment is ongoing; the needs of caregiving will change from day to day.

Night care: For some patients there is no clear distinction between night and day. They alternately doze off, then wake and want company, unaware of usual schedules. One person can quickly become exhausted. No matter how much you think no one else can take over, let someone help. Find volunteers who will be there several nights a week. Prolonged disruptions in sleep patterns have serious long-term effects.

Housekeeping: Even under the best circumstances, to keep a household running smoothly is difficult. When someone is sick and needing careful attention, laundry, cooking, cleaning, planning meals, and general maintenance tend to become overwhelming. Because most people have some experience with chores, the least skilled volunteers or those who feel uncomfortable caring for the patient can be assigned these fundamental tasks.

Finances: Ask someone to manage the various home care finances, which include budgeting, keeping cash on hand, making contact with insurance companies, and applying for Medicare/Medicaid benefits. Since many expenses involved in caregiving are reimbursable and/or tax-deductible, it is especially important to keep accurate records. If no one on the team is familiar with finances, ask a friend or the social worker or discharge planner in your hospital to help you get started on the recommendations listed in Chapter 8, "Keeping Records."

Advocacy: The person dying and the family need someone or several people willing to go to bat for them. Securing insurance benefits and information about the person's disease and medications, and solving other frustrations of getting what is rightfully yours, takes energy—far more energy than the patient or those closest to him will have.

Transportation: People who can drive are invaluable, especially when the home is some distance from shopping and other necessary resources. Errands requiring transportation are apt to be numerous and frequent and involve anything from picking up medications to organizing and transporting visitors. Set up at least one or two drivers who can be called upon in an emergency and as a backup. For further protection, check into the local ambulance, delivery, and cab services.

Telephoners: Volunteers are needed to make calls to inform people who want to be in touch and to answer the many calls that will come from relatives, friends, and neighbors. Family and friends have every right to be informed, although answering the telephone and making calls can seriously drain the energies of both the patient and the caregivers. For those living at a great distance, or for those who are not encouraged or able to visit, calls are critical. Contact made by the volunteer with these individuals should be particularly thoughtful and considerate.

Companionship: Reading, listening, sharing a hobby, playing bridge, gossiping, and confiding continue to be important to the dying person. Visitors bring with them facts from the outside world, memories, and "fresh air." Depending on the patient's mood and physical state, which can vary even from hour to hour, visitors are often a welcome addition to the daily routine. A new face or an old friend can lift the spirits of the family and patient and relieve pressure on the principal caregiver.

Supplies: Various members of the team can be responsible for procuring necessary supplies, everything from furnishings to clothing to drugs and medical equipment.

Emergency support: At the outset of home care, it is essential to establish an emergency around-the-clock support procedure, so that if a crisis occurs you know exactly how to handle it. During the course of the patient's illness, either you or the patient may become frightened or need emergency help. Talk over this possibility with the doctor, even ask what emergencies are likely to occur. Learn how to contact the hospital, whom to contact there, and how to transport the patient. If the household contains young children, plans must include emergency child care. Like a fire drill, an established procedure that everyone in the household learns will give peace of mind and will prevent undue confusion should a crisis occur.

At the time of death: As soon as possible after the patient dies, a physician must come to certify death. The doctor must be willing to come at any time of day or night. If the body is to go to a funeral home, arrange in advance whom to call at the time of death. If the body is being donated for research or for organ transplant, learn from the medical school or hospital what to do at the time of death.

SELECT PEOPLE CAREFULLY

Whether team members are volunteers or paid helpers, those who will be in your home for regular hours and perhaps for long periods of time must be easy to get along with. Someone who is tense or excitable, nervous or anxious, cannot give comforting care. People who offer help but then just stand around in the way can also be a terrible strain. You may be able to find errands for them to do outside the household. Be tough about choosing team members.

Talk with those who have volunteered to provide services. Explain in general terms what the dying person's care requires. Be direct, watch, and listen. Make your expectations of tasks and time commitments clear. Describe what this experience means to you and to the patient, and ask what the volunteer hopes to gain from it. Particularly with close friends and family, find out what they want to accomplish. Do they want to be helpful, say goodbye, assuage guilt, or seek companionship for their own grieving? None of these motivations is bad, but as the sole motivation they may get in the way of attending to what the patient needs. If someone really just wants to have a few minutes alone with the patient, help him to do that, and then see if he wants to help out.

Remember, you have the right to choose people who are kind and helpful. One of the most difficult challenges of home care can be answering the protest "But I am family," from a persistent but impossible uncle. Kinship cannot be the only criterion. Some relatives who want to help may make you feel tense or may make unnecessary demands. Be objective and honest with yourself about every member of the team. If you feel someone will not be comfortable to have around, be polite but insistent. If you don't have the energy to deal with that uncle, make it another team member's assignment.

ORGANIZING THE TEAM

Once you've assembled a group of capable and compatible people, assign each one a distinct area of responsibility. Given a somewhat confused environment, most will do best with some direction.

Tasks should be oriented toward attending to the dying person's needs and making the best use of the skills of each helper. Team members support each other best when they are not tripping over each other and know what others' responsibilities are.

Because every member of your team is an individual, with his or her own personality, work habits, point of view, and peculiarities, open discussion between team members is essential to a good working structure. The human variety that makes home care work and nourishes us as individuals can also create chaos, blame, and guilt. In haste or anxiety, the usual courtesies may be overlooked; it is not unusual for feelings to be hurt. Even though the mission is clearly worthwhile, harmony does not naturally and inevitably prevail.

Regular discussion permits team members to raise questions, adjust schedules, clarify their tasks, identify conflicts, and ensure that efforts aren't being duplicated. If possible, the patient should be involved in these discussions. Meetings allow team members to vent feelings, set new guidelines, and get to know each other. Sharing a meal together and planning a holiday or special celebration, which may even include the patient, are other ways of nourishing relationships, which is what home care is all about.

A few simple organizational tools can also help everyone on the team keep abreast of both the patient's and each other's needs. Post the following information in a handy, obvious spot, near the telephone or refrigerator.

Directory: Keep a central list of people on the team, their addresses and telephone numbers; list days of the week and hours they are available.

Schedule: Make a complete, clear schedule of all regular duties so that team members know what is expected of them and what they can expect of others. When necessary, break down tasks into their component parts; instead of simply listing "cleaning house," provide for dusting, mopping, vacuuming, waxing, etc.

Emergency procedures: Everyone who is in the house on a regular basis needs to know: (1) what to do if the patient exhibits a symptom that cannot be managed by the person in charge; (2) what to do if a trip to the hospital is necessary; (3) what to do if the patient lapses into a coma or appears to be dying; (4) what to do when the patient dies.

Good organization, with well-articulated procedures for informing others of what they should know, goes a long way toward stabilizing people's activities and feelings.

PROBLEM SIGNS

Persistent unhappiness calls for action. Duplication of efforts, incomplete or forgotten tasks, decisions not carried out, general grumbling, insufficient communication, gossip and rumors, scattered energies, and general feelings of hostility are all reasons for reassessment. Even under the best circumstances, remember that everyone in the household is under emotional pressure, and each is an individual, with different standards, speeds, and styles. When you sense that the team is faltering or that something is in the air, act quickly.

If someone is obviously out of sorts, ask what is wrong. Indicate that you sense a conflict and offer your help. Let the person talk fully, and don't try to correct facts or impressions. A full airing is very helpful. Gently ask questions and then guide the person to take steps to correct the problem. Maybe a break is necessary, or an apology, or a conversation, or a change of task. Remember that the point of airing problems is not to apportion blame to guilty parties but to work together to renew the bond you all share. Tension, frustration, and anger work against the team's reason for being.

The unusual stress of home care, complicated by the overtiredness it often produces, may cause members of the team to react in particularly bewildering ways. A broken dish may seem a major calamity; a suggestion will start a tirade; a team member may disappear for several days; another will begin mothering everyone. Such behavior is usually a sign of needing a change or even some counseling. Many people have trouble admitting that they have reached —for the moment, at least—their emotional limit. They imagine this to be a sign of weakness. It is beneficial for the team if members decide beforehand to help each other when they sense trouble, agreeing that they will gently identify for each other behavior that indicates stress and the need for a break.

The following can be used to identify and understand human behavior which can put individuals and the team under a strain.

Rigidity: When dealing with uncertainty, fear, and crisis—all intense emotions—one human tendency is to become rigid, to adopt formula for care. Our task as caregivers is to help and comfort, not to live by a set of inflexible standards. What works today may not work tomorrow. Resist setting up rules or procedures that will quickly become useless to the patient. Encourage team members to ask themselves, "How are things going *today?*" and provide care accordingly.

Being the boss: Team members as individuals or groups may have their own ideas of how the patient should be treated or should behave. One may want to "write the script" for everyone else, or try to impose his own standards on others. Remind others that the patient's needs and view of how they can be met come first. A social worker described the chaos which comes from not looking at care through the patient's eyes.

> When a patient has more than one caretaker, I've seen conflicts arise over what makes the patient comfortable and what she really means or feels, especially when the patient is not able to speak for herself. Particularly when a caregiver gets worn out, she tends to shut out the world and turn a deaf ear to the patient and the family. I advise people not to allow caregivers to be alone for long; it's too easy to lose perspective.

Remember, and if necessary remind the group, that the team exists for the patient's well-being and dignity. We are here to treat him and not ourselves, and care should therefore be given according to the dying person's needs and wishes, not according to the team's idea of what is right, necessary, or best.

Standing apart: People have a natural tendency to want to be appreciated individually. Under stress, someone may persist in an antagonism or unnecessary definition of a role as a way to be "special." By trying to stand apart, an individual reveals a need to be valued. Everyone can help by acknowledging frequently the worth of each contribution.

IT'S VERY HARD WORK

People in the "helping" professions are liable to suffer from a condition called burnout. We can benefit from lessons they learn, particularly the need to talk about feelings, to admit that working with someone dying is very hard work, and to take steps to give ourselves respite. Most people say their work with the dying induced important personal growth, but that this depended on learning to take care of themselves.

Some team members are experiencing dying for the first time; others are reliving memories of earlier deaths. Whether or not this is a caregiver's first death, it is not easy. Everyone's feelings and reactions count and need to be heard, either in team meetings or by confiding one member to another.

I guess I want to know that someone is going to care that this is hard work and that I am suffering. I want to know someone is going to listen, even force me to talk when I retreat. I may not be able to share these feelings with my mother. She's the one who is dying, after all, and I don't want to add my pain to hers.

After the patient dies, the immediate family will be the focus of everyone's attention. Others who have been intimately involved with the patient throughout the illness may now feel lost, as though they had no role to play. This situation can be extremely painful. Try to gather non-family members of the team together to talk and reminisce about the past weeks or months, to remember the sad things as well as the funny incidents. Have a meal together, and plan to go to the funeral. Write or give something together as a memorial to the person who died. Set a time and place for a reunion in a week or so. A special bond will always exist among you because of this shared experience, and you can begin to honor it.

In general, holding the team together and working in harmony depends on keeping the overall goals of home care in mind and reestablishing them whenever necessary. Of course, there will always be disappointments: a longtime friend may prove to be unreliable; a community agency may fail to provide a necessary service. But try to focus on the accomplishments, not the shortcomings. The team's value is based not on its perfection but on its humanity, warmth, love, and ability to share and give.

7
SUPPLIES

Successful home care includes careful thought for provisions that make the patient comfortable and ease work for the caregiver. Having certain supplies on hand in case any number of needs arise will give everyone some peace. You can expect, for example, to need several basic furnishings for preventing bedsores. Learn here what preparations are generally advisable and be sure to ask the nurse or physician to advise you.

When assembling equipment, remember that the quality of the patient's life depends upon his comfort and sense of independence and being cared for. In this spirit, take stock of your needs. Here are two caregivers describing their inventories:

Our doctor sent a visiting nurse to assess our situation and make suggestions. She thought a hospital bed would be useful, but my husband did not want that, nor did I feel it necessary, since his twin bed was high, and we made it comfortable with pillows and a board at the foot to raise blankets. We used an electric blanket, and when he complained of cold, I put a hot water bottle at his feet and a wool scarf around his head. He had a large table for his things, water, and a lamp. We didn't use much of anything else, but I had the assurance from our community drugstore that they would supply whatever we needed and deliver it to us.

Mom didn't want a hospital bed right away, so I tied pillows all around her bed to keep her from rolling out. I didn't want to rush her. We also had a portable toilet in the room, a clothes hamper, and a collapsible wheelchair, plus two chairs for visitors. I figured out how to arrange all that so we could move about the room easily. Beside her bed were her rosary, bell, glasses, clock, prayer books, notepaper and pen on a table. The smell of flowers seemed to bother her, so a friend gave us a dried arrangement.

Before you spend too much time and money obtaining new supplies, keep in mind that most people are satisfied with modifications of what they already own and like to use. In fact, the patient probably prefers the old nightgown and robe she's had for years; getting a new blanket you might think is more suitable or cheerful may not be her view. Be imaginative in adapting what you have on hand. For example, if the patient cannot help with her own dressing and you need nightgowns that can be removed easily, cut the back of one the patient loves instead of buying a hospital gown. Whenever possible, stick to the familiar.

THE PATIENT'S ROOM

"Make sure you get the room right, will you?" Liz was an active contributor to this book and included the author among those few people she wanted with her as she was dying. She lived alone, a librarian by trade and an interior designer by instinct. Bit by bit, she created her surroundings out of all the materials accumulated in her life. Since her illness caused increasing back pain, she had rented a hospital bed about a year before she died. After two months she was spending most of her time in that bed and asked her upstairs neighbors to move it into the sunniest room in her apartment. She wanted the light and the view: the tree outside the window was inhabited by several squirrel families that delighted her. She slowly gathered into that room (carrying little things by herself, soliciting help from visitors to carry larger objects) what she called her "best loved" possessions: her stone collection under the windowsill, her blue-and-red Indian blanket, rugs she had bought several years before, and her favorite paintings. Everything in the room had a history, and Liz recalled important people and events through them.

"And don't forget the cart." At the side of Liz's bed stood a wooden cart on rollers. On it were her telephone, magazines, scissors, Scotch tape, photographs she was sorting, letters to reread, medications, and personal care items, arranged in piles or in baskets. A work surface was essential to her, as she spent her days sorting through cartons to divide the many tokens of her family's life among her sons and others she felt should have them. The cart was where the action of her life took place, and everything on it—like everything in the room—was there for a reason. "The room is just the most important part, tell them," she said, "it's where we live."

As Liz suggests, caregivers should make sure that where the person lives is comfortable, cheerful, and familiar. Depending on the patient and his condition, the surroundings should encourage activity as well as provide quiet. Many prefer the living or family room to a bedroom, since it is apt to be sunny, large, and in the flow of activity. Curtains or blinds should be available on windows, however, so that light can be modulated. A bathroom should be nearby. Keep whatever room is used as normal in form and function as possible. As changes are made to accommodate the patient's needs, make sure to inform him and obtain his approval. Ask him what he would like to have in the room, on the walls, and by his bedside. A telephone should be within reach, preferably with a cutoff for the bell. Include something he associates with calm, such as a religious object, seashell, or picture of a sunrise. A plant or an aquarium provides a quiet sense of life and has the benefit of adding moisture to the air. Remember that his reach and vision are probably limited, so what is most important to him should be placed nearby. Place beautiful and simple objects such as a mobile, flowers, pictures, rocks, near the patient where he can see and touch them.

A few accessories which you can find in hardware or radio supply stores—or borrow from friends—will give the patient some independence and more options about how to spend time.

- Remote control or easy on-off switches for lights, fan, radio, television, humidifier, etc.

- Telephone amplifier, speaker, shoulder rest or handle for the receiver.

- Book holder with clips at the bottom edge and a mechanism for tilting.

- Glasses holder at bedside (or pin a holder to the pillowcase), chain for glasses around the neck.

- Alarm or bell by the bed and in the bathroom, on a rope or within easy reach.

- Radio or cassette recorder for music, tapes from friends, guided meditation; small radio with earphones for listening at night when others are asleep.

Keep the room clean and neat, according to the habit of the patient. Being too tidy is extremely annoying to some. One patient said that someone was always putting things away before she was finished with them. Another complained that the efficient home-maker was "wearing out the rugs" by cleaning too frequently. Housekeeping should be performed when the patient can tolerate it and kept to a quiet minimum. Sounds and smells of cleaning can be comforting some days and nauseating on others.

The temperature of the room should be kept fairly constant. During the winter rolled cloth or paper stuffed along the cracks of windows and under doors will help reduce drafts. If the patient is walking, a warm floor or rugs make trips to the bathroom more pleasant. If the floor is cold and she is too uncertain on her feet to risk rugs, then warm slipper socks or nonskid slippers will solve the problem.

Make sure the patient's safety is considered in all arrangements. For example, shorten electrical cords so that an arm or leg will not accidentally catch one. Check to see that clothing is not dragging, and turn hems up by two or three inches on full-length robes, gowns, or pajamas. If the person is restless and you fear he may roll out of bed, install rails or put the mattress on the floor. If he smokes, take great care to provide safe covered ashtrays and non-flammable garments and bed furnishings.

Some furniture may have to be removed or rearranged if the patient is using a hospital bed, wheelchair, commode, or walker. Hallways and passageways need to be cleared: bookcases and foot-stools especially tend to become hazards. Rugs may impede progress of a wheelchair or be tripped over. Either roll them up or put down plastic runners. Check the bare floor for nails, raised boards, or tiles which a shoe might catch. Keep the floors clean but not slippery-waxed. Since medication and general distress can be disorienting, the patient will rely on things to be in the same place from day to day. Rearranging furniture may result in a fall. We all remember getting up in the middle of the night in a strange place and tripping over something that wouldn't be there if we were home.

When it seems best to have on hand some "machine" that looks particularly nasty (oxygen tanks, for example), take the time to cover it up or put it out of sight. A screen in one corner of the room or a large straw basket will hide supplies and protect them from unintentional use. If young children are in the household, take whatever precautions are necessary to keep little hands out of trouble.

In all the adaptations you make, support the patient in his desire and need to be independent. Every day there will be some challenge in this regard, and his dignity is worth the effort to find a solution, either by a creative use of the existing environment or with a few special supplies. He may be well enough to prepare his meals but unable to stand to do it. The patient may want to go downstairs on a good day but be unable to walk. He may be able to manage being alone, but how can he let visitors in the locked front door if he is bedridden? Such problems have been conquered by others, and they can be by you. Assume a solution, and find it by asking people for help and ideas.

WHAT EQUIPMENT IS USEFUL?

Without making the living room look like a hospital ward, some special equipment may provide greater comfort and make life easier for everyone. When thinking about what you need, remember that the patient's basic requirements are simple: a place to sleep, tools for eating, ways to sit and move about, and provisions for bathing, toilet, and other personal care. Here is what one caregiver found useful:

> I bought an apparatus that looked like a park bench with suction cups on it that I placed in the bathtub so I could bathe Mom and wash her

hair. We used this until she couldn't leave her bed anymore. I used a wheelchair, a portable toilet, and eventually a bedpan. When Mom could walk a little, we had a walker. I also had dishes that held hot water, so food stayed warm. The dishes had suction cups on the bottom so they wouldn't slip off the tray. I bought a cup with a lid on it, so she wouldn't spill water if she reached for the cup at night.

If the patient is going home from the hospital, make an assessment with her and others on the team, nurses, and the attending physician to understand which hospital supplies would be useful. Ask for advice about what may be required later, as the illness progresses. Although you cannot know now everything you will need, you can at least assemble the basics and have them on hand to save the anxiety of having to find someone who will make deliveries at night or on a weekend.

Several questions should be asked of anything you contemplate obtaining: Is it safe? Comfortable? Easy to use? Easy to clean? Shall we purchase, rent, borrow, or make it? Will insurance or Medicare/Medicaid pay for it? How will it fit in the available space? Is it something I can operate? If any of the answers are negative or raise problems, then ask for ideas and help. Compromises may be necessary, and a well-negotiated solution is worth the effort.

RESOURCES FOR EQUIPMENT

Now you have a list of equipment you need, or at least of problems that need to be solved. Begin by improvising or borrowing as much as possible. Familiar furniture and household supplies can often be used as they are or with slight adjustments. Your own pharmacist, visiting nurse, home health aide, doctor, social worker, and friends who have been involved in home care are all good sources. Don't be shy about saying to a friend, "I need a bedpan for Dad. Do you have any idea who might lend me one?"

Request information from your church or professional group, United Way, Red Cross, or Chamber of Commerce. Local community agencies and clubs often have equipment. Local ambulance services, volunteer fire departments, or nursing homes may have oxygen and suction machines among other supplies. In this way, you can also become acquainted with other services they offer. Organizations that do not have equipment may be able to arrange discounts with suppliers. Whatever health organization is concerned with the patient's disease may have funds or supplies. Local chapters of the American Cancer Society, for example, may provide some supplies free of charge, as well as an allowance for equipment, transportation, and other assistance.

What you cannot borrow may be available for rent. Use the Yellow Pages to locate hospital supply firms. Most have catalogs they will send or will answer questions over the telephone. Describe exactly what you need, asking sales people to offer ideas and quote price ranges. Many suppliers have twenty-four-hour, seven-day service (although it may cost extra), and orders are normally delivered the next day. When you need an item quickly and it doesn't arrive when promised, call and check on it. Some companies will accept Medicare if the customer will pay the difference between what the benefit allows and the cost of the equipment; fewer accept Medicaid. A fee may be charged for delivery, setup, or service.

When you need to purchase equipment or want to know what is available, contact either hospital supply firms or large retail stores such as Sears and Penney, which will send special catalogs of health care items. Be warned that equipment for home care is a growing industry and that suppliers may put pressure on you. Salespeople may try to play on your guilt or feeling of inadequacy. Before you buy something you didn't mean to buy, call a friend or get some advice. The telephone company, plumbing or hardware store, vocational rehabilitation service, and variety or discount store all carry supplies that make life easier and may cost less than those from a hospital-supply firm.

Whether borrowing, renting, or purchasing equipment, in order to qualify for insurance benefits or to obtain the supplies, you may need a written letter of referral listing what you need, signed by your physician. In an emergency this referral may be possible by telephone. When obtaining physician referral for an agency, such as the American Cancer Society, ask your doctor to complete a request form allowing for "whatever supplies the home care provider or visiting nurse requests" so that he will not have to be contacted each time a new piece of equipment is needed.

Be persistent in looking for what might make life easier for the patient or caregiver. Once you get what you need, get used to it, learn how to operate it. You will soon become comfortable with provisions most people associate with hospitals.

A BASIC CHECKLIST

Bed

One of the joys of home is being in one's own bed. Often a patient's bed can be used as is throughout the illness, if it is functional and safe. However, if special care, comfort of the caregiver, or the patient's ease could be served by modifying the bed, many adaptations are available.

The height of the bed from the floor is one feature that can be quickly adjusted. As long as a patient can get in and out of bed, the height should remain where it is most convenient for his mobility. When he can no longer leave the bed, it can be raised to make lifting, feeding, and bathing easier. Most beds are 15 inches to 22 inches high, while a practical working height for most caregivers is 30 inches to 32 inches. An extra mattress can add the several needed inches to the height, as can wooden bed leg blocks (8 inches × 8 inches × the height desired to be added, with 3- to 4-inch holes in the top of each to stabilize the legs), which can be made, rented, or purchased. You can experiment with different heights by using cinder blocks or tightly bound stacks of newspapers, with a hole gouged in the top of each to stabilize the legs.

To avoid bedsores, a patient must shift position of the head, shoulders, and legs at least every two hours. Pillows and bolsters can help accomplish this, but adjusting them requires partial lifting of the patient, which may be painful for him or difficult for the caregiver. For everyone's comfort, you may wish to use a mechanical bed, which adjusts the bed height and the position of the patient's head and legs by motors or manually operated cranks. A variety of control combinations is available; some of the options available are: (1) manual adjustment of height, head, and foot; (2) manual adjustment of height and remote-control adjustment of head and foot; (3) no adjustment of height and a choice of manual or automatic head- and foot-position control; (4) completely automatic adjustment of height, head, and foot. While most models come as self-contained units, a few motorized flexible spring-and-mattress combinations can replace the spring and mattress in a home bed. Be sure you are getting what features you really need before you borrow or buy any of these models.

Bed Furnishings

Since the patient's bed is probably his primary location, attention to basic details will be very much appreciated.

A firm mattress: If firmer support is needed, a bedboard can be placed under the mattress.

Pillows: Three standard-sized ones are suggested for sleeping and for adjusting patient position; smaller pillows can be used to stabilize a position. Inflatable air or water-filled flotation pillows in various shapes help distribute weight of arms, back, head, and shoulders. Triangular pillows under the knees take weight off the back and legs.

Mattress pad: Whatever brand you use must be easy to wash and dry and should be fitted or firmly anchored at the corners to keep it snug and flat.

Sheets, pillowcases: Part-synthetic fabrics are easier to wash and dry but may feel too warm to the patient or not absorb sweat. Stains are easier to remove from all-cotton sheets. A hospital bed may be a different size from the household beds and require special sheets.

Blankets: Cotton thermal weave gives warmth and ventilation, is lightweight, and is easy to launder. Electric blankets should be used with extreme caution and must be regularly monitored. Some patients, and not just children, might occasionally find comfort in a sleeping bag, which gives the feeling of being pleasantly surrounded, cuddled.

Bed Accessories

Depending upon the nature of the illness and the needs of both the patient and the caregiver, consider the following bed supplies.

Drawsheets: An additional top sheet can provide wrinkle-free surfaces, give additional protection to bedding, and assist in moving the patient in bed. Either fold a flat sheet in half the long way or use a purchased drawsheet, which can be backed with rubber or plastic. Absorbent paper sheets can be placed over a drawsheet.

Supports for covering: It is often necessary to relieve the weight of blankets or other coverings on the feet, the legs, or the entire body of the patient. Frames that go under covers may be purchased or improvised.

Pulls and lifts: A trapeze-type bar can be suspended over the bed or chair, enabling the patient to raise himself, exercise, or shift position. Pull types attach to the foot of the bed.

Foam pads: For a softer bed surface, cover the mattress with either Eggcrate padding, made of soft, wavy plastic foam which provides ventilation, or a five-inch foam pad. Cover foam pads with a waterproof sheet, if necessary, and a mattress pad.

Bedboard: A bedboard can be cut of plywood or purchased, to fit under the mattress for firmer support. Some boards fold for storage.

Water mattress: Undulating water beneath a patient acts as a gentle massage to stimulate circulation and thereby prevent bedsores. Improvise a water mattress by filling a sturdy camping air mattress with water on top of the bed mattress, covering it with a pad. Hinged water mattress pads that flex with a hospital bed are available.

Quilted air mattress: Another therapeutic style of mattress features air channels that automatically inflate and deflate in an alternating pattern for mild stimulation of muscles and blood circulation. Many find the hissing sound it produces quite soothing. The motor can be turned off when motion is undesirable.

Side rails: Detachable rails provide security as well as a place to grasp for turning in bed; some drop down for easy access.

Sheepskin: Used fleecy side up, the wool fibers of a good-quality sheepskin distribute weight over a large area, reducing a standard mattress's tendency to produce localized pressure points and bedsores; its deep pile also lets air circulate and keeps skin dry. Synthetic sheepskin is cheaper and easier to launder but tends to be less resilient and reflects rather than absorbs heat.

Back support: Soft molded cushions for the back or a standard backrest will help relieve the patient's weight and provide a variety of postures. Improvise with a beach chair or a straight-backed chair placed upside down with legs in the air and the top of the back resting on the bed, covered with pillows.

Chairs

When the patient can move or be assisted to a chair, the change of view and position can help her total outlook, even minimize awareness of discomfort. Place the patient's favorite chair within easy walking or carrying range of the bed. Small pillows, a footstool, and a blanket add to the pleasure of an alternate location. Soft pads or cushions make the seat or chair back conform to the patient's position. A special harness jacket or set of soft straps can support the patient in the chair. Your medical supplier and team members can offer advice about what is available for your particular circumstances.

Adjustable recliner chairs: Such a chair will both extend the time a patient can spend in a chair and enable him to move about the house. Back and leg rests adjust to comfortable positions. Select a model with large wheels and a push bar at the back. A swingaway, self-storing table may be attached.

Wheelchairs: These are specialized equipment, with many available feature options: manually operated or power-driven operation, reclining back, detachable arms and legs, low or high back, narrow or wide widths, elevating leg rests, swinging and detachable front riggings, folding or nonfolding models, collapsible body for carrying from one room to another. An especially useful model includes sides that collapse for transferring a patient from chair to a car, bed, tub, or toilet. Accessories such as a tabletop and carrying bag can be added to a wheelchair to aid in the patient's independence and mobility.

Bed and Chair Surroundings

A patient feels more control if she can easily reach things she uses frequently. Be sure to place within easy range of vision a clock and a calendar to assist with her orientation.

Bedside/chairside tables: Provide a surface near the patient for her use. If she changes location during the day, a rolling cart may be a good solution.

Medicine tray: Keep medical supplies portable so they are not part of the permanent bedside environment.

Bedside bags: An accessory bag helps keep small items organized. A small paper bag pinned to bed or chair offers convenient tissue disposal.

Call signal: Some patients will be able to lift a bell and ring it, but an electric bell with a tap button may be easier to handle. A whistle is useful, if the patient can manage it. Electronic voice systems with many options for speaking and for monitoring sound are also available.

Over-the-bed-or-chair table: Adjustable, removable tables are optional but convenient for meals, activities, and placing supplies when performing medical procedures. They are available in utility and furniture models with a variety of features.

Footstool: A sturdy stool with rubber-tipped feet and a nonslip step surface will aid the patient getting in and out of bed.

Lighting: Indirect lighting is easier on the patient's eyes; caregivers will need more intense lighting for care procedures.

Screen: A folding screen shields the patient during a medical procedure or when resting. Across the doorway, it gives privacy to the whole room while providing good ventilation. Use a screen also to hide medical equipment.

Bathing

Normal personal hygiene should continue for as long as possible because such care is very important to anyone's well-being. Caring for personal needs is explained fully in Chapter 9, "Physical Care." Install hand-grip bars and nonslip strips or rubber mats in the tub or shower area. A hand-held shower head with a wall mount can be hooked up to the faucet so the patient can easily direct the spray or attach the unit to the wall. For soaking in the tub, use a soft polyethylene foam pad that rests along the back and bottom of the tub to allow the patient to recline on a soft, nonskid surface.

Even if the patient is unable to bathe himself, the tub or shower can continue to be used for bathing. A toilet chair or other waterproof chair may be placed or rolled into the shower; a sturdy stool can be used if the patient can sit alone. Soft straps will help position a patient safely in a chair. Another option is a seating unit that stands beside the tub with a swivel so the person can be shifted to a position over the tub.

Supplies required for a bath in bed or in a tub or a shower include:

- Bath sheet—a cotton sheet blanket or large beach towel

- Towels, washcloths

- Shower cap

- Soap or other cleansing agent

- Bath oils (but use cautiously: while pleasant and beneficial in moisturizing the skin, they make a tub or shower slippery)

- Lotion and creams

- Talc

- Nail care tools for fingers and toes

- Basin and protection for the sheets if giving a bed bath

Dental Care

The patient's own supplies can be used, unless special procedures and medications have been prescribed. For tooth and mouth care, you will need:

- Soft-bristled toothbrush

- Toothpaste or powder

- Glass of water

- Dental floss

- Mouthwash

- Basin

- Towel and washcloth

- Storage for dentures and denture cleanser

- Large cotton-tipped swabs for rinsing mouth if patient needs assistance

Shaving

A male or female patient will prefer doing his or her own shaving as long as safety and ability allow. If the caregiver is doing the shaving, it is generally easier to use an electric shaver, preferably battery-operated. For shaving with a safety razor, the following supplies are needed:

- Basin

- Soap

- Washcloth

- Razor

- Shaving cream

- Aftershave

- Styptic pencil

Care of Hair

Daily brushing helps keep the hair clean and stimulates circulation in the scalp. If the patient finds a regular brush too harsh, try a softer one. Shampooing should be done in a place and position most comfortable for the patient. If you wash a patient's hair in bed, you will need:

- Shampoo tray—improvised, molded, or inflatable

- Shampoo and, if desired, rinse and conditioner

- Pitcher of warm water for rinsing and a large pail of warm water in which the patient can soak and shampoo his hair if the water supply is away from the bed

- Several bath towels and washcloths

- Waterproof protection for the bed

- Large pail to catch waste water

- Cotton for ears, if desired

- Hair dryer

Having a professional hairdresser or barber come in to trim, style, or set a patient's hair is helpful and wonderful for the patient's spirits. If the patient is not well enough to enjoy a regular shampoo, or as a temporary measure, try a dry shampoo.

Toilet

The goal of whatever equipment is acquired to provide a toilet is the patient's independence. Each situation is different, so use your good sense and ingenuity to give maximum privacy. What is possible will depend on the patient's physical ability. Walking or even being assisted or wheeled to the bathroom is good exercise and should be continued even when it might be "easier" to keep the patient in bed. Almost any effort is preferable to a bedpan from the standpoint of the patient's dignity. A young woman described a sequence of measures she used to postpone use of the bedpan:

> I knew that the day my grandmother could no longer get to her bathroom was going to be awful for her, so we put it off as long as we could. When she became unsteady on her feet, I made a row of chairs from her bed to the toilet and she could grab the chair backs unassisted at first, and then with me at one side. Later, it took two of us to support her and, as this was impractical because she would occasionally have to wait for two people to be in the house, we brought in a commode chair which could be wheeled to her bedside. She cried the morning she realized her strength allowed only this much effort.

Solve the problem of getting to the bathroom in whatever way seems to work, with either supports or people. In addition, make adaptations to the toilet area itself so it is safe. In the absence of stable appliances built and installed for this purpose, an unsteady person will grab for what is there: towel rack, paper dispenser, hooks. Anticipate this need by installing rods that are designed for body weight. The physical therapist at the hospital or home health agency can advise about height and types of safety appliances. Rails mounted on the wall or a walker placed in front of the toilet will aid in sitting and rising. An adjustable-height toilet seat is easily attached, and a guardrail can be installed on the toilet seat for additional support.

If the patient can no longer walk to the bathroom but is still able to sit, a commode chair can be used. Improvise a commode by placing a waterproof pad under a bedpan on the seat of a very sturdy armchair. The bedpan and cover can be removed between uses. Portable commodes come in many designs: some look like regular chairs; others are on wheels and can be positioned over the toilet if the patient can be wheeled to the bathroom. Most models include a detachable plastic pail which is easy to empty and clean.

For the patient who must remain in bed, bedpans and urinals are a necessity. In addition to the regular contour-shaped bedpan, you can purchase a fracture bedpan with a low, wedge-shaped front that can be placed in position with very little lifting of the patient. Both models are made in plastic, metal, and enamel. The plastic units are not as cold to the touch; others should be warmed.

Hand-held urinals are made of metal, plastic, and enamel and come in both male and female styles. A day-and-night urinal is available for men and comes attached to a belt and connected by a tube to a collection bag. Some patients may want to use a catheter, a decision which obviously involves your physician. In any case, or at the last stage, the most comfortable method for patient and caregivers may simply be diapers and paper sheets.

Walking and Support

Moving about the home or even the room is very good for the patient's general comfort and self-esteem. Use your imagination about how to help him be mobile. The arm of a strong friend is good security; a cane or walker can also give the patient some freedom to move about.

Canes vary from simple wooden or metal models to folding ones to intricately carved conversation pieces. Footed canes have three or four feet and several kinds of handles, including forearm crutch types. Nonslip tips are essential for walking support and should be inspected regularly for dirt and wear; rotate tips to even wear.

If the patient needs more assistance, walker frames are stable, can be folded, and are adjustable in height. A sturdy wood chair mounted on ball-bearing rollers can also be used as a walking aid, assuming the patient is steady enough or is given support to control the amount of rolling. If the distance to be covered is short, strategically placed furniture will afford surfaces for support. A physical therapist in your community or hospital can advise what form of walking support will best suit the patient's needs.

Eating

Many ways of preparing and serving food which the patient can handle himself are described in Chapter 10, "Eating." Utensils and various supplies are also described there, but the following are major categories of eating equipment and some adaptations to them that can be helpful.

Tray: If the patient is bed- or chairbound, he will need a lap tray or over-the-lap tray for his meals. The tray can be simply made from a large sturdy cardboard or wooden box, or you may use a standard model. Paper tray covers are inexpensive and disposable, as are decorated napkins.

Cup: For drinking, a tippable child's cup with a handle and cover or a push-button thermal mug that reseals automatically, even if dropped, will prevent messy accidents. Other possibilities include a flexible straw, a snorkel cup with a built-in straw, and a cup with two handles.

Dishes: Nonskid bowls and plates with a soft rubber ring attached to the bottom are available. Many patients, especially those able to use only one hand, find helpful a scoop plate (a plate that is high at one edge and low at the other) or a bumper guard that fits on the plate. Keep foods warm with bowls and dishes that are insulated or heated by electric coil or hot water. Anchor anything necessary to the tray with soft rubber suction cups with a double-side grip, such as those sold to hold soap in the shower.

Utensils: Large-handled utensils and various modifications to knives, forks, and spoons are also available, including a fork with a knife edge.

Medications

Various ways of taking medications can be explored by the patient and caregivers. Most people want to do everything possible to forestall use of injections. Use ingenuity and ask your pharmacist for advice. Most caregivers inevitably try to crush pills or capsules and hide them in food. Because people who are dying tend to have enough trouble enjoying food, it is probably best not to complicate it with foreign flavors unless the patient agrees. Patients usually prefer to keep medicines and food separate, and this is what you can assume if the patient is not able to talk. Check with your doctor about solid and liquid forms for medications, and be specific with the pharmacist about what is easiest for the patient to take.

Liquids: You need to improvise or acquire whatever implement will help get the correct amount into the patient's mouth and positioned to swallow. Some use an eyedropper or a syringe. You may also buy a nonspill spoon, which has a hollow vial in the handle marked with measures from one quarter teaspoon to two teaspoons. Fill the vial to the correct dose and tip the spoon into the patient's mouth.

Pills: Crushing pills may help if the patient has trouble swallowing. You can try flavoring them with an extract or syrup. You can also buy a specially designed glass with a small shelf at its bottom on which the pill is placed; small slits guide the water to the pill and then into the mouth, reducing the likelihood of choking. If you have difficulty remembering what pills are to be taken when, devise some system of envelopes or small glasses, and count out pills into them when you have a quiet moment. One visiting nurse used egg cartons.

BE PREPARED

In addition to what we have described, other supplies can add to the patient's comfort and make care more convenient. You may not need all of them, and your imagination and ingenuity will lead you to add others. Don't buy them if you can borrow, improvise, or make do with what you have. Consult with the health professionals on your team, too, because no doubt your particular case has its own requirements. Many of these items will be used only when your doctor or nurse suggests, such as laxatives, suction, or catheter equipment. Keep adequate supplies on hand so you won't run out

at an awkward time. Many products can be returned if they have
not been opened.

- Bandages and gauze pads
- Tape
- Tissues
- Lip balm
- Bacteriostatic ointment
- Lozenges
- Deodorant dispenser
- Cotton-tip applicators (including some treated with glycer-
  ine and lemon or glycerine and milk of magnesia to moisten
  dry mouth and lips)
- Rubbing alcohol
- Cotton balls and swabs
- Body lotion and cream
- Oral laxative
- Mirror
- Rubber or plastic sterile gloves
- Bed socks
- Heel, foot, and elbow protectors
- Eyedropper
- Syringes
- Transfer or slipping board (for moving the patient without
  lifting; use with instruction and caution)
- Tongs
- Jars or other containers for cotton, etc.
- Disposable cotton sheets and diapers

- Flashlight

- Tongue depressors

- Thermometers (oral and/or rectal; solid state digital ther-mometers offer a forty-five-second readout)

- Humidifier (warm or cool mist)

- Suction equipment and supplies

- Urinary catheter and supplies

- Oxygen

- Ice bag or ice gel packs

- Hot water bags, nonelectric heating pad, Hydrocollator pack

With a good inventory and information about what supplies may be helpful given certain conditions, you will begin to feel more at ease with home care.

8
KEEPING RECORDS

Some people are naturally inclined to maintain records of daily routines, expenses, and appointments, and even keep a journal of thoughts and events. Others find this scrupulousness somewhat difficult or even distasteful. Keeping at least minimal records during home care will save time and worry about remembering important events in the patient's care and condition to tell the physician and other caregivers. It will also help later, when you need to recall purchases and other tax-deductible or reimbursable expenses. If you're already a careful record keeper, stay at it; if not, let this information guide you.

Critical information that you will want to keep track of throughout home care falls into the following categories:

- Emergency numbers

- Instructions for care

- Medications

- Daily care

- Equipment and supplies

- Expenses

- Travel
- Team members

If you set up standard forms or a recording system in advance, then making notations will be easy. Either follow the suggested formats in this chapter or develop your own. Find your own short-hand and ways to consolidate information. Your patient's care may require more or less record-keeping. The essential point is to have at hand information that is used often, and a record of actions that must be repeated. As home care gets under way, you'll begin to have a clearer idea of what data should be kept. Place the records in a loose-leaf binder, with colored tabs to separate each section. Keep the binder in an easily accessible place, preferably near a telephone. Teach other team members how to make notations and check the record book for information they need to know about caregiving, errands, or whatever their task is.

EMERGENCY NUMBERS

Telephone numbers of particularly important people on the team should be quickly obtainable by anyone in the household. Keep a directory posted by the telephone or taped to the cover or page one of the notebook, and include at least the following information:

TELEPHONE NUMBERS

NAMES	HOME	OFFICE	BEEPER
Home care nurse(s) *Visiting nurse association* *Physician(s)* *Hospital* *Ambulance service* *Pharmacy* *Equipment supply* *Family members*			

INSTRUCTIONS FOR CARE

When you first begin home care you will receive instructions about the patient's care. Those directions will probably be changed over time. Whoever is on duty must have the most current information. Directions will include how and when to care for an open sore, change a dressing, or adjust the position of the patient. Write the instruction clearly and legibly. Following is a simple format. When an aspect of care changes, make the new notation and use a colored ink to draw a simple line through the old notation. You will still be able to read the earlier instruction if you wish to refer to it, but all who glance at the sheet will know what is the current instruction.

CARE INSTRUCTIONS

DATE	INSTRUCTION	WHO GAVE IT	DATE CANCELED

MEDICATIONS

Medications are only as good as their success in promoting the patient's comfort. If you are to measure their effects with any precision, medications must be given as often as directed, in exact dosages, and according to all special instructions. Because many options are possible with respect to the dosages, combinations, timing, types, and manufacturers of drugs, your observations of how the patient reacts and feels after medication are valuable. They will allow the physician to make adjustments to the original prescription. While this degree of careful attention may not be necessary much of the time, prepare for such record-keeping just in case.

Make a chart for medications according to the following format. Make notations when changes occur. In addition to simplifying record-keeping, the chart also serves as reference for others providing care, obtaining additional supplies, keeping income tax records, or contacting the issuing physician.

MEDICATIONS

DRUG	DOSAGE	DATE BEGUN/ DISCONTINUED	PHYSICIAN/ PHARMACY	NOTES (PURPOSE, EFFECT, POTENTIAL SIDE EFFECTS/ANTIDOTE)

DAILY CARE CHART

A daily record of patient care may seem tedious and time-consuming, but it can serve as an important reference for caregivers, the physician, and home care nurses.

When we were preparing to leave the hospital, the discharge nurse made a chart for us to record my husband's fluid intake and output, his food, medications, and pain. I was very glad to know what information was important and useful to the doctor. Making the notations gave me a focus and something tangible to do.

Many functions are served by this record, and they may change. For caregivers, a daily chart may provide an important hold on reality beyond the small world of home care. Caregivers tend to experience a blurring of time and even though each moment seems memorable, facts essential to good care become confused.

Time came to be measured in naps, medicines, and juice preferences. The daily log became less a record of food and weight but slowly expanded to include hours of sleep, observations of pain, schedules for medication. The future disappeared. We were living day to day and focusing on what would provide the most comfort. I wouldn't have known where to begin if the nurse at the hospital hadn't handed me a log to keep.

Daily chart maintenance does, of course, involve a certain amount of time and effort. But it's probably not safe to count on your memory for what you have and have not done. Once you've established a routine for attending to it, you'll find that the record provides more than a simple log of daily events.

Use the chart to establish a schedule for the day. Whether or not you are the only caretaker, getting a routine will offer useful orientation for everyone. When other people are involved, some order is essential. A routine also creates a feeling of safety for the patient.

Establish a timetable for meals, bathing, sleeping, and other activities and write it down the night before or first thing each day. Follow it as best you can, altering it when necessary for the patient's comfort. If you find—and you may find—you need more time to accomplish tasks that involve the patient, allow for it. A dying person's pace is significantly slower than yours, and allowing time is one of the benefits for everyone involved in home care.

The chart also ensures consistent care. When more than one person is giving care, shift changes can be easier with a carefully kept chart. (It is also a much better use of whatever time and energy exist for conversation to talk between you about feelings or to change the subject away from the patient or illness.) Members of the team can come and go, and simply review the past few hours or days at a glance. The caregiver on duty can leave knowing appropriate and informed care will continue.

Draw up a daily care form that you feel will be easy to follow and will provide useful information to those concerned. Your doctor or home care nurse will probably have suggestions. Make entries of events that seem noteworthy—particularly small or large crises, food dislikes and preferences, moods and what preceded them (if anything), effects of medications, sleep patterns, unusual bowel or digestive functions, etc. Record major care events during the day. If you are trying a procedure, method, or tool for hygiene, record the function and degree of success. After a few days this record-keeping will become natural and you will know instinctively what is important. Ask others who relieve you to make notations also so that you will know what has occurred and can learn the details later. Asking others to help with this and other records underscores for them the significance of their contribution.

EXPENSES

Many of the costs of providing patient care at home are either reimbursable through the insurer(s) or are tax-deductible. As unpleasant or complicated as you may find the whole matter of finances, prepare now to keep a simple record of expenses as they are made so you won't have to recreate this information later. Keep all receipts, invoices, check stubs, and related scraps in a large envelope, file folder, or mixing bowl. Use the sample chart that follows for your records and be sure to take account of the following categories of expenses:

- Medications
- Equipment (purchases, rentals)
- Transportation for the patient (taxis, ambulance services)
- Supplies (paper products, lotions, bed sheets, etc.)
- Food prescribed by the doctor (such as protein supplements)
- Medical visits (doctors, visiting nurses, homemakers, etc.)

DAILY CARE

Date/Time	Care Given	By Whom	Medications Name/Dose/Effect	Activities/Sleep/Symptoms	Intake Food/Fluids	Output BM/Urine/Vomitous
6/20 1:30 A.M.	bed pan	DWL	1 T. cough med. Arrested symptoms	complains of pain in mouth. Alert, angry. Sat on couch. Watching TV	Asks for ice cream. drank 2 glasses ginger ale.	still no bm (5 days)
6/20 6:15 A.M.	mouth care and bath	ASQ		comfortable, confused.	3 spoons egg, 1/2 c. milk	
6/20 8 A.M.	bed pan	DWL	Demerol— 1 tablet 50mg. pain under control after 50 minutes. He went to sleep.			vomited 10:20 A.M.
6/20 10:30 A.M.	backrub	DWL	Alpha Keri, Marlox on bedsores	Agitated but calmer afterward. watch elbow sore.	two sips Apple J.	

EXPENSES

DATE	ITEM/SERVICE	COST	REASON/PRESCRIBER

AUTOMOBILE TRAVEL

Automobile travel to and from the hospital or pharmacy, or for transporting supplies, nurses, and other helpers is tax deductible. Keep a record of your mileage and encourage other drivers to do the same.

MILEAGE

DATE	FROM	TO	MILES	PURPOSE

"LET ME KNOW"

During the time you provide home care, many friends are going to step forward to offer themselves in a general way to your service.

At the moment assistance is offered, you may be distracted, or not know precisely what someone else could do, but train yourself to say, "Thanks. Can I put you on my list of volunteers?"

My husband had worked for a large company for years, and I am a teacher with many students. We were fortunate to have lots of people volunteering their time. I kept a running list of who was available for what, so if I had an errand to be run midmorning, for example, I knew who might be available.

You will receive not only such general offers of help but also specific goods and services. Everyone has something useful in his attic left over from Aunt Mary's gallbladder operation, and friends will soon appear with casseroles, magazine articles, and recommendations from so-and-so the expert. Don't turn any of it down, even if you can't handle another loaf of bread or don't need to try a new massage at the time. Keep a list of what has been offered so you can easily note these suggestions and go back to them when you have time or a specific need. In addition, create a master list or a card file system, whichever works best for you. For most people, something like the following will suffice:

GOODS/SERVICES

NAME	TEL. NO.	WHEN AVAILABLE: HOURS,DAYS	WHAT OFFERED

KEEP A JOURNAL

I couldn't have survived without my journal. It was my friend when I couldn't reach anyone else. In the middle of the night, for several minutes during the day, or whenever I was lonely or confused or overwhelmed, I would write down my feelings.

Many caregivers speak of the saving power of a diary. In the midst of a long day, or when it's 3 A.M. and you don't have the energy to make a telephone call, you have a companion. While writing is not a substitute for communicating with other people, it is a good tool, a way to learn to place problems outside your own door. Often the simple act of putting into words confusing or complicated feelings engenders a solution to dealing with them. Writing has the wonderful ability to take some of the power out of your fears. A social worker told this story:

Amy was twenty when she was caring for her mother. She felt acute isolation from her college friends and the life she had put aside. She began to keep a journal in which she wrote out her sadness about her mother's dying and her anger at being interrupted in her studies and separated from her boyfriend. "My journal really saved my life," she said. "I had someone to talk to at all hours of the day, someone who understood, just accepted it all. My thoughts and feelings became my friends and I lost most of my fear."

If keeping a journal is already a habit, stick to it. If this is your first experience with a diary, or with any form of personal writing, begin with a blank piece of paper, sketchbook, or notebook. Or treat yourself by buying a clothbound blank book. Write your name on the first page. Don't agonize over a suitable title or pseudonym or thought worthy of an introduction. Just begin. Write the date and then, "I feel. . . ."

Write whatever you want, whenever. This prose is for you, and the important thing is that it *work* for you. Spelling, grammar, punctuation don't matter. If it helps, pretend that you are writing to someone—your childhood friend, an imaginary confidant, yourself a year from now, or a grandchild. Write about today and what it is

like to be you today. You can even draw what you feel. Be honest.
Don't try to make sense; that can come some other day.

The journal is a safety zone. Think of it as a pile of feelings to
look over when you have more energy, a place to go and not be
disturbed, a garden which only you may tend. Much has been written recently about journal-writing and how to use it for self-ther-
apy. In *The New Diary*, Tristine Rainer describes how keeping a
journal can help transform emotional pain into positive energy for
self-healing. She suggests several types of writing which will lead
you through confusion and pain to safety.

Narrative: Tell the story of your day. Describe how you want to
remember the person you are caring for.

Lists: Make lists of things to do or to look forward to, of fears or
things to think about or tell someone someday, of what you can be
grateful for today, or of people who are important to you.

Philosophy: No one is going to dispute you, so write out your
thoughts about people, illness, death, immortality, or whatever concerns you.

Dialogue: If you are angry with the patient or a member of the
family, write out the dialogue you wish you could have—and perhaps can have—if you take some of the hostility out of the feelings
by rehearsing in your journal.

As Rainer shows, releasing pain through such writing will slowly
provide distance from it, making it more manageable.

Articulate as much as you can, even your barely formulated thoughts
and fears. Allow yourself to cry as you write, if you feel the need.
Write until you can write no more; write until you are exhausted.
Don't make judgments about yourself or your writing. . . . Don't be
afraid that you will uncover more pain than you are able to cope with.
You also need not fear that confronting and expressing the pain will
create more pain. [p. 117]

You may be confirmed in the strength diaries can offer by reading those written by other caregivers and close relatives of people

who are dying, such as John Gunther's *Death Be Not Proud,* Martha Lear's *Heartsounds,* or C. S. Lewis's *A Grief Observed.*

Keeping records is one of the many practical skills acquired in caregiving that you may find will become part of your life thereafter. "Survival" skills we learn out of necessity are often later seen as the gifts of a painful experience. Keeping track of expenses, making a schedule for your day, and keeping a journal of your thoughts and experiences are invaluable and may stay with you throughout your life.

9
PHYSICAL CARE

"Don't call this chapter 'Home Nursing' or use medical terms," suggested one of the doctors who advised on this book. "Keep it simple. Call it 'Physical Care,' and use words like 'might' and 'could,' not 'must' and 'should.' There's nothing rigid about caring for someone. Encourage people to learn body mechanics so they don't hurt themselves. Aside from that, just give them all the support you can."

Having a dying person in your care may often seem like having responsibility for a newborn baby. Depending upon the condition of the patient, you may be afraid to hurt him or that there is something critical you will or will not do. Relax. It's only natural to feel some degree of fear at the seriousness of the task that you've taken on. But the first rule of providing adequate physical care for a dying person is that the caregiver try to relax and be confident in his abilities to offer what the patient needs. It is very unlikely that you could do the "Wrong Thing" for the patient. Dying people, like babies, are resilient, and any "mistake" you might make will be far outweighed by the generosity of your warmth and simple human contact. In fact, anyone can in a short time develop the necessary competence for the physical requirements of home care. With minimal training, you will run the same risk as a student nurse or army medic of causing any serious harm.

This chapter is intended to teach you some skills that will be useful in providing care by explaining the basic principles and theories behind the procedures and thereby offering some typical applications. Feel free to add your own ideas, methods, and variations, which may be more relevant to your situation than what you read here. These skills are easy to learn and, like learning to ride a bicycle, they require only practice.

What is the purpose of physical care during a terminal illness? First and foremost, your aim is to provide comfort. This is from a doctor as he lay dying:

> The caregiver who cradles your feet, makes soft rings for your heels, removes wrinkles and crumbs from the undersheet, sponges you off with a skilled hand, she is an angel from Heaven. Efficiency and craftsmanship with just a touch of tenderness are what I am so grateful for, even though I can't express it. I know my field of vision is very small, so I appreciate your nursing me close to my face and sometimes talking so I can recognize you and feel the safety of companionship in my tiny universe.

Providing physical care for someone who is primarily confined to bed or unable to move requires familiarity with several simple techniques, the most important of which are how to clean up after a bowel movement, measure medications, and handle the person without causing him pain. Although the material in this chapter teaches you how to perform these tasks, you may turn to professionals for clarification, demonstration, and special problems. For example, ask a physical therapist to come to the house and teach you how to use your own body efficiently to move the patient, as well as simple massage techniques and passive exercises to alleviate the patient's discomfort from inactivity or paralysis. Ask the visiting nurse to demonstrate how to turn and bathe the patient, make the bed, and lift or support the person in such a way that you won't hurt yourself. Whatever special technical skills are required—monitoring oxygen, emptying a catheter bag, changing intravenous feeding bags, or giving injections—can be taught in the hospital or at home by a visiting nurse.

Preventing discomfort and even fear of pain and doing everything possible to enable the patient to be free of her body is your ultimate objective. Anticipate the patient's needs for a bedpan or pain medication; provide them before she is uncomfortable. Be sensitive and aware of the constantly changing condition and mood of the patient. At times she may want to be massaged and held; at other times, she may want only to be given medication and left alone. Do whatever you must do with a minimum of disruption; be unobtrusive, tender, and efficient. Make it clear the patient can ask for help at night, which is the most frightening, lonely time; knowing she can have company if she needs it will probably reduce the need.

Because the daily mechanics of giving and receiving care probably represent the principal activity of the patient's life, this task also offers an opportunity to share time together that should be exploited. Treat it as you would any other routine you may have shared with the patient in the past, like taking a drive or playing tennis, and let the patient participate as much as possible. Give reasons for everything and explain steps as you go, being aware that vision, hearing, and hand-and-eye coordination are probably blurred, so that even the simplest tasks can be misunderstood or frightening. Guard against compulsiveness; if the patient loses interest in a bath, don't insist on it. If a sore is extremely painful to clean, ask the doctor how necessary the procedure is. Since pros and cons exist for every treatment, make the effort to discover them and solicit help in weighing them. If the patient objects to what you are doing, try to understand his problem and make an adjustment; don't just ignore it by saying he is having a bad day. Ideally, in matters of personal maintenance, support the patient with time, equipment, and a helping hand so that whenever the situation permits he can take care of himself.

Physical care procedures should also be conducted in the flow of the person's life, taking into account her habits. Most people have a rhythm to their lives that should not be interrupted. Take into account when the person normally bathes, eats, naps, reads, and enjoys chatting or seems to need companionship. These routines can be modified gently to fit with others in the household. If there are a number of people who must be considered, plan to assess the schedules frequently to make sure compromises are working.

When the physician or nurse suggests a treatment which may cause temporary discomfort but then provide relief, discuss the options with the patient. If he is willing, negotiate a way to try the procedure, and be aware you may need to cancel it. The patient's comfort may also be enhanced by sticking to a schedule, such as turning him every two hours or giving medication at precise times. If this is the case, acknowledge to the patient that you know when or how you are giving care is not ideal, but if he is willing, the doctor feels the routine will make him more comfortable.

My grandmother's cancer was located along the gum on the inside of her mouth and spread down into her throat. For several months, the radiologist and visiting nurse concurred that keeping it clean and clearing away dead tissue would promote her comfort. She dreaded the daily visit for this procedure and often was so tired from it that she had to rest several hours afterwards. Who knows whether this treatment should have been done? At any rate, we did finally give it up because it made her so unhappy.

Honesty and constant review of the basic questions—what the person wants and what must be done to keep her comfortable—will keep the focus of your physical care plan where it should be.

BED CARE

Since the bed is likely to be the center of the dying person's life, make every effort to see that it is comfortable and in a good location. The bed will probably be situated in the patient's room or in the living or family room, near household activity and accessible to caregivers. Most people decide not to have the patient above the first floor, to save everyone the effort of climbing stairs. Experience shows that a firm mattress raised to a height easy to reach without stooping and a location away from walls for quick access makes care more efficient. The bed should be protected with a plastic sheet or plastic mattress cover. You may also protect the pillows, but plastic covers for them can be noisy and not very soft. Alternatives for protective coverings are Chux and disposable cotton pads, which reduce laundry but add to expense. Make sure that whatever coverings you select do not create an odor or texture that is uncomfortable and do not make the patient sweat. Several layers of sheets or a cotton cover may help alleviate this problem.

Changing the clothing and bed linen of a person who is either immobile or has limited strength is a skill you will develop with practice. The basic strategy is to strip and change half the clothing or half the bed at a time. To change clothing, begin by having the person remain in one position. Loosen and remove the clothing from the side of his body not resting on the bed, and replace it with clean clothing. Then turn him to the opposite position, remove the remaining soiled clothing, and finish putting on the clean.

Making the bed with a person in it works on the same principle. (Follow the illustration on page 119 if you need clarification.) Step 1: Move the patient on his side to one half of the bed, taking care to cover any feces or urine with a protective sheet beforehand. Step 2: Untuck and roll dirty linen toward him, so that it lies along his back. Step 3: Put clean linen on the bed up to the line of dirty linen. Steps 4 and 5: Taking care to flatten the folds of linen as best you can, gently roll the patient over the line of linen to the clean side of the bed and complete the job. Try to prevent wrinkles from forming, since the patient's skin will have become extremely sensitive and even slight irritations can cause a break in the skin.

Positioning

Within reasonable limitations of the caregiver's physical ability and the patient's comfort, the inactive patient's position should change every two to three hours. He should be turned from side to side and from his back to his chest unless his illness prevents one of these positions. If there are areas of redness on the side which has been facing the bed, they should fade in five minutes. If they take longer to fade, position changes should occur more frequently. Frequent shifts in position will promote circulation, prevent joint stiffness and bedsores, and help to maintain enough strength to move and be moved so that eating, toilet care, and other necessary activity will be able to continue as comfortably as possible. Most people will naturally select a curled position, favoring one side, both for warmth and to relieve pain. While the person may not want to be moved, explain why it is important to change position and that he can return to his favorite side in a few hours. Negotiate trade-offs if necessary: "I'll read or sing to you while you lie on your stomach."

When the patient must change positions or move for any other reason, have him help to whatever extent possible. Explain to him what you are doing. Loosen bedcovers and get all obstacles off the bed or out of his way. Coordinate motions by a voice signal, such as "Ready, set, go" or some variation. Use the signal even if you are the only one moving, so he is alerted. When he cannot be of help to you, use a draw sheet and principles of body mechanics (which are explained below). Always use a helper when available.

When you settle the patient into a new position, check to see that vulnerable parts of his body are properly protected:

- Support the back with pillows or towels to follow the natural curve of the spine.

- Support the joints to prevent strain. Place pillows under knees, ankles, and elbows to position the limbs carefully so they are not touching and are flexed. Keep weight off the protrusions by, for example, placing a small pillow under the calf of a leg to keep the heel elevated.

- If the hands are kept closed, place a roll of several dry washcloths in the palm.

Using a Drawsheet

If the patient is unable to help you move him, learn how to use a drawsheet, which is the most comfortable way for the patient to be moved, is easier on the caregiver(s), and may even make it possible for one person to change the patient's position in the bed. A drawsheet may be a sturdy crib sheet or a regular single sheet, folded in half and laid on top of the bottom bedsheet. It should be long enough to extend a few inches above the head and below the hips, and wide enough to tuck into each side of the bed. Since the patient is apt to slide down in the bed, it may be necessary several times a day to slide him gently back up. Try the following procedure: Roll each side of the sheet close to his body. If two caregivers are pres-

Making a Bed with the Patient in It

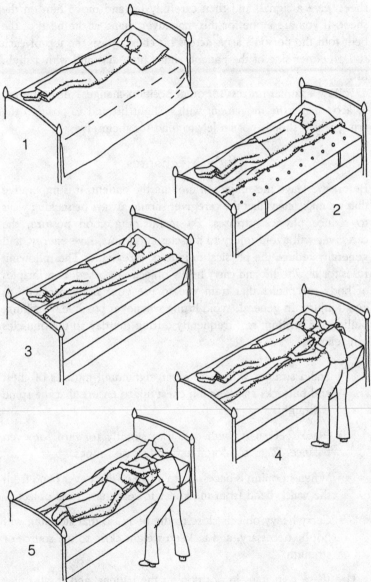

ent, they should stand at either side of the bed, hold the ends of the sheet, give a signal, and then carefully lift and move him on the sheet. If you are alone for this maneuver, stand at the head of the bed, fold the person's arms across his chest, grasp the top of each roll on either side of the patient, signal him, and pull with a slight lift.

Follow a similar process for other position changes, remembering to accompany the movement with a slight lift and to position the arms, which should not be left to fend for themselves.

Body Mechanics

Before we leave the subject of moving the patient, it is imperative that we make clear that the caregiver should always be seeking ways to reduce physical stresses. By maintaining good posture, the caregiver will avoid injury to muscles and joints, save energy, and generally reduce the physical fatigue of caregiving. The following rules for how to lift and carry heavy objects are based on principles of body mechanics that train you to use your body correctly to avoid injury. In general, avoid lifting whenever possible by rolling, pulling, or turning; rest frequently during the day so that muscles can relax.

- Stand straight with head erect, tightening muscles of chest and buttocks and keeping chest up, to ensure that the spine is straight.

- Place feet apart, with one foot slightly forward for even balance. Wear comfortable, firmly based shoes.

- When stooping is necessary to move or lift, never bend from the waist; bend from the knees to reach and raise objects.

- Carry heavy objects close to the body, so that stooping will not be necessary, and to keep weight close to the source of strength.

Use these principles in positioning the patient, and in all other physical activities of caregiving.

TOILET CARE

At first my husband could be walked across the hall to the toilet, which had a six-inch raised seat of plastic. He could grasp the towel rack. I cleaned him after pulling him to a stand. Later I ordered a commode for his bedside. We managed this by swinging his legs over the side of the bed, then pulling him to a sitting position by grasping his hands. When his feet touched the floor I could swivel him a quarter turn to sit on the commode, which had a strong chromium back and arms. He would return to the bed by reversing this maneuver. To protect the bed, I made a drawsheet from cutting a whole sheet in thirds and used a soft plastic sheet under the bottom sheet. In the last two weeks, I used invalid diapers, which my husband never needed but which gave him reassurance. He used a urinal. When he couldn't tolerate the bedpan for a bowel movement I spread several thicknesses of newspaper beneath him, which I could fold and dispose of easily.

For everyone's sake, the patient should continue to use the bathroom for his toilet needs as long as possible. Not only do alternatives surrender some privacy but they are also a reminder that the patient is quite limited in physical range. Not "making the effort" to get out of bed may seem like giving up. Walking on the arm of the caregiver or with the aid of a walker or holding on to a row of chairs—these are some of the many ways independence can be maintained. A point may come when none of these remedies will be enough. Anticipate that this transition will be very tough. Some caregivers struggle for a day or two with trying to arrange to have two people in the house to help the patient, but soon this, too, becomes very difficult.

Alternatives

Several alternatives are recommended for patients who can no longer get to the bathroom. It may be possible to use a bedside commode, either a regular chair with a bedpan flat on the seat or a commode chair. For the person who cannot leave the bed, a variety of bedpans, fracture pans, male urinals, and bottles is available. Call the local medical-supply firm or visiting nurse agency, tell them your specific problem, and ask for suggestions.

If the patient cannot sit up by himself, try to help him to an upright position, which will make elimination easier. Give him privacy by leaving the room if he will be safe from falling or rolling over. Or, you can cover him, or stand behind him or on the other side of a screen. Your imagination and specific demands of the situation will help you toward a solution.

The patient should be cleaned after a bowel movement to prevent irritation and infection. Use soft toilet paper, disposable wipes, or a warm, wet washcloth and mild soap. Make this as simple for both of you as you can, again by using your own good sense and asking for ideas.

If the patient is very thin or has bedsores or for any other reason cannot manage a bedpan, alternatives are available. You can use disposable cotton sheets, diapers with a plastic sheet underneath the patient, or, as more than one caregiver has suggested, newspapers. Remove them when they are soiled, and make sure to wash and dry the person thoroughly. Apply a medicated cream or a "barrier" cream around the anal area to protect him from irritation or infection.

Incontinence and Constipation

For urinary incontinence, several options are possible. First, a catheter can be inserted and its collecting bags made portable, so that if the patient is mobile, or has to be moved, the whole system can travel with him. While this procedure is simple enough to manage at home and can be a good solution, it is not without complications. Some patients feel restricted by the tubing or find its presence intolerable. A confused patient may try to pull it out. Also, any foreign object in the body increases the chance of infection. Talk it over with the patient, weigh the pros and cons, and if you decide to give it a try, do it just for a short while. An alternative for men is a condom-style catheter. Designs change all the time, so it is worth taking the time to call a good medical-supply house and ask about the newest developments.

If incontinence is occurring at the final stage of the illness, the amount of fluid produced may be so small that the discomfort of a catheter would not be worth the "trouble" it saves. You may then wish to use pads between the legs and underneath the patient, changing them frequently. Keep the patient as dry as possible by checking pads, sheets, and nightclothes and changing them as often as necessary.

Because of the nature of the diet (or too little food or fiber), lack of exercise, and the general slowing of body functions, bowel movements may be sluggish or infrequent, causing the patient some concern and discomfort, especially if he is used to being quite regular. Constipation can also precipitate urinary incontinence in a person whose control is fragile. Explain the possible causes, and offer gentle natural laxatives or laxative herbal teas, which are available from health food stores. If the problem persists, your nurse or physician may suggest an enema or suppository. Disposable enemas are safe and easy to use. Ask the visiting nurse how to administer the enema, or follow directions on the package.

In general, try to reduce the patient's anxiety by establishing with the physician a regimen such as: "If there is no bowel movement in forty-eight hours, do XXX procedure; if there is no bowel movement in twelve more hours, do YYY procedure; if this does not produce a result in four hours, call the physician." With a little experimentation, you should be able to work out a regimen that works.

More details about caring for constipation can be found in Chapter 11, "Care of Symptoms."

MOUTH CARE

Dry mouth, fissures of the tongue, and bleeding gums are very painful and typical conditions faced by a dying person, but they can be avoided by careful attention, as can the accompanying embarrassment of bad breath. Keeping up the usual oral hygiene routine will promote general comfort and a sense of well-being and do much toward preventing bad breath and sores. Give the patient equipment, a small cup of water, and a small basin for spitting. If he is unable to brush his own teeth, use a soft child's toothbrush or cotton applicators and do it gently for him, using a mildly flavored toothpaste or hydrogen peroxide mixed with baking soda. If the patient cannot spit, use applicators for cleaning and rinsing. A mouthwash of warm water and a half teaspoon of salt or baking soda in a glass will freshen taste and breath. Observe mouth, teeth, and gums for sores or bleeding. If there is extreme bad breath, consult with the nurse, because it may indicate a medical problem.

If the patient's lips or tongue are dry or blistered, use a finger or cotton swabs to apply petroleum jelly or a mixture of either mineral oil and milk of magnesia or glycerine and lemon. If the mouth is generally sore, use a topical anesthetic such as viscous xylocaine, 2 percent Cetacaine spray, or Cepacol lozenges with or without benzocaine. Follow directions on the package of these preparations for the most effective use. Elixir of Benadryl swished around the mouth and then swallowed also acts as a mild local anesthetic and sedative, as well as a mild deterrent for nausea.

If the patient wears dentures and wants to use them, help him to care for them. You may be tempted to discourage him from using dentures, since they seem a bother, but they probably help him look and feel better and will help in eating. If he becomes unconscious, however, they should be removed.

FOOT CARE

Being in bed or immobile for long periods takes a particularly severe toll on feet, which depend upon activity for proper circulation, especially in older people. If the patient has diabetes, the feet are at even greater risk; consult with the physician for special advice. Encourage exercise by flexing, extending, and twisting the knees, ankles, and toes. One at a time, hold the ankle off the bed and move the foot in a circular motion. Massage the feet firmly to stimulate circulation. In addition, prevent discomfort by cutting nails regularly, keeping feet free of perspiration by using medicated powder, removing dead skin with a pumice stone, and softening skin with a lanolin lotion.

BATHING

Some form of daily bathing is recommended for hygiene as well as a sense of well-being. Even if the actual preparation is slightly disrupting, the patient will usually feel better for the effort.

The location, duration, and degree of assistance needed for bathing will vary with circumstances, which will probably change over the course of care. To the extent that he can help, or even bathe himself in a tub or in bed, let him have the freedom to get the exercise. If the patient is immobile, bathing and drying provide an opportunity to do range-of-motion exercises (see page 127) and for stimulation of joints and muscles. During the bath, watch for changes in skin condition that may have occurred. Red areas that do not fade, breaks in the skin, sensitivity to touch or the flexing of a limb, or anything else that concerns you should be reported immediately to the nurse or physician.

If the patient is not able to leave the bed, use a basin on the bedside table; otherwise, use the tub or shower or sit beside the bathroom sink. Offer the bedpan or toilet before bathing. In any location, keep the patient covered when possible and heat the room. Allow plenty of time, and provide as much privacy as possible. Test the temperature of the water so it is comfortable to your wrist. If you use a basin for a bed or chair bath, change the water several times. Provide mild soap, washcloths, and plenty of towels. A big bath blanket will provide both warmth and privacy. When the patient is clean and dry, apply moisturizing lotion and care for any breaks in the skin. Have the change of clothing nearby. If the patient is bathing himself be discreet but don't go far away. He may tire quickly, so be ready to help him out of the tub and with drying and dressing.

SHAVING

A man will probably want to shave or be shaved every day. Women patients may want to shave legs and underarms. If at all possible, they should do this themselves. Simply supply a basin and mirror. An electric shaver may be best if the patient is not very strong, or if you do the shaving. To use a safety razor, use a favorite lather and a warm washcloth, and take care. The patient will probably want to direct you in shaving a preferred way, so listen for directions. Supply cream or after shave, depending on preference.

SKIN CARE

Adequate fluid and nutritional intake along with frequent turning helps prevent breakdown of the skin. Since these measures will become more difficult as illness progresses, you need to learn alternatives. Massage the skin, especially where bones protrude, using a good moisturing lotion such as Alpha Keri. Sheepskin, a flotation pad, or an air mattress will relieve pressure. Be aware that, if they do form, bedsores will probably not heal, because they are ulcers and the patient no longer has the physical reserves to promote healing. Relief is possible, though, and information about how to care for bedsores and ease their discomfort can be found in Chapters 11 and 12, "Care of Symptoms" and "Pain."

HAIR CARE

Brushing and caring for the hair each day will stimulate circulation in the scalp, feel good, and improve morale and appearance. Try to wash the hair when the patient expresses a desire for it or once a week. If the hair cannot be washed in the sink, shower, or tub but the patient can sit up, ask him to lean over a table. If the patient is bedridden, position him on his back in bed so that his shoulders are on the bed and his head is over the edge, securely supported by your hand or the hands of an assistant. Use a basin to soak and soap the hair, then pour clean water on the hair to fall into a waste pail on the floor. Waterproof sheets will protect the bed and floor. Dry shampoos in spray and powder are simple to use if the patient is just too tired or uncomfortable to move. For patients with very long hair, consider braids or a bun to prevent the discomfort of tangles and mats.

EXERCISE

Any recreation will release anxiety for both patient and caregiver. A focus on some activity outside the illness can be both a release for tension and a temporary relief from worry. If the activity can be in any way physical, it will also stimulate the appetite and promote elimination of body wastes. If the patient is able, drawing, coloring, playing cards or an instrument, writing, or doing a handicraft are beneficial. One patient enjoyed working in soft clay on his over-the-bed table. Even passive activity, such as selecting and listening to music, reading or being read to, watching television, or supervising children playing, serves to exercise the mind and stimulate the senses.

Exercise is widely known to be good for mental as well as physical health. Getting out of bed for meals is an obvious choice and is very good for the spirit as well.

As long as the patient is able to brush his own teeth, care for his hair, feed himself, and go to the toilet, these activities will ensure his independence and provide a beneficial amount of good exercise. People primarily confined to bed but with some mobility are encouraged to have short exercise periods in which they move feet, head, hands, arms, and legs to the best of their ability, alternated with several minutes of imagining a favorite activity, such as swimming or walking.

When a patient reaches the point of virtual immobility, brief sessions of passive exercise—range-of-motion exercise that the caregiver can provide—will help promote comfort, maintain what flexibility is possible, and prevent the stiffness and pain caused by inactivity. Before you undertake any routine, consult the medical people on your team to be advised of possible problems and limits of exercise. The caregiver's time and the person's interest can determine the frequency of the activity; one exercise session is easy to provide in the course of a bed bath.

Before you begin to exercise, talk with the patient about what you are going to do and how he can help. Tell him you will move slowly and steadily, supporting the weight of each body part as you move it. All he needs to do is relax. Tell him you will exercise joints to the extent possible but want to know if anything you are doing hurts him. Untuck sheets and blankets and arrange clothing so that he is warm and covered, but allow enough room to move about.

Each joint has its own natural path of movement, and the aim of passive exercise is to grasp the associated body part firmly and move it surely and slowly in all possible directions. Begin with the neck: grasp the head in two hands and move it from side to side, forward and back, then rotate it from left to right. Repeat these movements several times. Support the upper back with a pillow so that the patient need not bear any weight. Maintain a firm hold of the head throughout the exercise; the patient probably cannot comfortably hold it himself, and you want to build his trust so that these exercises will be relaxing. Apply the same principles to exercise shoulders, elbows, forearms, wrists, fingers, thumbs, hips, legs, knees, ankles, and toes.

Back rubs and massage are good for decreasing tension and provide an ideal opportunity for the patient to be cared for in a more benign and intimate way than other activities of physical care allow. Massage also stimulates circulation, which prevents breakdown of the skin and reduces general pain and aches. Use a good massage oil and keep the person warm as you massage. Make sure to work sore places gently, gearing the pressure you use to her comfort.

BE ALERT

In giving care, you are the closest person to the patient and this carries the responsibility to be watchful as changes occur: fluctuations in breathing, a rise in temperature, or a rapid or slow pulse. Important changes will normally be obvious simply from observing the person: he will be flushed or quite pale, breathing very heavily or intermittently, quiet and withdrawn, or agitated. Usually there is no point in routine taking of temperature, pulse, or blood pressure, but if for some reason the doctor advises you to take vital signs, you can easily learn how from a visiting nurse.

Being alert is an important way to learn about the patient and what might be helpful to him. Changes in physical well-being, his mood, and his description of symptoms and pain may mean thought should be given to a new treatment or an adjustment in medication.

As a matter of security, you may want to have a regular call-in time with the physician to report the patient's condition. However, if at any time you become concerned about a change, do not hesitate to call the nurse or doctor to talk about it and ask for advice.

10
EATING

People feel better when they eat, and this is why we need to be concerned about nutrition for someone who is dying. Many undesirable symptoms can be caused by a poor diet. Malnutrition can lead to skin breakdown, dehydration, bedsores, irritability, constipation, and other discomforts. One of the many benefits of home care is that it offers a dying person the greatest possibilities for attending to diet.

At home, the patient can select his favorite foods, they can be prepared when he is interested in eating, and they can be served in a pleasant and familiar atmosphere. Family members and friends can join in meals. The combination of food he enjoys and the opportunity to spend time with loved ones will probably make him feel better, improve his strength and endurance, and help prevent complications.

Most dying people reach a point where they no longer can or wish to eat solid foods. As the patient becomes less interested in eating, provide her favorite snacks—or anything that is palatable—and don't worry about a balanced diet.

I met with the hospital nutritionist to learn how to prepare a soft and liquid foods diet, because her disease was in her mouth and throat and chewing and swallowing were very painful. Eggnogs, custards, and a daily pint of protein drink were about it. We tried different flavorings, including brandy, but nothing tasted very good. An old family cook brought special soups and soft vegetable dishes. A small glass of wine was suggested to stimulate appetite, but it didn't really work.

Try to suspend any judgment you have about "good nutrition." The usual attitudes about food and how eating promotes health need to be discarded when someone is dying. If the patient is exercising at all, and feeling fairly good, then eating well-balanced meals may be possible; otherwise, whatever he eats will be beneficial. If all he wants is apple juice, or raspberry ice cream, then take the rebuff to your meal-planning gracefully, and serve up gladly what he wants.

Avoid the "eat a little bit more" urge, or any appearance of trying to force a patient to eat. Meals should be pleasant and not opportunities for performance. No one "needs" to have a dying person eat. Allow him as much autonomy as possible over the preparation, selection, amount, and combination of foods, as well as the duration of the meal.

Until the last twenty-four hours, I was able to bring my husband to a sitting position with feet dangling over the side of the bed to eat. I served his meals, which gradually became only a few mouthfuls. He fed himself from a tray table. His lack of appetite and increasing weakness alarmed me. I tried many kinds of enticing foods, but he lost his sense of taste. In the last two weeks all he had was liquids.

Dying people worry about their diet and sense the concern of others about it. A common tendency is to think, "If only I could eat, I would get better." Keep this fear in mind when a patient is agitated about not eating, and reassure him that missing a meal is all right. Another attitude to guard against is fatalism. Family and even nurses know intellectually that the person will die regardless of what he eats. But when someone says of the patient, "He hasn't eaten in days," avoid the temptation to respond with some version of "It doesn't matter; he is going to die anyway," even though it may be on your mind. Optimism in each small task of caregiving is important for everyone.

For some, it is over this very issue of nourishment that the truth the person is not going to get well is confronted. Since everyone shares the myth that nourishment means recovery and good health, relaxing about food may bring into sharp focus the reality of his prognosis. Make sure that individuals who are seeing this truth for the first time have a chance to talk, ask questions, and express their feelings fully.

Be aware that even if the patient does eat, her body's use of food is probably not optimum. She may have poor absorption of vital nutrients, an intestinal blockage, or metabolic disturbance. Some of the physical symptoms of her disease—feeling full or bloated, fatigue, general depletion—will act against her enjoyment of a meal. In addition, depression and anxiety, radiation and chemotherapy treatments, and other emotional and physical complications will affect eating desires and habits. Radiation can destroy flavors, change the way things taste, and result in enough pain that appetite is reduced. Chemotherapy causes nausea, vomiting, loss of taste, and pain. Surgery or the disease itself may affect some element of the digestive tract: mouth, throat, stomach, or bowel. Remember, the body controls appetite to allow only what it can handle. If liver or renal weakness is a factor, for example, too much food will create discomfort; with other conditions, too much water can cause problems. Appetite often does not fare well with illness for good reason.

Your medical team can help anticipate how appetite may be affected by these variables, advise about ways to counteract these effects, and provide information you can use to help the dying person with food. For example, studies have shown that a strong correlation exists between taste and experience. Whatever a person eats before chemotherapy he may never want to eat again. Foods that were favorites—sweets, meat—may now taste bad or have no taste at all. By listening well and asking questions, you can learn what he would and would not be willing to try.

Although chances are the patient's food preferences and mealtimes will be difficult to incorporate into the family routine, try to encourage him to continue to eat when the family does. This will help him stay connected to others and orient him to times of day.

Whatever your situation, don't let food become a battleground. Cajoling or forcing the patient to eat will only make him more anxious and alienated. Planning food, preparing it, and eating can be pleasurable if done in a positive spirit.

EAT WELL

Within the limits of what the patient will tolerate, a high-calorie, high-protein diet is the most beneficial for maintaining weight, proper chemical and fluid balances, and a feeling of being nourished. Ask your doctor if vitamin or other nutritional supplements would promote comfort. Do what you can to entice the patient to eat, beginning with providing his favorite foods and flavors. If there are snacks and desserts which have been off limits in the past for weight control, now is the time to dig out the recipes and serve them up. Yogurt, cheese, peanut butter, nuts, lunch meats, and sandwich fillings are some choices, and treats made of cheese, eggs, and milk are good sources of protein and calories. Add skim milk powder to cakes, breads, puddings, and gelatin desserts.

For cancer patients, proteins found in meat, eggs, poultry, fish, legumes, whole grains, milk, and other dairy products help repair tissue that has been damaged by treatments. Anemia commonly occurs with cancer, and concentrating on iron-rich foods such as liver, egg yolks, meats and seafood, whole grains, green leafy vegetables, legumes, dried fruits, and nuts will help restore energy.

The patient may not tolerate this regimen, in which case the goal should simply be to keep her from becoming seriously dehydrated and provide foods that she will find acceptable enough to eat, be able to swallow, and retain in the body long enough to absorb a sufficient quantity of calories, proteins, vitamins, and minerals. Calories are more important than a balanced diet: the patient should have all the ice cream she wants.

Small meals with high-protein snacks in between may result in a greater protein and calorie intake than trying to serve three "well-balanced" meals each day. Have foods handy that the patient likes and that can be prepared quickly. Keep a snack at the bedside like a milkshake or protein-supplement drink that can be sipped over several hours.

Liquid protein supplements can also be used as snacks to augment the nutritive value of meals. Supplements are available at drugstores without prescription. Some are in powdered form to be mixed with milk; a number come in different flavors, or flavors can be added to them. Your doctor may recommend one brand over another or suggest that you look for certain vitamin contents. Supplements normally taste better cold; if they are milk-based, they should not be left at room temperature too long. Experiment and see which variety the patient prefers. Adding a raw egg, mixed in very well, or ice cream, whipped cream, nonfat dry milk, or yogurt will give them more flavor and add protein.

While these manufactured protein supplements save time, they are expensive and usually "homemade" variants taste better. Experiment with blended mixtures of yogurt, eggs, ice cream, milk or powdered milk, fruit juice, wheat germ, bananas, honey, and the like to concoct a high-calorie, high-protein supplement. Instant breakfast preparations, high-protein powders, and brewer's yeast added to blender mixtures also boost nutrition and calories.

Use *double-strength milk* when making a liquid preparation in place of water: add one cup of dried skim milk to a quart of whole milk, or make powdered milk with milk instead of water. Mix very well and strain out any lumps. Double-strength milk as an ingredient will improve benefits of soups, cereals, desserts, creamed foods, mashed potatoes, or any combination of fruits.

CHEWING DIFFICULTY

Many dying people have various difficulties with chewing and swallowing, owing to the disease, treatments, and other causes. If eating solid foods is painful for the patient, resist the temptation to puree everything unless absolutely necessary. With some thought and care, most foods can be prepared in a way that is manageable for the person but not limited in variety, texture, taste, and appearance. Meats can be cut into small pieces or ground, then creamed, combined with noodles or rice, or used in a hearty stew. Fish is soft when baked, or use it in creamed or casserole dishes. Cheese can be grated and used as sauce or melted over vegetables. Make soups with meats, beans, rice; for extra protein, drop in an egg or add strained baby meats. Fresh fruits and vegetables may be served by mashing, shredding, fine-chopping, or using a blender or food processor; cooked fruits and vegetables can be served chopped or mashed. Cooked cereals, ready-to-eat cereals, and toast can be served with milk. If these techniques fail and you must resort to pureeing, use a blender or a food processor, which will turn anything into soft or liquid form. Freeze soft foods in ice cube trays to serve at subsequent meals.

Because the patient will probably at some point either prefer or require food in liquid form, try to develop a repertory of liquid snacks. If lumps present problems, a strainer or cheesecloth over the serving cup will catch pieces the patient may choke on. Use eggs, fruits, juices, milk, wheat germ, vegetables, ice cream, yogurt, and other foods the patient likes in combinations that can be prepared in liquid form. Add seasonings such as chocolate, vanilla, fruit flavors, mint, and cinnamon. Snacks can be served hot, cold, or frozen, depending on the season or the mood of the patient. Serve them in small amounts of one-half cup to one cup.

MAKE MEALS PLEASANT

You can encourage a patient's appetite by taking special care in the selection, preparation, and serving of food. Begin by considering various appliances and special utensils that make food preparation and eating easier. A toaster oven, juicer, ice crusher, and blender or food processor will help in the kitchen. For the bedside, a bed tray, cup with no-spill top, coffee mug, straws, and dishes that keep foods warm will help with serving. If the patient is active or dishes slide on the tray, use a rubber mat or dishes that have suction cups. Keep a thermos of her favorite high-protein drink by the bed. A hot plate in the room will allow the caregiver and visitors to serve the patient and themselves without leaving the room.

Here are some guidelines gathered from experiences others have had with caregiving. Translate these ideas into your particular situation and the patient's abilities and personality. Caregivers said experimentation often provided a welcome change and when rewarded by the compliment, "good meal," was very satisfying.

Before mealtime:

- Arrange pain medication schedule so that the patient will be comfortable at mealtime. Although some medications are intended to be given at mealtime, when possible keep food and medicines separate.

- Offer the bedpan, and let the patient wash her face and hands with a warm, wet washcloth.

- If at all possible have her change position, sit on the edge of the bed, sit at a table or chair in her own room with her back to the bed, or move to another room. If she cannot move, tidy the bed area, smooth sheets, and adjust the backrest.

- Serve a small glass of white wine or sherry to stimulate the appetite (check first with your physician to ensure that alcohol will not react badly with other medication).

Selection of foods:

- Have the person choose what he wants, and be flexible and inventive with foods he likes.

- Use familiar family recipes.

- If the patient no longer enjoys foods he used to love, try new foods or combinations, since taste has probably been altered by medication and treatments.

- Plan a meal that looks good, with a mixture of colors and textures.

- Avoid foods the smell or sight of which the patient has shown he cannot tolerate.

- Avoid tart, acid, spicy, or highly seasoned foods.

Preparation:

- Keep the kitchen door shut and windows open to eliminate odors. The smell of food cooking, especially the smell of red meats, can make the person feel nauseated.

- Select foods that will help and not irritate troublesome symptoms, such as constipation, diarrhea, and nausea (see Chapter 11, "Care of Symptoms," for specifics of foods to encourage or avoid).

- Use mild distinctive seasonings such as lemon juice, basil, mint, and particular favorites to improve taste and aroma.

Serving meals:

- Serve foods in familiar dishes; avoid extremes in temperatures.

- Serve small meals and small portions so the patient can clean her plate; offer second helpings on request.

- Make sure the bed tray or table is clean and attractive, and include a flower or card. Try playing background music.

- Serve food at regular intervals, not only when the person says she is hungry.

- Create a mealtime atmosphere and, if others are in the room, avoid alcohol, cigarettes, and other smells that detract from eating.

Mealtime:

- Be sensitive to the patient's desire to do as much as he can by himself. Buttering, pouring tea, cutting, salting, and eating should be done by him alone if possible. Let him arrange his dishes and place his napkin.

- When you help, do not use a bib or scrape his chin with a spoon. Ask his advice before you do anything to assist. If others are around, be discreet in preparation: for example, cut food in the kitchen.

- Eat with the patient when possible, and eat what he eats. Pay attention to him, don't rush, and be sensitive to signs that he is feeling too ill to continue, or needs help.

- If the patient is insisting on being fed, and you know he could be feeding himself, it is probably a sign that he could use more attention. Try to provide visitors as an antidote, so that he will be encouraged to retain autonomy over eating.

- Don't criticize the patient when removing unfinished or unwanted servings.

FEEDING A PATIENT

Usually toward the end of the patient's life, his strength, coordination, disorientation, and other factors make eating difficult or impossible. More and more assistance will be necessary.

When you are going to feed the patient, prepare for the meal in the same way that has worked when the patient was feeding herself. As long as she is able to eat or drink anything independently, using fingers, a straw or a cup, make sure to provide some foods each meal that she can manage herself. Before you begin, make sure the patient can swallow and that you have her attention and cooperation. Allow plenty of time so you won't be rushed. Make sure the food is a comfortable temperature, and then serve it in small amounts to avoid choking. Do what is possible to make your help easy for the patient to accept, by letting her guide your hand, signal when she is ready for more, and tell you what she wants to eat.

For spoon-feeding, fill the spoon two-thirds full, scrape off the underside of its bowl, touch the spoon to the patient's lower lip, and tilt upward to allow the food to run into the mouth. Make sure she has plenty of time to swallow before serving the next portion. If she is able to eat by sucking through a straw, place one end in her mouth and the other under the surface of the liquid so that no air is swallowed. If she can drink from a cup, support her head by putting your arm under the pillow on which her head is resting. Hold the cup, allowing her to guide it to drink at her own pace. Alternate flavors, and if the patient is eating some solid food, alternate liquids with solids. If the patient cannot see, tell her what each mouthful is. After the meal is finished, remove food and implements, wash the patient's face and hands, and provide for dental care.

Books and theories on nutrition, diets, food, healing, and related subjects abound; check your local library or bookstore if you want to read further. If it does not become a source of conflict, eating can be satisfying, social, and a support for the patient's comfort. Ask for all the help you need from the doctors, nurses, and hospital or community nutritionists to make eating as pleasurable and healthful as it can be.

11
CARE
OF SYMPTOMS

We cannot repeat too often that the whole key to caring for someone dying is to pay meticulous attention to every detail of the patient's well-being. This means ministering to the multiple general miseries of dying, including mouth sores, discomfort from lying immobile, catheters and other tubes, nausea, lack of appetite and malnutrition, secondary infection, heartburn, abdominal distention, constipation, incontinence, itching, bedsores, shortness of breath, difficulty with vision, and body odors.

This chapter is concerned with treating these physical symptoms of dying. While considered "secondary" to symptoms caused by the illness, they often create greater discomfort. Attention to them is called palliative care. Such care is not simply hand-holding, nor does it mean turning your back on medicine. Its purpose is not to render the patient passive or euphoric or to find the drug that will provide relief by taking away awareness. The goal is to give the patient back his life from the doldrums of pain.

Palliative care depends on the willingness to listen and attend to each ache and pain. Some patients are able to describe them in such a way that you know what needs to be done; others are not, and so you must rely on observation and asking questions. Some symptoms are more easily identified than others. As you care for one symptom, another will probably occur or become clearer. As each appears, inquire about it and take action. If one solution doesn't work, seek out and try another.

Palliative care is an ongoing process. Attention to symptoms will probably be necessary until the moment of death, and recalling the little victories of such care is often a source of peace for the survivors.

> I guess what helps me the most is knowing I did everything I could and that as we figured out ways to make her comfortable we got closer. It was really a good experience. All the little tricks I learned—padding her bed with sheepskin, arranging pillows, making a frame to keep blankets from touching her sore feet, giving medication so it didn't hurt her mouth—showed me I could really make a difference.

What follows is a list of typical symptoms that plague someone dying, with ideas about how to ease them. Try out the suggestions, but don't stop there if the patient is still uncomfortable. Ask people on your team for help.

THIRST AND DEHYDRATION

Many patients have trouble swallowing, don't have the energy to ask for enough liquid, or for some other reason become dehydrated. Encourage the patient to drink plenty of liquids, since adequate fluid level in the body will promote comfort. Some drink a lot of water, others very little. If the patient will drink liquids that are nutritious, such as milk, eggnog, protein drinks, and fruit juices, so much the better. If she prefers soft drinks, provide all she wants.

Even though the patient may be very thirsty, he may not be well enough to recognize that sucking or sipping would relieve discomfort. When he cannot take liquids independently, special care is necessary. Use a mouthwash every two hours, and lip salve or Vaseline frequently to prevent chapped lips. Remove encrustations and swab the mouth with a gauze swab soaked in a water-soluble lubricant recommended by your pharmacist. Lemon or other citrus candies, pineapple chunks, and artificial saliva will stimulate saliva production. Remove dentures or other foreign objects because they will irritate the mouth. Ice chips, sips of a favorite beverage, or frozen slushes should be given as often as the patient will take them. If the patient cannot sip, try various methods of administering liquids, including straws or eyedroppers. Be sure to tell the patient what you are doing so you have her attention and compliance.

If in addition to dry mouth or dehydration the patient has unusually bad breath, or you detect something unusual in the mouth, consult the nurse; there are a number of conditions that can be treated with a topical anesthetic and mouthwashes or solutions containing chlorophyll.

If the patient is unable to swallow liquids on her own, intravenous (IV) feedings to improve fluid levels can be arranged at home, although few people elect to do so. Another option is for the patient to spend several days or hours in a hospital for this purpose. Since IV treatments may prolong life, the decision for an IV should be made in discussion with the doctor, patient, and family. The doctor may suggest other ways to ease the discomfort. Families often observe and accept that the patient's willingness and ability to take in nourishment diminishes as her illness progresses. As a person comes closer to death, the body slowly stops nourishing itself.

SWALLOWING DIFFICULTY

Dry or sore mouth or throat can make swallowing excruciatingly painful. Soften and moisten foods by dipping them in coffee, tea, milk, or broth; melted butter, gravy, cream, and cream sauce are also good moisteners. Soft and liquid foods should be fed slowly or may even be frozen onto a stick. While some use a syringe successfully, nurses are apt to discourage its use because a weakened patient may inhale the liquid. Have the patient take a swallow of beverage before each bite of food. Discomfort from swallowing can also be eased by using a straw or tilting the head back. Water can be offered as ice chips or in a damp sponge placed against the lips. Soothe the throat with slushes, watermelon, or ice cream. Stimulate saliva production by having the patient suck candy or mints. Rinse the mouth frequently to keep it moist, especially before meals, with a solution of a half teaspoon of salt and one teaspoon of baking soda to one quart water.

ANEMIA

Many dying people, especially those with cancer, will be prone to anemia and its accompanying fatigue. A diet high in iron and proteins is suggested and your physician may recommend a vitamin supplement. This condition is probably not fully correctible, however, since it is rarely caused by deficiencies in the diet, but by treatments and the disease. Do what you can to encourage and help the patient to eat, and serve small, frequent meals.

NAUSEA

Vomiting and nausea may be caused by the disease or anxiety or be a side effect of treatments. Your physician can suggest drugs to counteract nausea, changing to other medications, and an antiemetic in the pain mixture.

An effective way to combat an upset stomach is through careful meal planning. Try small meals every two to three hours. Serve carbonated beverages, like cola, ginger ale, club soda, or spring water; let them stand for a short time before drinking so they lose some carbonation. Avoid sweet foods; try salty foods, dry crackers, and toast. If the smell of certain foods is a problem, do your best to keep odors in the kitchen. Eat plain foods that are boiled, steamed, baked or broiled; keep fatty or fried foods to a minimum. Use prepared foods that can be warmed in a low oven or do not require cooking at all, such as cottage cheese, cold meats, sandwiches, fruit. Encourage the patient to relax, eat slowly, and chew foods thoroughly to minimize the effects of a tense stomach. Have her drink clear, cool liquids an hour before or an hour after meals to keep low the amount of food in the stomach. Review Chapter 10, "Eating," for further ideas.

Various herbs, such as peppermint and chamomile, may be helpful in teas. Some have found marijuana useful in easing nausea, balancing side effects of drugs, and stimulating appetite. Be sure to obtain marijuana through friends who know its purity, subject to the legal restrictions of your state. If the patient cannot smoke, the drug can be cooked in foods. If this is all unfamiliar to you, seek advice. Your physician may be helpful, but will probably leave you to your own resources. While some patients respond very well to reassurance, careful diet, and antacids or other drug treatments, others who cannot tolerate food at all may finally have to take only soda water or suck plain or flavored water frozen in a manageable size on a stick. Whatever the patient is able to eat and retain will keep him more comfortable than going without food.

CONSTIPATION

A lower intake of fluids, inactivity, medications, and insufficient nourishment are likely to result in the patient's not maintaining his usual bowel schedule. This change may be more upsetting to the patient than you expect. Older patients may even become frightened by this change in a lifetime habit. Caregivers should reassure patients that daily elimination is not necessary since diet and activity level have changed. However, if the patient complains of bloating, cramping, and discomfort or has a hard abdomen, you can ask the physician for help.

The problems of severe constipation are easier to prevent than to cure. Plan ahead by having the physician describe for you a regimen to follow, beginning with whatever dietary supplements—such as bran and other roughage—the patient can tolerate. Encourage him to drink fluids. Follow his usual toilet schedule, giving him all possible privacy, and providing whatever he suggests may help him move his bowels. Let him know you want to help and listen to his complaints; the patient may have trouble because of his physical condition or because the act of moving his bowels itself creates pain.

If recommended, commercially prepared enemas are readily available and easily administered, following directions on the package. Glycerine suppositories act to stimulate the bowel and can be used at the same time every day to help the patient keep a schedule if this eases his mind. Stool softeners and agents that attract moisture to the intestines are other solutions. Some caregivers have found that a slight increase in pain medication timed to give the patient extra relief so that a suppository can be administered comfortably solves the problem of pain experienced with a bowel movement. Again, consult your medical team before you use any of these preparations.

DIARRHEA AND CRAMPS

Among the many troubles a dying person experiences within his stomach and intestines is diarrhea, gas, and cramping. Limit foods that produce discomfort, such as carbonated beverages, some spices, artificial sweeteners, gum, cabbage, beans, and onions. Limit cold beverages and ice in beverages. Serve low-fiber food.

If the patient has persistent loose or uncontrollable bowel movements, ask the physician's advice. Make sure the bed is well protected with Chux or papers that can be easily removed. Keep the patient clean and dry, and use lanolin lotion or a barrier cream such as Peri-Anal to prevent skin irritation.

BLEEDING

Although bleeding seldom occurs, your team can be prepared for the possibility. If the patient begins hemorrhaging, try to keep calm and apply an ice pack or pressure to the location as quickly as you can. A good supply of Chux and tissues should be at hand so that you can dispose of blood cleanly and efficiently. Try to prevent the patient from being aware of the quantity of blood lost. While you may feel more comfortable calling your physician when bleeding occurs, probably little more can be done for the patient than what you do at home. If the bleeding is severe or continuous, it may be frightening to the patient or family, and you may want to consider a short period of hospitalization. Admittance to the hospital will probably not be necessary for the patient to have a transfusion, if this is desired. Your doctor can arrange for the patient to receive blood as an outpatient in a local medical facility.

FEVER

If the patient is comfortable, you probably need not be concerned with fever, since measures you may take to control it can be disturbing to him. If the patient is not comfortable, consult your physician about treating the fever. Sponging, giving fluids as often as possible, and administering acetaminophen or aspirin, will help control temperature. The patient will probably alternate sensations of hot and cold, so be prepared to cover and uncover him. A light covering is advisable at minimum. When he cannot seem to get warm enough, lying beside and holding him can be a wonderful comfort.

SEIZURES

Although the possibility of seizures is remote, fear of them is common to both patients and caregivers. Learn from the doctor whether or not they are a likelihood, how to recognize signs, and what precautions to take. If you observe jerky, uncoordinated movements—early indications of seizure—your physician may want to provide an anticonvulsive drug to reduce chances of a major episode. Because this medication has a sedating effect, however, patients may choose a minimal dose and slight seizure activity, gambling on the likelihood of a more serious episode in the interest of maintaining alertness. Ask your physician if there is a drug you should have on hand in the event that a major seizure occurs.

If the patient has a seizure, turn her head to the side to prevent her from strangling from secretions in her mouth and throat. Protect her from sharp objects, falling off the bed, or harming herself in some other way. She may be incontinent and lose consciousness briefly and will probably be quite drowsy afterward. A seizure should not last more than two to five minutes. If it continues, call the physician. A drug can be administered that will stop the seizure.

BEDSORES

Perhaps the most persistent problem of dying is the susceptibility to bedsores, which are caused by confinement and inactivity. Although in view of the patient's general health they may seem trivial, bedsores are extremely painful and can create more misery than the disease itself. Since the patient has little resistance to infection, they can also lead to more serious complications. Bedsores are caused by constant pressure, poor nutrition and dehydration, and a general rundown condition. Circulation is sluggish, the patient is usually thin, and body tissue has no resistance. Particularly susceptible are prominent parts of the body—the tailbone, ankles, heels, shoulders, elbows, and hips—where the pressure of weight decreases blood flow and therefore food supply to that particular area of skin.

Again, preventive care is infinitely valuable. A firm mattress that provides for even distribution of body weight is desirable, especially when used in conjunction with foam rubber doughnuts to keep pressure off trouble spots. Alternating air mattresses, water beds and water mattresses, and anything else recommended for distributing weight are worth considering. Smooth out wrinkles in the bedding, and see that folds of the drawsheet do not irritate the skin. Washable sheepskin with the woolly side placed next to the patient's skin, or chamois placed under the affected part of the body —such as the hip, shoulder, or ankle—will help absorb moisture, relieve pressure, and protect the skin from irritation. Have several of the leather skins on hand, since they must be changed often and need to be air-dried for softness.

Change the patient's position every two or three hours, massaging those areas most recently under pressure. Getting the patient to shift from his favorite, and probably most comfortable, position is more difficult than you may imagine. Often caregivers give in to the patient's need for rest or his resistance, thinking this is the most humane treatment. However, this is one aspect of care to which you and other caregivers really should apply the word "must."

When you shift the position, look for red marks. If they are apparent and do not disappear within a minute, gently rub them with lanolin lotion to stimulate circulation until the redness disappears. Baths and back rubs also help with circulation. Make sure folds of skin are dry, especially if the patient is sweating.

Products sold at the local drugstore can also help. Applying powders and lotions assists with keeping the patient clean and dry, a major preventive measure. Toughen red or susceptible spots with tincture of benzoin, which is sticky, but preferable to an open sore. Skin that is dry and cracking, and the area around the site of a recent operation, should be lubricated with vitamin E lotion, Betadyne, Vaseline, or lanolin lotion.

If you notice that a persistent red spot does not go away with massage, dab the stomach de-acidifier Maalox or another recommended preparation on the spot, and do everything possible to keep weight off that area. Wash the area twice a day with mild soap and warm water, taking care to dry the skin thoroughly, and reapply the Maalox. If it seems to be getting worse, ask one of your health professionals for advice. If a break appears in the skin, report it immediately so that treatment can begin.

ULCER

When the patient has a skin sore or ulcer, special solutions and dressing will be required, and your visiting nurse will advise you on the necessary routine. A regular bath or shower helps the patient feel better and reduce odor. If a smell becomes particularly unpleasant, you may want to use charcoal pads or a room deodorizer.

ITCHING

A constant sensation of itching can happen because of skin breakdown, medication, or any number of other causes. A patient can feel quite crazed by this symptom if it goes unrelieved. Use lanolin lotion in caring for the skin; Caladryl lotion may provide some anesthetic relief. The physician will be able to prescribe medication or a topical cream if discomfort continues.

BREATHING DIFFICULTY

A dying person's respiration may be irregular or labored, and even pause occasionally. He may not necessarily be distressed or even aware of the changes. Whether or not the patient is worried, caregivers should remain calm to prevent the patient's becoming frightened. If you do notice the patient gasping for air or otherwise experiencing trouble with breathing, gently bringing him to an upright position with pillows, or holding him in a sitting posture may alleviate his distress. If the physician has advised oxygen, learn how to use it and when it should be administered. Because increasing the humidity in the room will help with loosening fluid blockages, you may want to borrow or purchase a humidifier or vaporizer. Suctioning will keep airways clear and prevent choking, but this is an uncomfortable procedure and may prolong life. As with other such decisions, you, the patient, and the physician may want to discuss the options.

AIRWAY SECRETIONS

The patient may develop secretions in her throat or a rattling sound, which may or may not trouble her. You have heard this referred to as the death rattle. Family and caregivers may find the noise very disturbing. A variety of drugs can treat this condition, depending on its cause. Keep calm and reassure the patient if she is frightened, providing fresh air and positioning her in a comfortable, raised posture.

HICCUPS

Because of general turbulence in all the body's systems, one of the reactions can be hiccups. If this occurs, have the patient rebreathe air into a paper bag, hold his breath, or use whatever other family remedy has worked in the past. If this does not relieve the symptom, consult your physician, who may want to prescribe a medication such as Valium.

CONFUSION AND RESTLESSNESS

For any number of reasons, including the disease, emotional upset, and medications, the patient may be agitated or lose sense of present reality. He may not understand what he is doing, or what time it is, or who people are. He may be fidgeting or wanting to climb out of bed. This behavior can be difficult for caregivers. Ask your physician to recommend any of various drug treatments to help with the sense of disorientation or with restlessness. Interaction with other people often has the greatest benefit. Draw the patient's attention to objects around him that are familiar. Keep photographs nearby. Put a calendar and a large clock with a lighted face near him. If he can be near a window, sit and point out people and simple activities on the street. Gently and repeatedly identify the time and day or a familiar event that will soon take place. Give the patient a visual tour of his surroundings, guiding him around the room with his eyes. Hold a little celebration commemorating an event he remembers. If the patient continues to be restless, ask what you can do to help him relax, then try having him breathe slowly with you, and listen to his breath.

HALLUCINATION

As the body and its chemistry break down, and because of medications and other factors, it is not unusual for some hallucination to occur. If a patient seems clearly to be hallucinating, do not try to humor her, because she is probably rational enough to be aware of what is happening. If you ignore it or say she can't possibly be imagining things, she will become anxious. Correct her gently by describing whatever is really there, explaining she is imagining the problem, and that medication is probably responsible for her confusion. Advise the physician of the patient's symptoms so he can consider medication alternatives or treatments.

INSOMNIA

If the patient has trouble sleeping, try to determine what physical or emotional distresses may be responsible, and try to have the patient talk about them. He may fear sleep and need companionship at sleep times. Drugs can help, and it is important to keep to the most effective schedule for pain medication. Your physician may recommend a sedative or some change in the routine narcotic dose if the patient is unable to sleep through the night because of pain. Other solutions may be a well-timed bedpan, a warm water bottle, alcohol, soft music, a hot milk drink, quiet and shaded light, changing position, or a back rub.

Remember to take the patient's symptoms and each expression of distress seriously. How the patient feels right now, today, is all that matters. Your attitude of attention, and willingness to take action and try solutions until relief is felt, will provide more comfort than any specific application of care.

12
PAIN

___

As far back as I could remember, my grandmother had prided herself on taking the minimum amount of medication recommended. "You never know when you might really need it," she'd say, breaking an aspirin in half. She should have been able to collect on all those undermedicated headaches.

The last month of her life, all we could think about was her pain. We hammered pills to a powder to mix them with applesauce when she could no longer swallow them. Then we switched to medication available in liquid form and fed her with an eyedropper. Gradually the difficulty with swallowing increased, and even when we switched to injections, pain was not controlled.

"You are all liars," she said to the doctor. We pleaded for stronger medication, not knowing what was available or even what relief could be expected. He repeated, "We have to be patient, these things [meaning *dying*] take time, we don't want to give her anything that might be addictive or put a strain on her heart." I remember following him down the stairs, screaming, *"What are you saving her for?"* We argued about dosages and frequencies for the next three weeks until she died. "I know what you are asking me to do," he would say in accusation. I wanted to free her from pain, whatever kind it was. I knew she wanted to be free of pain, whatever that relief precipitated.

Even now, I see her face with jaw set, teary red eyes. "I want to die," she would say in a voice that was not hers but pain talking through phlegm and a throat so sore she could no longer swallow. In the still house, long after she died, I could hear the repeated moans, "Help me, help me," as in refrain of the last chorus.

This true account of unsuccessful pain management was the impetus for writing this book. Soon after my grandmother died, I talked with health care professionals about the experience of caring for her and my frustration at not being able to convince her doctor that more or different medication was needed. In these informal interviews, I came to realize that my despair over her discomfort, our respect and even fear of doctors, and the isolation of home care as I had experienced it had all achieved the effect of immobilizing me from pursuing satisfactory solutions to her needs. Since I had been overwhelmed by the circumstances, I figured that others experienced the same frustration and could benefit from some facts and support.

I soon learned the greatest fear most people have about undertaking home care is that they will not be able to control pain. Anticipation of this failure can make even the patient's slightest twinge a source of unbearable anxiety. But with proper preparation—gathering information and the necessary medication—and continued vigilance, chances are very good that pain can be controlled, and without leaving home.

In fact, many people become increasingly comfortable in home care. As the patient resolves relationships, relaxes in his own home, and is assured of caring and attention, he often feels better. One caregiver said her husband seemed in the last few weeks to be unaccountably more comfortable. "There weren't any changes in medication and the doctor couldn't explain what had happened. When I asked him if he was comfortable, he said, smiling, 'Yes, why not?' "

Any amount of pain suffered by a human being is too much pain; terminal pain especially has no purpose or justification. Nothing is to be gained from experiencing it, either physically or spiritually. Though we are all accustomed to speaking of the bravery of a patient who suffered in her dying, families and patients must confront and refute this myth for what it is. As friends and relatives, we must be determined to seek and serve the comfort possible for every dying person with the proper care and medication. "Suffering builds character" has no place here, nor does the attitude that because pain may not appear to have an obvious cause it can be disregarded as "just emotional."

Proper medical care in terminal illness is providing drugs sufficient for comfort, and with few exceptions nearly everyone can be made comfortable. Medication, including narcotics, should be given in frequencies that anticipate pain, and in sufficient doses to reflect the decision that pain relief is not merely a goal, but *the* goal. In this way, severe pain is not allowed to become entrenched; as a result, for most patients general comfort will be managed with the lowest possible doses of drugs. Many patients want to be as alert as possible and this means carefully monitoring drugs and comfort for the best balance.

ERRORS IN PAIN MANAGEMENT

Because of the changing dynamics of pain, it isn't sufficient to settle on a program for pain control and then blindly follow it. If at any point during the regimen you've established the patient becomes uncomfortable, all expertise must be summoned to assess and, if necessary, revise your strategy. Options should always be examined, and the following stories, which are all too common, offer good examples of what happens when they are not:

Our doctor, in consultation with a Boston specialist, agreed to maximum doses of Prednisone, which my husband could tolerate more than other drugs, although he had uncomfortable side effects from swelling. He had occasional severe leg pain which was treated with Darvon. As time passed, the leg pains became more frequent. I could support my husband walking with my hands under his armpits, to a chair where he could be more comfortable. Darvon took an hour to bring relief. Then I would walk him back to his bed. In the last six weeks, he was too weak to make the trip so he had to bravely endure the pain until Darvon took over. I would sit and talk quietly to divert him. Looking back, I wish I had pressed the doctor for a better solution to his pain so he wouldn't have had so many long hours.

Pain medication was often inadequate, and I have never been satisfied by the doctor's explanation for that. The hospital provided good telephone advice. We kept the house warm and my wife took diligent care of her colostomy. I believe that our love alleviated the pain. But I still think she was more uncomfortable than she should have been.

What are the reasons that pain is not treated successfully? In most cases, the fault lies mainly in not enough discussion and an unwillingness on the part of the dying person, family, and medical professionals to try out the different solutions. Dr. Robert Twycross, a British physician who has devoted much of his career to advancing pain relief methods and is a colleague of hospice pioneer Dr. Cicely Saunders, believes in educating families and medical professionals. He describes some of the erroneous attitudes, insufficient communication, and misguided actions that lead to unsatisfactory pain management.

Mistakes made by the patient and family:

- Patient believes that pain is inevitable and untreatable.

- Patient fails to contact doctor.

- Patient misleads doctor by "putting on a brave face," or family places false emphasis on the patient's "courage."

- Patient fails to accept or take prescribed medication or does not "believe" in drugs.

- Belief by patient or family that one should only take medication "if absolutely necessary," not knowing now is the time.

- Noncompliance because patient or family fears "addiction."

- Noncompliance because of a belief that tolerance will rapidly develop, leaving nothing "for when things get really bad."

- Patient stops medication because of side effects and fails to notify doctor.

Mistakes made by the doctor and/or nurse:

- Doctor ignores patient's pain believing it is inevitable.

- Doctor does not appreciate the intensity of patient's pain; fails to get behind the "brave face," or challenge the family's pride in his "courage."

- Doctor prescribes a drug that is too weak to relieve much or any of the pain.

- Doctor prescribes medication to be taken "as required."

- Doctor fails to know or inquire about combinations of medications and doses necessary to relieve pain.

- Doctor fails to give patient adequate instructions about how best to use medications.

- When necessary to switch from one medication to another, doctor is not aware of equivalent doses necessary to maintain relief.

- Doctor fears patient will become "addicted" if a narcotic is prescribed.

- Doctor regards morphine and heroin as drugs to be reserved until the patient is "really terminal," and continues to prescribe inadequate doses of less successful drugs.

- Doctor fails to institute adequate follow-up to monitor patient's pain and response to medication.

- Doctor has lack of knowledge about other drugs that can be used with narcotics to make them more effective.

- Doctor fails to suggest nondrug solutions to pain when appropriate.

- Doctor fails to give adequate emotional support to the patient and family.

As drugs improve and more information is assimilated about how they work, physicians are becoming more confident about caring for terminal illness and its suffering. Assuming the home care team and patient are agreed that comfort is the primary goal, the challenge becomes clear: to relieve the dying person of distress. When possible, most want to be liberated from their pain but also clear-headed enough to be present in their lives.

WHAT IS PAIN?

Pain is a subjective complex sensation that can have physical, emotional, spiritual, and social aspects. The dying person hurts physically, of course, but she is also anxious and sad or depressed. She is troubled by her own suffering and may be wondering how she can endure it and what it means to her life. She is concerned about the future for her spouse, children, and friends. Each facet of her pain is important, and caring for each begins with listening. A patient's word on the subject of pain should be taken as final, and our task is to understand it in order to help.

The sensation of pain begins when certain nerves are stimulated, researchers presume, by a chemical substance released when cells are injured. The nerves send a message through the spinal cord to the brain that tells it you hurt. Pain is therefore primarily a warning of disorder.

The intensity of that warning depends on many "nonphysical" factors. For example, anger, fear, isolation, fatigue, and depression make pain feel worse. When someone has diversion, is rested, and feels cared for, pain diminishes. The emotional modification of pain —how a dying person "feels"—is one of the critical tasks of terminal care. A patient who theoretically should be in terrible pain but in fact feels calm probably is a person well cared for.

The sensation of pain may also vary according to the background of the sufferer. Individual histories with pain, the experiences of families and friends, and cultural differences are contributary factors. Studies have shown that a loud noise, hypnosis, or a major distraction will raise the threshold of pain by as much as 45 percent, while fear, stress, and fatigue will greatly lower it.

> The doctor had provided us with pain medication of various strengths as my husband's condition worsened, and when he asked or acted as if he needed a shot, I gave him one. He had much less medication at home because he was happy, alert, and diverted by all our activities. I think our playing cards with him and reading aloud did more than the pills.

This is not to say that the patient's pain is the result of boredom or inattention, only that diversion can be good medicine.

UNDERSTAND THE PAIN

If a dying person hurts or uses the word "pain" to describe his condition, think of it as a sign and your task to discover in which of many directions the sign points. Look directly at the sign, analyzing all the possibilities. First, seek solutions to what he can specify: treat a painful bedsore, massage his aching legs, soothe his chapped lips. What the patient may present as an unspecific but all-inclusive sensation of pain can be divided into specific symptoms that can be treated one by one. In fact, treating one will probably allow another to become clear, diagnosed, and treated. In this way, slowly, the patient's comfort can be ensured.

When you are aware that the person is suffering and not clear about its source, sit down and listen. Help her to ask the right questions if she seems to have lost her way in the misery and fear. Find out what her disease is doing, what are her symptoms, and if she is taking medications, which are working and how. Bring in the physician to understand what is happening physically, and to learn what symptoms can be relieved. Talk with the patient about what in addition to being comfortable is important to him, what he would like to be able to do. Is eating a priority, or drinking alcohol, or having friends and family nearby, or watching television, or having a card game, or being able to talk to a son? Help him figure out how these things might be accomplished, and do so in the spirit of believing that they *can* be accomplished.

Some caregivers said their patients at some point become "berserk" with pain or literally "terrified" of dying, even when taking some amount of pain medication. Such extreme emotions may be just pain, but are usually a sign that a person needs to talk. Case after case shows that when patients are able to express themselves fully, even to confirm their worst fear—namely, that they will die—relief is almost immediate. Within hours, the spirit improves, pain subsides, and the dying person even appears more comfortable.

Instead of surrendering to vague misery and grief, attending to symptoms gives caregivers and the patient a change in focus. As pain is eased, replace the attention paid to it with equal amounts of warmth and activity, which will help keep further pain in abeyance. In soothing the patient, talk about something positive, have him think about the pain as on wings, leaving him. Help him see himself as a whole person, secure, and distinct from the pain which comes and goes with a life of its own.

ISSUES OF PAIN CONTROL

Most physicians agree—at least in principle—that for a terminal illness relief of pain should take precedence over any concern about addiction to medication. While nonnarcotic analgesics should be tried first, if they fail, opiates such as morphine and heroin may be necessary—and, in fact, are not uncommon. Make it clear to your physician early on that you want narcotics used if necessary.

One subject that may be a matter of debate is when and how much medication should be administered. Thinking on this issue has changed considerably among those who insist on comfort for the dying. The dosage and frequency of medications should be administered to anticipate pain and not only when the patient expresses a need for it. You will learn too that the patient may require more medication at certain hours of the day or less medication on some days. By asking and observing, you will know what adjustments need to be made and when. The patient need never and should never be aware of the potential power of her pain. Such "preventive medication" does not mean that the caregiver can decide that the dying person should be more tranquilized than is necessary. While that impulse may seem motivated by concern for the patient, it may be a reaction to the caregiver's own fear.

Encourage the patient to help you know how much medication he wants. Explain that most people are able to strike a balance between comfort and alertness. If the patient does not want to be alert, he need not be, and you should not be insulted if he chooses sleep or to "check out." But if he wants to be slightly uncomfortable for a time in order to transact some important business (for example, some patients will ask for a lower dosage of sedative if a close relative is visiting), this is fully his choice.

Guard against the tendency to allow medication to become a

source of power used against the patient or among members of the team. Fear of retribution, not wanting to antagonize or badger the caregiver, and similar worries can cripple the dying person and keep her from freely making her own choices. Be sure to listen well to the patient. If there are others around, make sure they are included in discussions about how medications are to be used. While everyone involved in home care may have a different opinion on pain management, the patient's view is the important one.

A final consideration is that certain drugs, even when given principally to alleviate symptoms, will prolong life. Use of antibiotics for infection or medication to stave off pneumonia can be accurately thought of as palliative care, but may in fact have as a side effect the extension of life beyond the person's wishes. In most cases, such drugs can be rejected and symptoms that arise handled with alternate medication. Chapter 19, "Some Hard Choices," explores more fully this and similar difficult issues of treatment.

EASING EMOTIONAL PAIN

Stress and tension have been shown to prevent or delay effects of pain medication, as well as to increase susceptibility to pain. For this reason, taking into account all the factors that contribute to a dying person's pain—including thoughts, feelings, and attitudes—can in many cases result in a reduced need for medication. Less anxious patients tend to require smaller doses of analgesics. Dr. Balfour M. Mount, in the Department of Surgery at McGill University, has written extensively about pain management for terminally ill patients. He reported that patients in the hospice unit of the University's Royal Victoria Hospital, where the emphasis is on treating all sources of pain, received significantly more pain relief from the same doses of medicine than patients in general medical wards and private rooms. He attributed this success to simple acts of treating pain before it is acute, listening, and attending to various physical and emotional needs.

For the terminally ill, feeling cared for can be worth more than any number of medications. Giving the patient ample opportunities to talk will release a lot of tension and also give you ideas about how you can help. Think of ways to play with the patient—puzzles, word games, "Do you remember when . . . ," and other stationary activities completely unrelated to pain or illness. Most patients love to be read to. Such distractions are often enough to stop anxiety from accelerating into discomfort.

Dying people also need experiences of being cared for without being in pain. Let the patient know she is important and spend relaxed time with her on good days, so she doesn't feel she must be in pain to get attention.

At all times, the presence of a caring person helps prevent anxiety. Simply sitting with the patient, placing a cold washcloth on his forehead, and firmly holding his hand are effective pain remedies. Be sure to keep the patient warm enough, give massages, and pay attention to less obvious irritants like the feel of his clothing and the weight of bedclothes. Do things with him that are relaxing and even engage him in a little fantasy. Writing poetry and sketching simple images express and summarize connections with people, the past, and the future. Sharing music and happy memories will also stimulate warm feelings not related to illness. As a general rule, a patient who feels he is living in the present with more than dying on his mind will be more comfortable.

RELAXATION AND VISUALIZATION

The patient's pain will also be eased through simple exercises that promote a sense of calm and offer him ways to help himself. If the exercises seem to help, repeat them often. The patient can be encouraged to do them on his own, if he is able. One such practice is the relaxation response, created by Dr. Herbert Benson.

The patient should lie or sit in a comfortable position in a quiet room. He should be conscious of the rhythm of his breathing and should repeat quietly or silently a word or phrase. As thoughts and distractions occur, they should be disregarded. Dr. Benson recommends practicing this meditation for ten to twenty minutes at least twice a day, or whenever anxiety occurs or the sensation of pain is beginning.

Studies show that practicing the relaxation response reduces blood pressure, rate of heartbeat, and consumption of oxygen; stabilizes blood flow; and increases the production of alpha brain waves, which are associated with relaxation and calm. These physiological effects can make a big difference in diminishing the patient's sensation of pain.

Try another exercise, in which the patient visualizes pain leaving his body, based on the theory of Carl and Stephanie Simonton, who use visual imagery for healing. Choose a quiet setting and make the patient comfortable. Ask him to become aware of his breathing, and with each exhalation he can repeat silently or aloud, "Relax . . . relax . . . relax." Join him at first in the breathing and chanting if this will help. Next, tell him you will begin the relaxation with his face. Ask him to form an image in his mind of tension, such as a clenched fist; ask him to relax his face using another image, such as a cooked noodle. As his face relaxes, encourage him to note the ease he begins to feel in the rest of his body. Have him move step by step down his body, relaxing in the same way each part, muscle, joint, limb. As he lies limp, ask him to picture himself in a favorite setting, such as a beach. Stay there and bask in the warmth. After a few minutes, have him make a mental picture of the pain as weak and confused cells, surrounded by strong, healthy ones. Picture the strong cells attacking the weak ones. Picture medication diffusing the cells, scattering them, flushing them away. Watch this cleansing, and picture the soothing flow of comfort from the pain outward to other parts of his body. Have him imagine the relief and praise himself for the effort and the success. Finally, invite him to slowly open his eyes and return to the room.

PAIN MEDICATION

Many kinds of medications for pain are now available, and every day more is discovered about them and how they work. Much of the challenge of palliative care is determining how to strike balances among a large array of medications, their side effects, and how well they treat symptoms. Constant assessment—in fact, a daily report—of a medication program may be necessary until the patient is comfortable. Persist in trying options until a solution is found. It is easy to get discouraged by failure, but make the assumption that there *is* a solution, and all you and your physician need to do is find it.

A discussion of pain medication should take place quite early in the course of home care, so that supplies and backups, if any, will be in the home. If special equipment or instructions about injections are also needed, they, too, should be arranged in advance. The doctor should state specifically what drugs she expects will be useful or necessary, in what sequence she expects them to be required, and what information she will need about the patient's condition or response to medications in order to know what drugs to use at what dosages. Often a patient will start out on one medication but later require a stronger drug or combination of drugs, and then in the last hours or days need less medication.

Different sources of pain require different solutions. Physicians who are involved in terminal care agree that treatment of pain is best accomplished through a medication composed of several agents chosen for their desired effects and for their ability to counter side effects. The usual ingredients of a pain mixture are an opioid (useful in treating mental as well as physical pain), an anti-inflammatory drug, an antidepressant, and a tranquilizer. In the United States, morphine in cherry syrup, administered with Compazine and mixed with whatever is necessary to control side effects, is often used. Alcohol is also thought to be of great benefit with persons who are weary and confused. Bone pain has been the most difficult to control, but mixtures of analgesics and antianxiety and antidepression medications have proven very successful in easing this pain for many patients.

Side effects vary for each person, but nausea, disorientation, and constipation are the most common problems. (See Chapter 11, "Care of Symptoms," for information on how to treat these ailments.) Keeping doses as low as possible diminishes side effects, but it is recommended that you begin with a slightly higher dose than may be necessary to gain the patient's confidence in the drug. Once he is comfortable, a lower dose will probably suffice.

"You don't have to kill the patient to kill the pain," says Dr. Cicely Saunders, pioneer in palliative care and director of St. Christopher's Hospice outside London. Her research shows that when patients are medicated *before* they feel pain, so it does not become entrenched, they can be quite alert and comfortable, usually with low doses. Give medication not only before the last dose wears off but to calm the patient even when no specific expression of physical pain has been made. Do exactly what comfort requires. At the end of life, physical pain is often less a problem than restlessness, irritability, and impatience; nonetheless, these conditions are as important to medicate.

According to Dr. Saunders, studies show that the proper administration of pain medication seldom results in drug tolerance or an inability to bring relief, even though these are often cited as reasons to hold back on doses. When pain is under control, usually only low doses are required, so that addiction occurs only rarely. If physical dependence does occur, emotional dependency seldom accompanies it; when the latter does occur, it rarely complicates the person's outlook, according to Dr. Saunders.

Advances in pain medications and in physicians' understanding of how they can be used and combined are a great boon to home care. As Dr. Saunders says, most people can be made quite comfortable. The key to comfort is that you and your physician approach pain with the determination that you will be able to find a way or ways to ease it. Chances are very good that you will.

ADMINISTERING MEDICATIONS

The first rule of administering medication is to follow the direction of the patient, who knows when he is and is not comfortable. Either directly or indirectly he can tell you the strength and frequency he needs. Allowing the patient's comfort to dictate medication can be a major issue with the physician and nurses, so be sure to express it as a requirement early in home care.

A major problem with terminal care generally and also with home care has been that medication has not been given frequently enough. The standard procedure for hospice management is to give regularly scheduled doses, usually every three to four hours, depending on what the dying person wants. With some practice, she can determine the amount necessary to balance control of her pain with a comfortable level of relaxation and alertness.

In order for the patient and caregiver to maintain the right amount of medication, get specific instructions from the attending physician about how much, when, and by what method drugs should be or can be administered. Equally important, learn how the drug works, how long it takes to work, and its side effects. Medicines have very specific properties and actions. Some work immediately, some after several hours, and some only cumulatively over several days. Some must be taken with meals, others only just before or after a meal. Since your home care physician may not know what drugs previous doctors have prescribed or whether adverse effects or allergies have been experienced, make sure the physician knows the patient's drug history. Tell the doctor also what the patient is currently taking and in what dosage. This information is important because most drugs work differently when mixed. Prescription drugs as well as over-the-counter products, and even aspirin, have different effects in combination.

In addition, don't hesitate to consult your pharmacist, who is a professional trained to help you take and administer medications properly and to give you information about drugs. The pharmacist may, in fact, be more current on forms of drugs than your physician and can make good suggestions you can then discuss with the doctor.

Some drugs come in pills or capsules, others in liquids; a few are available in either form. Make a point of learning also what drugs may be taken rectally or by injection, since the patient may not always be able to swallow. Discuss particular administering difficulties with your physician and your pharmacist. If alternatives are considered, be sure to ask about determining equivalent doses. For example, prednisone pills may make the patient feel nauseated because they are very bitter and hard to swallow. They can be exchanged for Decadron, which is a liquid, but a conversion scale is necessary to make the substitution.

Some caregivers said they tried to disguise medications, but the patient usually caught on to the game quickly and rebelled. Sneaking medications into foods is probably not in the patient's best interest. Ask his help in knowing whether or not disguises are desirable. Suggest that you can put pills, crushed or whole if they are small, in honey or applesauce, or mix them in protein drinks. In Chapter 7, "Supplies," you can learn about various other ideas that may help.

Usually a point is reached when the patient simply cannot swallow, and pain may not be controllable by drugs available for rectal use. If you have to resort to injections, be aware that they have some particular disadvantages. The greatest is often the caregiver's fear of giving them or unwillingness to "inflict pain," especially when the patient is very sick. Finding adequate sites for giving injections on an extremely thin person is also difficult. However, if swallowing or taking liquids is beginning to be a problem, you may be advised to learn the simple skills. It is not ordinarily possible to have a visiting nurse present each time medication should be given, so take the time to be comfortable with the idea and practice before injections are unavoidable.

> My mother was on a schedule determined by how frequently the visiting nurse could come to give her injections. She had her shots about eight hours apart, and eventually they had to give her bigger doses to last that long. Then the drug would wear off and the two hours before the nurse arrived were agony for both of us. I finally swallowed my fear and learned how to give the injections myself.

Try also to schedule pain medication so that the patient will not have to be awakened to take it and the caregiver can get a good night's sleep. If medication is necessary only every eight hours, try 10 P.M., 6 A.M., and 2 P.M. Close to death, most people sleep much of the time and are not very conscious of day or night. At this stage, patients are apt to do best on lower doses of medication taken more frequently (usually every three to six hours). A three-hour interval is not often needed, but if it means the dying person will not wake up in pain, be sure to do it. Awakening him for medication is far less disruptive for the patient and caregiver than sleep interrupted by pain. Some medications must actually be given at set intervals in order for the full effects to be felt, so that what seems like kindness —not "disturbing" a patient—may actually be counterproductive.

Finally, know that while the chemistry of the medication is constant and can be measured, the chemistry of the patient is not. Her mood and disease, the vagaries of the day, or a distraction of the moment will influence how the medicine takes effect at any time. If a dosage of medication that has been working does not seem to take hold in the usual way and the patient is restless or obviously under stress, try calming him by sitting close and holding his head or hand. Have the patient breathe with you, or sing a lullaby, or go through a progressive relaxation ritual. If you can break the focus on fear, he will probably drift slowly into a calmer state. Continued agitation means it is time to confer with the physician to reevaluate the medication.

OTHER SOLUTIONS

Depending on the types and locations of pain, you may wish to consider various alternative treatments for relief, including acupuncture, hypnosis, biofeedback, radiation, and surgery to cut the involved nervous pathways. Palliative surgery, such as a cordotomy or nerve block, can provide dramatic relief. If pain is or is expected to be acute, explore alternatives with your physician and others specializing in pain relief. Whatever works against pain works. No one needs to apologize or feel embarrassed by any source of relief.

Talk about particular symptoms with friends, visiting nurses, and others who will offer invaluable nuggets of advice and simple solutions, often full of warmth and good humor. In this spirit one caregiver spoke of the comfort she managed to bring her husband, who was suffering from back pain, through "a careful deployment of pillows." In addition, remember it is often the little things—a smooth sheet, a dry nightgown, Nivea cream on dry elbows—on which the success of a day may turn.

Control of pain is really the heart of terminal care. People do not fear death so much as they fear unrelieved pain and being alone with their suffering. Be determined to do everything you can to ease the pain and assure the patient you will not leave her in her pain. With this commitment, solutions for each symptom will be found.

13
HOSPITALIZATION

Over the course of the patient's illness, chances are some amount of time will be spent in a hospital. Even after the decision for home care has been made, the doctor may recommend admittance to gain information that will assist pain management. Another common reason for hospitalization during home care is that the patient or caregiver become so alarmed by pain or another frightening symptom that they need temporary relief from responsibility.

Emergency hospitalizations usually come at the end of a long night during which everyone has gone beyond their limits from the stress of seemingly uncontrollable pain, intractable seizures, bleeding, vomiting, or breathing difficulty. If you experience such a period—night or day—call your visiting nurse or physician and talk about what is happening so they can offer suggestions. Pick up the telephone before you wear yourself down by hours of anxiety. You will probably be reassured that there is not a medical reason for hospitalization, and offered a solution that can be provided at home.

Despite the reasonableness of caring for symptoms at home, there may well be a point when the patient or family feel they cannot cope, or the caregiver is exhausted. A night or even a few days of hospital care may be needed. The patient's medication can be adjusted, the family can get a break, and then home care can continue.

In making the admittance, you need not fear that you will be victimized by the hospital, or that heroic "saving" measures will be taken, or that the dying person will be pumped up or wired to machines. With the help of your physician, you can make it very clear that the admittance is for acute symptom relief only. Make sure that your doctor has communicated this to all necessary round-the-clock staff and written it on all orders. Do not hesitate to double-check everyone's awareness and compliance as soon and as often as you can.

However, you will need to take charge of the quality of life for the patient. To illustrate the importance of constant watchfulness, here are several not isolated incidents that occurred in the care of two terminally ill patients in a semiprivate room of an excellent teaching/research hospital. The two men were patients of the medical chief of the department in which they were being treated.

- Supper was delivered to the wrong room and the patient, who could not speak and had been without food for twelve hours prior because of testing, had to wait an additional two hours for a replacement meal.

- Restraints were placed on a confused patient who became agitated while trying to rearrange sheets he had fouled and left to lie in for over an hour.

- A patient was given no food for eighteen hours in preparation for a test that—unknown to nurses on the floor—was cancelled the night before.

- Bedsores on a patient's elbows were ignored, despite repeated requests from the family for moleskin, massage, medication, and frequent position changes. When the caregiver asked for an Eggcrate mattress, which the staff could have recommended but had not, the answer was that it would take four to five days for delivery. When she insisted, the mattress arrived and was fitted to the bed within two hours.

- A patient was involuntarily urinating and would frequently lie for several hours in wet sheets. Staff did not requisition any alternatives nor did they register concern for the patient. The family finally got the courage to ask if there were a better option, with the result that all agreed diapers were the best solution for the duration of the hospitalization.

What we learn from such observations is that "nonmedical" consideration is simply impossible to guarantee in a hospital. The staff is busy, emergencies interrupt routine checking, and the general focus is on matters truly more life-threatening than a wet bed or a missed meal. While the patient may well benefit from a temporary admission for the technology and skills provided, someone in the family or a friend, and preferably many people taking turns, must take responsibility for other aspects of the patient's care. Be courteous in your presence at the hospital, but don't hesitate doing for the patient what needs to be done.

The elements of care that have been important at home—frequent turning, rubs to prevent sores, bed changes, toilet care, favorite foods, plenty of encouragement to take liquids, and providing stimulation and intimacy through activity and conversation—are essential. In our experience, for example, the hospital staff will not consistently encourage a patient whose appetite is poor to eat and select foods he likes, yet such assistance can as much as double a patient's intake. If the patient is able to walk, or ride in a wheelchair, or sit up in a bedside chair, someone must make sure these things happen. You can even watch as your requests are written out to care for these needs, but a query the following day will show that orders for care not considered critical are no guarantee. A team of caregivers to work in shifts providing these services can make all the difference.

Do not be surprised if you sense that little coordination of medical care is being provided. Doctors are extremely busy and distracted. They may not always follow through on a conversation, do not always talk with each other as often as might be advisable, forget things, and are not most concerned with the patient's peace of mind or yours. Ask questions, make demands, trust your common sense, and keep uppermost the purpose of your stay. Taking an aggressive position does not mean you don't "have faith" in the doctor. Most doctors appreciate active participation, and no doctor has time to worry for long about how his patient feels about him. Trusting the doctor's dedication to physical care, you can also trust your own commitment to the patient's emotional and spiritual needs and your understanding of how these can be served in a hospital. Never shrink from exercising your right and responsibility to understand what is being done and why, and to ensure that what you have been told will happen happens. In other words, be assured that the hospital exists to serve you and that neither you nor the patient need to be its victims.

14
A CHILD
IS DYING

Maggie rested on pillows in a large red wagon—the one in which her big brother had pulled her around the neighborhood the week before. "There isn't anything we can do now besides keep her comfortable," her mother said. "When you are at home, you can take advantage of the good hours because you are always there." During the past few weeks, her family had read her stories and taken her to her favorite movie twice, and she'd slept between her parents in their "big bed." Maggie woke and waved at her mother, who said a few words to her, and she dozed off. Later, her eight-year-old sister suggested she might like a bubble bath. By evening, Maggie appeared to be unaware of others. "I told her it was going to be all right," said her mother. "I told her she would always be with us, that we would always think of her and always love her. I told her it was all right to leave, that we would be okay." Moments later, while Bob cradled his frail daughter in his arms, Maggie squeezed his finger one last time and peacefully died.

Perhaps the most difficult experience for anyone is caring for a dying child. For all parents, this is the most horrible nightmare come true. The shock, depression, and anger experienced by a mother and father—and their families and friends—when their child is diagnosed to have a terminal illness is shattering and affects the rest of their lives. The only solace lies in doing whatever they can to make their child's life today as comfortable and secure as possible. This most likely means caring for the child at home.

Being at home means he can sleep in his own bed, pet his dog, eat his favorite food, play with his own toys, and be teased and delighted by his siblings. It means, too, that his parents can continue to be parents. Terrible helplessness, which is an unavoidable condition of being a parent of a dying child, is somewhat assuaged when parents are responsible for care, for they at least have the satisfaction of knowing they can be fully caring and actively involved with the child. Studies have shown that parents who have cared for their dying children at home have experienced less difficulty with grief after death, as have other family members who have been involved in daily routines of a terminally ill child.

Parents with a dying child face multiple special problems, including guilt, since they are used to thinking their children's well-being depends on them. When suddenly they cannot keep a child from harm, they may even blame themselves for the disease. (We could have lived in a less polluted environment, fed her better foods, had more careful prenatal care, etc.) Compounding this situation are the day-to-day strains of a family in crisis. If the dying child has siblings, they will no doubt act out their rivalries and resentments. Friends and relatives will hear parents' anger and fear, feel powerless to help or put off by it, and back away. Parents are apt to experience difficulties in their own relationship as a couple. Even the most solid marriages are challenged by the emotional and often physical exhaustion that accompanies having a dying child.

The truth is, your problems may seem unsurmountable. Fight the natural tendency to take on the whole matter yourselves, or to assume no one can help or understand, and ask for and accept what relatives, friends, and others offer, even if it seems too little. Try doing the best you can just for today, to care for your child and involve others in maintenance of family life. In addition, read here about how to handle the most difficult issues facing you: talking with your child about his illness, handling stress yourself and in the family, and providing care and activity for your child. While information supplied elsewhere in this book can be adapted to care of children, supplement it with specifics offered in what follows.

TRUTH-TELLING

What should a child know about his illness? A great deal of evidence shows that children who are informed about their disease benefit from the frankness, are more agreeable about treatments and routines, and are better able to go on about their lives to the extent that they are physically able. Continued pretense may seem to serve the child better, but it often really answers only the short-term needs of parents who fear their child's reaction.

Another argument for honesty is that much of the emotional pain of illness can be treated with talking. If they have been open with their child about her prognosis, parents will be able to help her deal with the reality of her situation and can provide comfort by offering her activities that draw the focus from things she cannot change. The medical care, too, will be more effective, since the physician will be free to ask direct questions and thereby carefully address symptoms without pretending to cure the disease.

Once a diagnosis is confirmed, parents must collect themselves, learn about the disease, and develop trust in several medical people who will support them throughout the illness. If possible, discussion with the child about the diagnosis should take place when his condition is stabilized; the anxiety level is then lower, and he will have more physical and emotional energy to digest information.

In general, children should be told as much as they ask for and can understand. If it is difficult to interpret what this means for your child, seek professional help. Above all, resist the temptation to erect a wall of secrecy around her. Children have big ears and bigger imaginations. Failure to be honest and direct will undermine your relationship with the child at a time when everyone very much needs for it to thrive.

There is no one perfect way to describe to a dying child what is happening to him. However, the American Cancer Society's "Parents' Book on Leukemia"* does offer a general script for beginning such a conversation. The following language, offered by the society

* Available by writing American Cancer Society, 777 Third Avenue, New York, New York 10001.

as a model, can be adapted to your child's age, condition, disease, and ability to understand and converse:

Jamie, we think you want to know what's wrong with you. You know that we've done several tests to find out what is wrong. Well, now we're sure what the problem is. You have a disease called leukemia. Have you heard of it?

Several preliminary factors should be kept in mind during your discussion. Remember that the child will grasp only as many facts as she can handle, and the more important assimilation is the emotions of the parents and others around her. She can be reassured or frightened or misinterpret what is said, depending on the emotions conveyed by the speaker. If the tone of voice expresses anxiety or fear, she may hear that instead of the facts. Timing is also important. If the child has been concerned about a friend, or is having trouble with a sibling, or is learning something exciting in school, her reaction will be affected. Head off possible difficulty by being especially sensitive when talking and listening.

Don't be hurt if she appears at times not to listen; watch your child as she responds. Determine what she knows and what she fears. Explain in terms she can understand what the disease is, how it works, what effect it has on her body, and how she will feel. Tell her what discomfort, symptoms, and slowing of body and activities will happen. Assure her the most important thing for everyone is her comfort, and that the doctor and you will do everything possible to keep her from hurting.

If your child asks if anyone dies from this disease, be honest and say that sometimes people do die of it. If the question is more specifically directed to himself, tell him that he may die but for today he is alive and very much loved and needed. But if he is ignorant of the possibility of death, or until there is certainty that the child will in fact die, don't burden him with information that will make his life a daily struggle against the odds. Tell him only as much as he needs to know not to be frightened or confused by what he experiences today.

Once you learn your child will die, slowly work in the truth about what is happening. Your child is probably more concerned about what will happen when he is actually dying than he is about being dead. Death on television is quite terrible, and this is probably his view of it. Discover his fantasies about death, and help him by giving him facts. The nurse and doctor can tell you and your child what will probably happen. Explain and demonstrate at every opportunity that everyone is working hard to help him not hurt, and that the doctor cares about him and wants to help. Tell your child he should describe fully how he is feeling so the doctor will know what to do.

Expect your pediatrician and others on the medical team to be friends to your child. Ask them to answer whatever questions your child has. A child may be able to vent feelings with her doctor that she cannot share with others, and this opportunity must be offered. The doctor can also counsel on support groups for terminally ill children. A great deal of help is available from child care workers, teachers, and mental health professionals who have experience with helping children to assimilate information and express feelings.

A CHILD UNDER STRESS

Because you know your child very well, you will to some extent instinctively know what needs to be said and done. Much of the behavior the child will exhibit in reaction to his symptoms and what is happening to his life and activities will be familiar, if somewhat accentuated. He may "act out" in ways you thought he'd outgrown. The adaptations the patient and his family must make will not be easy.

In caring for your child, keep in mind your own knowledge of his or her ways of coping with stress, fear, or disappointment. These very general characteristic responses of different ages can be used as a guide.

- An infant's fears are simple: she does not want to be separated from her parents.

- A preschooler worries about the pain of a treatment or symptom. Memory is short, and anxiety may not be evident except possibly in sleep disturbances. The finality of death is not understood.

- From age five to nine, death is remote but may become personified in fantasy images of ghosts and demons. Children in this age group may begin to grasp the concept of death's permanence. Illogical thinking will reveal anxiety, and the child will also exhibit anger, though probably not very directly.

- After about the age of ten, the child is likely to be aware of the reality and finality of death. The older the child, the greater his comprehension about his illness. A child who is old enough to understand the diagnosis often handles it better than his parents.

- Because teenagers as a group tend to be under stress anyway, their anxiety will be compounded. Parents may be faced with frustration when their adolescents do not want to talk about their feelings. Teens will need to be treated as adults in managing their own lives and care.

At all ages, but especially with increasing maturity, the child must be allowed to develop her own way of living and describing her illness and needs. While this is painful, everyone benefits in the long run. A social worker told this story:

I had a case of a thirteen-year-old girl whose mother was upset because her daughter refused to wear a wig when she lost her hair. Dying children must be left alone to work out their own problems. Sometimes they will toss out cues, indicating they want to talk. This girl later said, "I won't be here next summer," and instead of talking around the hint, her parents were able to follow up. The child said that she didn't want her family to miss her and made some suggestions about her funeral and about donating her organs. As the family learned to talk about her inevitable death, more intimate sharing became possible.

One father talked about how his teenage daughter took charge of her own care and even sought out her own doctor. "There really wasn't much I could do, and she didn't make any pretense about that." His daughter made all the decisions about treatments. When her family would hear her throwing up in the middle of the night, she would send them back to bed and go into her brothers' rooms to let them know she was okay. "All the kids got quite close. I guess I felt rather helpless, but now I see it was a good lesson for me."

In addition to letting your child handle the disease as she will, you can also be sensitive to what will be difficult for her. What are the causes of stress for a dying child? First, the physical symptoms of her disease, including lethargy and pain, will frighten her and make her feel not quite connected to the people around her. Side effects of treatments and medications and changes in physical appearance will frighten or embarrass her. Hospital admittances, treatments, and even nursing care will have taken their toll, so that she may be suspicious and fearful of even the gentlest care. Changes in the emotions of people around her will also create uncertainty. She may feel somehow at fault or confused if her mother is crying or there is tension in the household.

While you cannot control many of these factors, you can help the child understand and accommodate them. Continuous personal care and counseling by parents and professionals can be accompanied by empathy, patience, and truth. Just being with him will go a long way. Show the child that the family is very sad and angry about the illness, but not about him. Tell him you are ready to adapt to whatever he needs. Don't deny the obvious, and even point out the presence of friends, favorite toys, and other things he loves that are with him always. If the child is angry or upset at not being able to join in something, encourage him to express his emotions and acknowledge them. Tell him you are sorry or frustrated not to be able to change how he feels. Include the child in all decisions about her illness, what to eat, what she will do today, but don't force her participation; urge her to take on the responsibility of caring for herself. It will not help for her to defer always to the doctor or a parent. Provide opportunities for her to be in control.

In handling the stress that will inevitably be one of the symptoms of a terminally ill child, use your own instincts to provide him with every possible way to feel safe. If you get overwhelmed by the pressure of his behavior or the extent of his needs, have someone take over for you for a day, or seek professional help.

HOSPITALIZATION

What should be your concerns if your child needs to be hospitalized? First, do your best to use a hospital where you can stay with your child. You and your child will be happier if you continue to perform usual functions, such as bathing and feeding. Try to be present to make even the smallest decisions regarding care, help with treatments, and accompany your child in any medical procedures. You can play a critical role in helping the child to understand what is being done for him and in making his wishes known to medical personnel.

Children have special fears of institutions. A hospitalized child under five often regresses to bed-wetting and fear of strangers and may resume old, unpleasant behaviors. Older children may become angry and aggressive as a result of hospitalization and may have trouble concentrating or getting along with peers. For children with some social or psychological disadvantage, such as having only one parent, further signs of disturbance may be evident. A certain amount of disturbance is normal and will pass with time; however, if the child seems to be experiencing a severe trauma related to the hospitalization, consult a professional.

If you can anticipate the hospital stay, prepare your child for what it is like and what will happen for him there, how it will help him feel better. Explain where he will sleep, go to the bathroom, and what he will eat. Ask him what he wants to take with him. Tell him when you will be visiting or that you will be staying with him, if this is possible. Explain the procedure that he will have, and give him the opportunity to ask questions. Ask the doctor to have a chat with the child about what will be done. If pain will be involved, this should be explained, and the child should be reassured that it will be treated. Do not discuss anything in the child's presence without his being active in the conversation.

Counselors suggest that as part of the preparation young children's parents should play doctor or hospital with them. As your child plays, do not direct her; listen and encourage her by playing parts as she is "writing" them. This activity will provide clues about what you can help her understand. Pay particular attention to expressions of feelings, acting out of fantasies, and any factual inaccuracies. In addition, you might want to read the many excellent books written for parents and children on going to the hospital, some of which are included in the bibliography of this book.

While your child is in the hospital, try to have his routine as close as possible to the way it is at home. Siblings and friends may be entertained for short visits. Have on hand some of his favorite toys and snacks. Depending on the age of the child, providing music or singing familiar tunes can quickly help him feel safe. Even when you cannot prepare your child fully, simply providing the constant presence of someone he loves will get him and you through the ordeal with minimum difficulty.

CONTINUITY

What you can ensure by maintaining control of your child's care and having him at home as much as possible is continuity. Since he is no doubt confused by the strangers who have been providing medical care, by how his body feels, by the effects of medications, and even by the changes in moods and routines of those closest to him, whatever can remain unchanged should be maintained. A child needs to know where he is and have familiar people around him engaging in their usual activities.

The family should continue its usual routines of work, school, Sunday drive, evening reading and baths, or whatever is familiar. The only change you may want to make is to become more flexible: take shortcuts in chores or even let one activity go temporarily so that on a day when the child is feeling strong enough, everyone can spend time together.

On a good afternoon, the child may enjoy a wheelchair or wagon ride, being carried to the park or the movies, or just having someone sit with him and talk quietly, perhaps while looking out a window. Whether or not he is able to participate fully, the child benefits from being included even as an observer in the activities of his family. Follow your own good judgment as parents about what activities are best for your child. Because there is little you can do to "harm" him, try not to overprotect him from contact with friends and siblings. Let his comfort be your best guide.

Use good sense about where and when your child should rest, and this will vary from day to day, even hour to hour. You can let the child tell you where he would like to be. Many families put the child's bed in the living room. This makes him feel special and ensures that he does not feel banished or punished by being in his bedroom. His playmates may want to visit, and this is another good reason to have the child in a "living" and not a "sleeping" area. If your child can be moved, let him rest outdoors or in another part of the house. Changes of scenery are diverting and enrich a day.

In addition to providing continuity in playmates, activities, and surroundings, most parents make the choice to continue—as the child is physically able—to train and discipline him. He can continue his studies or undertake more sedentary hobbies related to his interests. Continue teaching the child to read if that is the stage of development he is in. Parents of a terminally ill two-year-old boy persisted in toilet training and teaching him words. "He was really proud of accomplishing short sentences," said his mother. "I was sure he would be happier if he kept learning." An older child can have some tutoring at home, by either a parent or a teacher, using familiar materials from school. This stimulation will add to the quality of the child's life, even if only minimal concentration is possible.

Remember as you make these decisions about what your child can do, that she will feel most at ease when her life is most like what she knows. Continuity will strengthen everyone in the family.

EATING

An important aspect of continuing care you can offer your child is nourishment. Pain must be controlled for him to have any appetite, and even when comfortable, your child may not be hungry. Avoid expressing concern about what and how much he eats, because tension can turn meals and snacks into a nightmare for you both. Let him make his own selection of food. He can drink and eat whatever he wants, and whenever, although if he can enjoy being with the family at meals he may eat better.

Dehydration and dry mouth are very painful, so adequate fluids make the biggest difference in his comfort. Any liquids will be fine, although an extra boost can be achieved by liquids that have some nutrition, such as eggnogs, yogurt mixtures, milk shakes, and the protein drinks described in Chapter 10, "Eating."

Make food tantalizing and easy to enjoy. Your child no doubt has her favorite foods and flavors. Here are some tips that other parents have followed, with success.

- Sweeten whatever foods your child prefers, or use flavorings such as vanilla, lemon, or strawberry.

- If he doesn't like meats, substitute fish, chicken, eggs, or cheese for protein.

- Cold foods may be more inviting, even more comfortable if there are mouth sores; offer ice cream, semifrozen yogurt, or slushes.

- Serve foods that can be picked up with fingers, such as raisins, popcorn, nuts, breadsticks, balls of fruit, animal crackers.

- Make little balls out of wheat germ and peanut butter or cooked pasta and cheese, for easy-to-eat protein snacks.

- Offer spicy foods like tacos or pizza, even Chinese-style sweet and sour sauce with meat, if the child can tolerate these foods.

- Color hard-boiled eggs like Easter eggs.

- Serve food on a child's tea set or other toy.

- Have a picnic in the backyard or on the living room floor.

- Small meals and plenty of rest between them may encourage a lethargic child to eat.

CONTROL OF SYMPTOMS

Be careful not to underplay the seriousness of symptoms. Stomach upsets and crying, for example, are so common in children that the severity of pain or vomiting and the emotional discomfort the symptoms involve may not receive enough attention. "It goes away if he is doing something he likes" may be true, but activity is only a partial answer to the multiple pains of terminal illness.

Seek individual symptoms and their causes. Insist that the physician attend to symptoms, and seek advice from him and others about the latest medications. He should be alert to side effects and care as much about your child's comfort as you do. There is no excuse for untended disturbances of sleep, or appetite, or spirit. It is the task of parents and the medical team to listen and question until causes are found. "Psychosomatic" causes of discomfort should be treated with careful medication and informed sympathy. Emotional and spiritual pain for children—as for adults—needs to be treated as seriously as physical pain. Low doses of pain medication given every few hours in anticipation of distress, and not when the child complains, will relieve the fear. As is true with adults, withholding medication because it may be addicting is ridiculous. What difference does it make? Even when you may feel the child is becoming dependent on a drug, chances are her plea for help is quite genuine and she is seeking and deserves adequate pain control.

Although it will be impossible and not even advisable for the family to be continually cheerful, your realism, humor, and serenity will help the child feel safer. Finally, talking and providing opportunities for him to express himself and feel the love of people around him will do more than any dosage of medication. Because children are easily distracted, they respond particularly well to games and diversion. Even if he cannot physically participate, a child will play with his eyes when in the presence of interesting activities. The greatest relief for most children is just to be in the middle of the family's activity where they can watch and join in when they are able.

DEATH AND GRIEF

We cannot pretend to advise on how to be with a child when death is near. Know that simply being with the child is what counts, even though he may not be able to communicate or acknowledge your presence. Maybe it also helps to know that, as for adults, death itself is rarely frightening. One mother told us her son's breathing became very slow while she and her husband sat on the couch holding him. His head was on her lap and his feet on his dad's. He just stopped breathing and died peacefully.

After the child dies, his body can remain in the house while the family says goodbye and makes arrangements. The physician needs to come to certify death. When the time is right, parents can take the body themselves to the funeral home or make arrangements for transportation.

Parents will need a lot of support from the physician, social worker, clergy member, and friends in the period immediately after the death of a child. This can be an acutely lonely time, when even the partners will feel isolated from each other. Friends, not knowing what to do, may simply want to stay away, but it is at this point that parents most need someone who will sit and listen for hours to memories about the dead child, the circumstances of death, and the pain they are experiencing. Each parent will react differently: one may decide "to get on with life"; the other may need weeks to talk and recollect. Friends can help them as individuals by supporting the specific needs of their grief. As with all grief, there is no timetable or formula for getting over it, and most people will benefit from some degree of professional help.

While the short-term effects of a child's death will be particularly acute, repercussions will be felt the lifetime of a family, regardless of how "well" or "poorly" the event has been faced. A parent never forgets loss of a child; siblings never look at their own lives as before.

I learned of my thirteen-year-old son's diagnosis soon after I became pregnant with his brother. The night I gave birth to Charlie, Bill was admitted to the same hospital vomiting blood. I was afraid he would see the baby as his replacement, and I must have overdone it because Bill said to me, "Mom, don't you think you should hold the baby more?" Bill died when Charlie was five months old. About a year later, my husband told me if I didn't stop mourning, he would divorce me. I got some help, and I've been able to go on, but it's hard. Charlie is now eight and his biggest problem is his fear that he will die of cancer as his brother did. He's afraid of his thirteenth birthday.

Overwhelming feelings may last several years, and periods of intense sadness will continue beyond, especially on birthdays and holidays and at times of the year that trigger memories. The majority of parents experience some marital difficulty because one or the other fails to tolerate or understand the other's reaction. A wife, for example, may resent the seeming ease with which her husband picks up his work. If they are not working, mothers without other children need to become involved in something outside the home. Professionals suggest that becoming pregnant too soon after a child's death will only put off the grief, which may recur later in harmful or less direct ways, including resentment or overprotection of the "replacement" child.

Parents can try to hear the care and concern of friends and accept offers of help and even listening. Tell the story of your child's illness and death as often as you need to. Talk about your child and seek reassurance that you did everything possible.

Remember that grief does not begin or end for any one reason or by a deadline, and it does not involve "correct" ways to act or feel. The healing takes a lot of time and willingness to keep going even when you don't see the point. Parents often say their recovery began when they stopped asking "Why?" and accepted the fact that their child had died. Slowly they developed lives and conversations separate from the dead child.

When you learn that your child has a terminal illness, contact a local support group or one with a nationwide network of chapters such as Compassionate Friends, Inc. (P.O. Box 1347, Oak Brook, IL 60521), Share (St. John's Hospital, 800 East Carpenter, Springfield, IL 62769), and Candlelighters Childhood Cancer Foundation (2025 Eye Street NW, Suite 1011, Washington, DC 20006). A chapter of one of these groups may be nearby. During home care and later, grieving your child's death, you can be helped to cope and eventually to recovery through association with other parents.

15
SELF-CARE

While the previous chapters have not disguised the fact that providing home care is difficult work, we want to address directly the multiple problems and their sources: caregiving, emotional strain, and physical exhaustion. This chapter is intended to help you care for yourself. Begin by posting this list on your bathroom mirror or the refrigerator door.

> Assume great things of yourself and others
> Treat yourself well
> Ask for help
> Be grateful for small things
> Do not isolate yourself

Remember that this period is temporary, and while you should give it what you are able, survival is every bit as important as caregiving. When the patient dies, you will need to move on to the next phase of your life, taking with you what you learn.

Home care can cause serious physical and emotional damage to the person responsible for care unless a very determined effort is made to prevent burnout. It cannot be emphasized too strongly that the caregiver is more at risk than the patient. Burnout is a very real physical, emotional, and spiritual crisis, and it occurs most frequently under the intense demands of a one-to-one relationship.

As caregiver, you are carrying a number of specific stresses: you are probably emotionally close to the person dying; you may be working at a job or maintaining a family; you may have many personal sources of tension. The caregiver—usually the last person on the list for everyone—worries about the well-being of the entire team, forgetting or putting off her own needs. Every caregiver needs to learn to set limits.

It is widely acknowledged among people in the "helping professions" that good care is simply impossible unless the caregiver's needs are provided for. Doctors, social workers, nurses, and others are learning how to prevent the exhaustion that can follow attending to a steady run of people whose needs and demands are limitless. Time off, engaging in hobbies and sports, and regular sessions with a therapist or peers to let go of feelings and get help and perspective are ways professionals maintain their own equilibrium.

The same care must be taken—and is even more important—for "amateur" caregivers. Begin by avoiding two especially crippling misjudgments: that care cannot go on much longer, and that no one else can provide it as well as you can. These considerations are not necessarily wrong and may in fact be quite true. However, understand that the patient often lives longer than anticipated and that the point is not really whether you are the best person to do the job, but that in order to continue even a passable job, you need an occasional respite.

As you read in this chapter about burnout and stress, ask others for help and ideas. Identify with others and learn from them. You can also learn from yourself: your own body and reactions are an excellent barometer for what you need to do for yourself. Survival skills acquired in caregiving are invaluable for the rest of your life.

SIGNS OF STRESS

Detecting stress by observing signs in your behavior, body, and feelings is the first step in taking care of yourself. Ask a close friend to help you keep watch and let you know when signs of trouble appear. If you are worried, or friends are worried, then some cause for worry exists, and it is time to take some action.

Be aware of any changes in your normal habits or general ability to cope with the events of each day. If you find yourself becoming anxious about an "overreaction" to something, or about the amount of alcohol you consume, or an upset stomach, don't just assume it's nothing or that it will go away.

Here are some other emotional and physical signs indicating stress.

- General irritability, depression, hopelessness
- Impulsiveness, emotional instability
- Crying or wanting to run away from the situation, feeling keyed up
- Inability to concentrate, disorientation, forgetfulness
- Accident-proneness, dropping things, bumping into things
- Vague, unspecified anxiety
- Being easily startled or moving about with no reason
- Trembling, involuntary tic
- Feelings of unreality, weakness, dizziness, fatigue
- Stuttering or other speech difficulties
- Pounding of the heart
- Dryness of throat and mouth
- Grinding teeth
- Insomnia or waking too early
- Nightmares
- High-pitched, nervous laughter
- Sweating
- Any changes in bowel or toilet habits, "stomach trouble"
- Pain in the neck or lower back, headaches
- Premenstrual tension, missed menstrual cycle
- Loss of appetite or excessive appetite
- Increased smoking or use of medications, alcohol, or drugs

In addition to these symptoms, caregivers talk about various mental states that at times overwhelmed them, indicating to them that they were under stress and needed help.

Guilt: When something goes wrong with the patient, and it could be anything (a slight choke, loss of appetite, bedsores), you feel responsible. Even if a visitor tires the patient or a smell from the kitchen makes her feel nauseated, you will take it out on yourself. Thoughts such as "If only I had been there" and "If only I hadn't given him *x,* he wouldn't be *y"* are real traps and you can watch out for them.

Suffering servant: Some people—even members of the patient's family—are so good at articulating sorrow that they can even succeed in manipulating you to take on their pain. It is not uncommon for the caregiver to feel the pain of the dying person or to allow herself to be the receptacle for everyone else's guilt and grief. Handling your own is more than enough.

Waiting: The patient will not die on her own schedule or at a time when everyone is prepared, and it often happens that death comes later than predicted, or even after a short period when the patient actually looks and feels better. You may find yourself wishing it were over, or constantly looking for signs, or putting everything in your life off. Waiting can produce frustration, anger, boredom, even denial that the patient is dying. A constant awareness of waiting or of all life revolving around the patient's death stops any normal life and needs to be corrected.

Abandonment: Lack of understanding and support from others in the family or outsiders is a serious problem. Sometimes it is imagined; more often it is real. People make demands on the caregiver's time and energy, asking for support for their feelings about the dying person, and then do not reciprocate. Medical-team members seem to come only to give orders, perhaps without giving a complete explanation of the medication they have prescribed or of the person's condition. The result is that you will probably feel trapped, attacked by others who make suggestions but leave you holding the bag. Demand companionship and information from people around you.

Odd person out: Often as caregiver you are the one person closest to the patient, and you probably have the best understanding of his needs. Yet others on the team or in the family discount you as too close to the situation, too emotional, too tired, or lacking age or experience, and knowing less than you do. Others will make decisions that affect you and the patient. You may feel very angry or apologetic with other people, or ready to explode. Try to talk with friends or a counselor before you become overwhelmed.

Hurt and embarrassment: You may find yourself taking personally the patient's moods. Often the disease or medication creates behavior changes, so that the patient may not behave in ways that are familiar to you or may do awkward or hurtful things. You may feel the patient doesn't really want you to be there, that you aren't appreciated, or that you have overstepped some invisible boundary, or that you are somehow not sensitive or good enough. Remember you are in a very vulnerable position and the patient will have periods of not being "rational." Keep one foot in reality by talking with others about your experiences.

Recognizing signs of stress is the first step in caring for yourself. Ask someone or several people close to you to read this section so they can help you observe danger signs. If behavior and feelings of stress arise, call someone you trust and start talking.

RULES FOR SURVIVAL

Coping with stress, or even preventing or minimizing it, requires some discipline and a willingness to live according to several basic rules. These rules for a balanced, sane life are derived from many thoughtful advocates, from caregivers to mental health professionals. Apply them to your own situation.

Ask for Help

Lesson number one is, recognize when you need help with all the chores that have to be done, and never hesitate to ask for it. People will overwhelm you with good advice, and some will offer assistance. Write down their suggestions and offers to refer to when there's more time available or a specific need to be met. Some tasks will probably be best done by you, so do them yourself. But be willing to turn over whatever else you can to others.

Time Management

Do only what work is most essential today, and put off the rest. Make a schedule for the day and stick to it; don't waste time trying to figure out how to do that one more thing. Arrange to do similar tasks at the same time, running all your errands in one trip, for example. If you have some nasty tasks, like tracking down an insurance agent or going over bookkeeping, either decide this is the day and just do it (preferably, first thing) or break the task into small units and do one each day. Delegate responsibilities: if you can afford it, hire someone to do things you don't like to do. If necessary, learn to say no to yourself and others.

Organization

Cultivate a spirit of efficiency and look for shortcuts wherever possible. Opportunities for saving time are everywhere: keep medical supplies together and near the patient; know what food and household supplies you have and keep a running list of what you need to restock; let other people run errands; keep the patient's personal items where she can reach them; buy and make food in quantity and use prepared food.

Medical Support

Having the telephone number(s) of medical professionals available around the clock will serve as your safety valve. Know where you can get help when you need it. Acquire practical knowledge and skills about caregiving.

Check in regularly with the attending nurse or doctor, preferably daily, to reassure yourself about the patient's care, to seek advice about whatever symptoms are evident, to ask about medications, or to pose any other questions that have arisen during the day. Touching base each day, especially on days that are difficult, will ensure that you have much-needed company. You will feel more confident that both you and the patient are getting the help you need.

Emotional Support

Stress provides opportunities for personal growth not available in everyday life, and many need help and direction at such times. People who work in the helping professions generally use what is called "supervision," a check-in session (usually weekly) with a counselor or group of professionals that allows them to make certain they are keeping a perspective on their work and express their feelings. As a caregiver, you can benefit from a similar check-in with someone outside the immediate home care environment who can observe your own physical condition, sense of balance, and emotions. Set up your own regular supervision with a close friend or with a social worker, minister, or other professional referred to you. During periods of great stress, when you detect warning signals that you are overwhelmed, seek out someone—a friend or a therapist—who will pay attention only to you. Stress, caretaking, and death can loosen our most hidden knots and with the assistance of a trained therapist can produce important self-knowledge and great personal growth. Remember that meeting your own emotional needs frees you to help others.

Good Sense

Get enough rest, good food, and conversation with friends. Take breaks, avoid excessive use of alcohol or drugs, relax your grip on perfection, don't make the patient's well-being your only source of self-esteem, and count your blessings. Use your humor: hold a contest or celebrate something. Remember there are many things you cannot control, including the patient's illness, moods of others, your own feelings.

> God grant me the serenity to accept the things I cannot change, the courage to change the things I can, and the wisdom to know the difference.

Take time to plan and reflect, as well as time to confer with other members of the team. Take the advice you would give a good friend in your situation. Divide your day into manageable segments of, say, forty-five minutes each, and reward yourself with a break between each work period to play a game of solitaire, write in your journal, make a telephone call, take a shower, sketch a scene outside the window, practice an instrument, read a chapter. Ten- or fifteen-minute breaks to shake off a task and refocus yourself can make all the difference.

Exercise

The physical labor involved in caregiving can also be a very therapeutic way to take a break, somewhat like gardening or cleaning out a closet. When you feel stuck or realize you are thinking or analyzing too much, get up and do something. Moving furniture or supplies so they are more convenient, changing the bed, giving a back rub, or any other activity that requires attention and produces visible results will clear out the cobwebs and use up some energy you might otherwise turn in on yourself. Keep up your own regular exercise program or take a fifteen-minute walk each day.

Physical Care

Avoid reaching the point of exhaustion, since being tired will make you more susceptible to physical and emotional upheavals. An upset stomach, catching a cold, or crying without apparent cause is a good indication of not enough rest. If you are unable to sleep soundly, try a glass of warm milk before bed, then ask for help from the doctor; concern about not sleeping well will only result in extra strain. Learn a relaxation or meditation method from a friend or from one of the many books on this subject. Eat well-balanced meals at regular times, take a multivitamin and "stress" tablets. If necessary, ask your physician about ways to care for yourself.

Waiting Skills

One of the biggest problems for caregivers, especially if they are used to a bustling routine, is boredom. (This will *not* be true, of course, if you are also managing a large household.) Home care involves a lot of sitting, watching, and waiting; the patient's pace in speech and activity can be excruciatingly slow. Dying can seem to take forever. Think of things to do in short periods of time that will provide a sense of accomplishment, such as phone calls, crafts, easy reading or writing, reorganizing a bookcase. You might choose to make a pillow or another handcrafted object which will recall this experience in the years to come.

Setting Limits

Despite your best efforts at self-care, you may be unrealistic about how much you can manage. You may need to set limits for both physical and emotional reasons. When you are having a difficult day, ask someone on the team to come and stay for a few hours so you can get away. Probably no one will be close enough to you each day to step up and call a halt for you, so it is a skill you must learn.

Live Your Life

Keep up as much of your own life as possible. Do what you can to retain what is important to your well-being, including good grooming, eating, and sleeping habits. Stay in touch with friends. You need to be able to get away from the house, or at least from the patient's room, for an hour or two every day. Don't give up your regular bridge or tennis game. Get a "sitter" so you can go to a concert, take a walk, or enjoy some other leisure activity. You are not a robot, or a paid nurse who comes and goes. Home care is very hard work, and one person cannot do it twenty-four hours a day. Many find they occasionally need a few days away, and that this break does everyone good.

Say No

One of the most important things a caregiver must do is to say no. If you don't know how yet, this may be a real personal gift to you.

- When you are afraid to be alone with the patient for whatever reason, call someone in.

- When a nurse calls to say she can't make it and asks if you can manage, say, "No, you will have to find a replacement."

- When the patient wants everything done by you ("You are the only one I trust," "You do it the best," etc.), tell her other people have to help out because you have something else to do, or are tired, or whatever.

- When a task or day or mood overwhelms you, try to do some simple task and let the mood pass by. If this doesn't work, stop and write it down, or call someone and talk, or call someone and tell her you *have* to call a halt for a few hours and could she cover for you.

- When the patient is angry or despairing and it's getting to you, ask someone else to be there for a while and just leave.

DETACHMENT

Caregivers talk about the lessons they learned from home care, and there are many. Among the most useful is how to detach from what is not in your control. While you will be able to help the patient by understanding the disease and its symptoms, and by providing physical and emotional care, you must acknowledge to yourself and to everyone else, including the patient, what you can and cannot do. Without detachment, the experience can be quite devastating. Too often we set ourselves up for misery through the motivation to be helpful. We want results—a smile, a sign of improvement, gratitude, a change of mood—and in many cases they will just not be forthcoming.

I remember the most awful moment when I realized that all the efforts I had been making only put pressure on my grandmother. I was trying to get my own results. I wanted what I did to make her well. One morning after many mornings of the same routine—me trying to get her to drink a heavy protein drink that she hated, while giving her a pep talk about building up strength so we might go for a walk—she looked up at me with tears in her eyes. "I just can't . . . I'm sorry, I just can't. I know you want me to, but please understand. I'm just too tired."

You can learn to accept the boundaries of what you can control, and this does not necessarily mean removing yourself physically or emotionally. The patient does need your presence and understanding. But your goal should be to accompany him, not to try to do anything for him, or change his outlook, or even "make things easier" for him. Just do and say what seems natural, stand by him, and don't think about the results.

Detaching yourself from the results of what you do will ease the strain of not getting what you want. Detachment also means the patient does not have to pretend to be cheered or relieved when—through no fault of yours—he isn't. Detaching yourself also gives you the freedom to attend to your own care, so that you live each day in a way that ensures your own peace. The patient will be nurtured by the serenity of the caregiver, and so will the rest of the family. Consciously make emotional investments in others around you; acknowledge other important relationships. Even in the midst of the most demanding circumstances, setting out your own schedule and limits will help you secure your own individuality.

I guess I thought my husband needed someone to die with him, as if I could take some of the load. Advise others to fight this natural tendency. The distinction between me and my dying husband became blurred. I felt as though I were dying, too. I ate his food, slept on his half-hour intervals, felt his confusion and pain. Anything that happened in his presence I observed as if I were dying. When he died, I was still there. I felt caught, like the one left standing at the end of musical chairs. I couldn't begin to say goodbye to my husband for months, because I thought I should be dead, too. It took me a long time to live again.

One final word about detachment: keep calling yourself back to the present. You can handle this moment, and that's all that's required. It is awfully easy to slip into generalizing about the past or how difficult the future will be. Wandering away from present reality is bound to lead you to anger, resentment, fantasy and the "poor me's." Living in the present heads off the crippling fears and obsessions about caregiving, questions like, "What will the patient be like tomorrow?" "Will I be able to cope with the next phase of her dying?" "How can I live without her?" "Will I be with him until the end?" and so on. Stay with today; it's plenty to handle.

Think of yourself as being in an accelerated survival course, much like the solo experience in survival training programs. If home care often seems like being alone on an island with three matches and a fishing hook, you are correct: this is a challenge, and your life will be richer for the experience.

16
FAMILY AND HOUSEHOLD

When the patient is part of a family or household, the decision to remain at home—preferably with everyone's agreement—affects the life of each member. Special care needs to be taken to ensure that the stresses on each individual and the family unit are not overwhelming. In addition to emotional factors, necessary day-to-day adjustments in everyone's routines are bound to be difficult. Being alert to the effects on a household of one member's dying will help you sense trouble before it becomes too great. This chapter is addressed to problems of households. While we usually cite examples from the nuclear family, issues raised apply equally to all households—friends, communal families, and others. Readers should translate freely to fit their own situation.

How one family rallies around a crisis will be very different from another, and comparisons are to be discouraged. In the same way, each member will behave differently. Often one or two will tend to be relied upon; another one or two never come through. However your family is organized, try to keep a sense of perspective, even humor, and recognize the real strengths because they are certainly there.

ACKNOWLEDGING THE TRUTH

The first challenge is to understand what it means that the patient is home or has decided to remain at home and not return to the hospital.

The family will provide care because cure is no longer possible. The realization by family members that the patient is dying may come directly from the patient or doctor, or it may be a slow acceptance in the face of undeniable evidence. For one family member, the truth came clear one morning at the breakfast table:

> She and I determined, with our inherited Yankee dependence on right-mindedness, that patience, effort in the form of following a medical regimen, mild exercise, and attention to nutrition, would somehow turn this persistent deterioration around. We went for walks, had stimulating discussions to balance the naps, talked of taking a trip in the fall, acted as if she'd be back on the golf course in no time. I know that she let go of this myth sooner than I. I was mildly aware that I was fighting her, trying to turn her will around. Not the will to live—that wasn't the issue yet—but the will to overcome some obstacle set by her physical limitations. I began to see that I had set a standard, which was not shared, by which to measure the success of each day. I was very stubborn.
>
> One morning as I outlined the day's regimen, she began to cry. "I'm not getting any better. You've got to believe me." It was then that I began to accept her as she was.

The truth may just mean giving up the false hope that enough good cheer, or medication, or time will cure the disease. Some feel that bringing the person home is a sign of giving up, and they fear criticism from friends and other relatives who don't understand.

Acceptance may come simply as everyone sees and learns the reality of the situation, and acknowledges the medical facts. "The hardest thing," said one social worker who works with families considering home care, "is when the family asks what we will do when the lungs fill up, and I suggest 'nothing,' and even talk about pneumonia being a dying person's best friend. The truth hits families when you describe what is likely to happen to the patient within the next few days or weeks."

An infection persisted in the raw area of her mouth, which had been operated on and then irradiated. Ten days on the antibiotics and ten days off, we seesawed through the spring. These repeated exchanges of discouragement and hope were exhausting. Each time the infection recurred, we had to resurrect the phrases we had acquired to feed our optimism. Morning treatments by the visiting nurse were painful, and my grandmother had to rest for several hours afterward. They often shattered the spirit of an otherwise good day. Somehow I kept thinking these events would end or we would overcome them.

The nurse finally told us this was "the way it would be." Somehow I hadn't thought death would be a slow erosion. How could a sore mouth mean death?

No one easily accepts that someone is dying. The patient may even help the family to keep up the fantasy that she will get well.

I thought she might have wanted to believe a lie. I had to change the sheets all the time because she was vomiting, yet I didn't want to admit to her she was dying. Did she know? Yes, I'm sure she did. She kept apologizing for being a burden, for puking blood. Now I know it would have been easier for us both if we'd talked about it.

Often the patient acknowledges the truth but allows the family to develop a myth to sustain itself—though one patient responded to his family's well-intentioned denial by keeping his hearing aid turned off.

One social worker who counsels families caring for patients at home said that some deny the truth so strongly that they see the chance to go home as a hopeful sign.

Even with all the evidence at hand, families and patients blind themselves to the truth and want to think they might be getting well. I try to arrange a family conference where I encourage people to ask questions and to project what may happen. I bring up truths and questions like, "The calcium level may go up, and these are the symptoms. This is what we could do, what do you think is best?" I try to get them to take on the truth and manage themselves.

Once you begin to provide home care, and as time goes by living with the daily reality of how the patient feels and the gradual deterioration of ability, everyone in the household will come to their own acknowledgment and accommodation to the truth.

THE FAMILY

A major change in the well-being of one member is bound to disturb the balance of the family, changing the way individuals interact in surprising ways. Things we take for granted that promote security in a household become clear when one of the people no longer plays the usual role. This occurs when an adult member loses a job, for example; when someone is critically ill or dying, the effects are startling. Even seemingly routine matters are now difficult or painful to carry out or are somehow not quite right. Not only will unconscious rituals like dinnertime, getting ready for church, putting the dog out, bathroom habits, and going to work be thrown off, but also the more critical elements that bind the family together. You can expect these activities to change and perhaps carry some stress:

- Discussing and solving problems

- Making decisions and setting priorities

- Dividing responsibilities and chores

- Expressing feelings

- Relating to others in the family and outsiders

- Spending and budgeting money

- Understanding of religion

- Scheduling daily activities

- Planning even the immediate future

- Providing for privacy and social needs

In addition, the family must negotiate new interactions because of the illness. Relationships with physicians, nurses, hospital personnel, and other providers will have to be worked out. Family members will need to provide some care and perform some tasks themselves. Some may be asked to take part in care that calls for a level of intimacy or reliability hitherto not part of their relationship with the patient.

As the patient is dying, the family lives each day with hope and despair, fear of a change in symptoms or in his mood, concern over the cost of treatments and continuing care, worry over loss of income, and other difficult feelings. If these tensions are not successfully dealt with, family unhappiness and discord can stimulate and even aggravate the patient's symptoms and generally create an emotional environment that is unhealthy for everyone.

Assessing the family for signs of stress is an important part of home care. Real trouble, if left unattended, will recur, and long-term emotional pain may result. An individual member may need reassurance or help; another may be stuck on a problem that is not the real issue and need to be gently redirected. A young child may be constantly picked on, or his playmate may be annoying everyone. If a family member has been suffering on some low level from a long-term emotional problem, this unsettled environment may bring it out in the open. For everyone, home care will release patterns and symptoms of stress. For further understanding of burnout, read Chapter 15, "Self-Care."

When you approach the matter of how the household can be helped to cope with the strain of home care, begin by observing its existing strengths and weaknesses. When professional counselors assess a family's ability to cope, they look at such characteristics as how members communicate; whether members support, encourage, respect each other; whether the family has a larger community from whom it will accept and ask for help; and whether individuals show flexibility toward each other and allow privacy and independence.

Seek the objective view and advice of a social worker, a counselor, or even a wise family friend. Take what you learn to help members know how they can strengthen their roles to be useful and satisfying, to share and support others in the household.

Regular family meetings are recommended, to serve as forums where medical news can be conveyed and fears can be shared and aired. A social worker or close family friend can participate and offer an objective view of strains and stresses. If the family is unable to meet, talk, organize itself, and feel generally satisfied about how well it is managing, then professional help should be sought.

In trying to promote everyone's well-being, remember the tendency to fix roles within a family: one cries; another holds the tissues. Patterns such as this need to be spotted and acknowledged. Everyone should have a chance to vent emotions and to soothe them. Family members can learn and accept what is really possible or logical for another person to do. Everyone can look for ways to be available to others, particularly to the caregiver. Nothing is so helpful as when someone else in the family takes a genuine interest in learning how to change a dressing or give medication.

In the process of coping with this disruption of their lives, families discover individuals' strengths and how to care for weaknesses. They learn to seek help for things they are unable to manage alone. A young child, for example, may initially need counseling from a social worker to help her adjust to the growing incapacity of her mother. Families may turn to friends and community services for a homemaker, "meals on wheels" program, day camp, or day care.

In short, the family will acquire new coping skills and develop resources and a willingness to shorten sights, live a day at a time, and ask for help. These are skills well acquired. When families look back on the experience of home care, many say they learned a better way to live and a certainty about what family ties and rituals were most important.

THE PATIENT

I am tired all the time, and yet I want to be a part of the family. I am exhausted and feel guilty because I can't help do the household chores the way I used to. I want to get good and sick so I won't have responsibilities, or so people won't ask anything of me.

When a person returns home to die, he is coming back to familiar surroundings in which he played a fairly well defined role. But because of his illness, that role will be substantially changed. A mother, for example, may be able to direct menu-planning but will not be able to do all the cooking; everyone knows that mother's recipes—even when duplicated word for word—just aren't the same by someone else's hand. Adjusting to the multiple changes in tasks—step-by-step acknowledgment that she cannot do what she once did—is tremendously upsetting.

Relegated by illness to an increasingly passive state, the patient will find that her mental attitude comes to depend largely upon how she is treated, so that to some extent she becomes a victim of those around her. Because she cannot play her usual role, the patient must also face not being connected in accustomed ways. A mother can no longer tuck the children into bed; a father can no longer shoot baskets with them after lunch; a child can no longer be affirmed through a good grade.

> I am afraid that the presence of illness in the household upsets everyone. I roam around the house at night and keep my husband awake. I have constantly to ask for help, with changing beds, cleaning, cooking. I hate it because I like having these things done my way, and yet my husband is the one who has to do it. I'm home all the time now, so I worry about everything more. I don't want to seem like a nag, so often I just end up hurting because I do it myself.

As the family begins to feel the patient's reliance, members may withdraw out of fear or confusion. Further complicating the patient's crisis is the fact that family members are also under stress, having had to make significant modifications in their way of life. These adaptations take effort and can be quite painful, and the patient may experience real or imagined emotional isolation as a result of family members' resentment, whether it remains hidden or is stated directly.

More tangible familial problems will also contribute to the strain. The issue of physical care is probably the most frequent battleground, for rarely will the family spend more than twenty-four hours with a treatment and care plan before someone is dissatisfied. Another challenge involves individual dynamics, which are such that the patient may be angry at his disease at the same time that the family is denying that it is serious; or the reverse may be true. The patient may feel guilty and the family resentful over a sacrifice that has to be made, such as a delay of vacation plans. Even when the family does its best to make life easy, the patient may not respond or may in fact make life more difficult. He may turn others away, or shut himself off from the world so completely that it will be nearly impossible to break through. This remoteness is especially sad when, for example, a child needs to be reassured by a parent or another member wants to settle an old grievance. The patient may manipulate everyone in petty ways: she may be angry with the sound level of the television, chain-smoke, complain about the smell of foods, or demand snacks, pills, company. She may not want to share the bathroom; she may not want to be left alone.

When the behavior of the patient becomes unreasonable, it is time to sit the entire family down for a talk, including the patient. Opening a discussion—no matter how uncomfortable or how much worse it might seem in anticipation—is always the best solution. Reassure the patient that everyone is trying to help. Explain that the only way the family can really offer the support she needs is by knowing what she wants and her cooperating as best she can with their efforts. It may also be that the group will benefit from special counseling. Often simply asking the hospital or community social worker to attend a family meeting will be enough to clear the air and get everyone refocused in healthy ways.

As much as possible, help the patient to be in control, to undertake independent activities that are valued by others. Mending, reading to children, bookkeeping, or brushing a child's hair can be done in bed. Sick children can be given simple chores such as watching a young child in a playpen or helping a sibling learn the alphabet.

My husband would sit for hours in his lawn chair watching the children playing in the yard or advising the neighbor on mechanics of his car. He wanted to be at home so he could be around us all and insisted on a business-as-usual attitude. The kids played their rock music, and I think he even gained some appreciation of it. His door was always open to the wonderful confusion of a large family, and the children's friends would come over and ask him for help with their homework.

Finally, the key to the patient's security in a family is to give her the feeling that everyone needs and has time for her. Her illness makes her look at the world differently, so that she requires a good deal of reassurance that she is okay and cared for. Since her functions and responses have probably slowed down, allow her plenty of time to react and answer. She also values time in which people are simply quiet and present. Someone reading or working in the room, or available to sit silently with her, separate from routines and anxieties, will produce security and calm. Above all, the family has wonderful instincts for what to do and how to listen to what the patient needs. Following these instincts will be very rewarding and reassuring.

DAY-TO-DAY ORGANIZATION

While caregiving won't last forever, at the time it is being provided each day may seem to take just that long to pass. No one can predict how long the person will live, and many make the mistake of believing it can't possibly last more than a week and become exhausted after a month of unrelieved care. Because the term of care is indefinite, caregivers must make special efforts to see that family life goes on—complete with arguments, enjoyment, weddings, and gardening—because it is just this regularity that individuals need from families. The easiest way to accomplish this is to keep the routines whenever possible: going to church, visits from close friends, playing games, the weekly drive and ice cream cone. If the patient cannot participate, do them anyway, and try to bring some of these rituals to the bedside.

Standard tasks in families also have to be done, no matter how bothersome they may now seem. This may mean temporarily making specific assignments. Review the functions listed below and determine which are relevant for your family. How are these duties completed normally? If the task has been done by either the patient or the primary caregiver, someone else will have to do it, since both have been "reassigned" to the illness. If the patient is able, be sure to include him in planning and performing chores. Some can even be done in bed. If he cannot help, no harm is done by his seeing the willingness and ability of others to fill in for him.

Meals:

- planning and buying supplies
- cooking, serving, and dishes

Housework:

- cleaning
- laundry

Household tasks:

- errands
- pets

Child care:

- preschoolers: bathing, dressing, feeding, bedtime routine, discipline, supervision, transportation
- schoolchildren: school, lessons, homework, clothes, transportation
- adolescents: transportation, supervision

Family activities:

- television, movies, reading
- sports
- vacation
- entertaining
- church

In addition to the usual household chores, patient care must be apportioned. All family members need to participate in planning the dying person's care so that the schedule and division of tasks will be generally understood. Again, the patient should also help with plans whenever possible. Needs and schedules of family members should be respected and adjusted only when necessary. Planning can be reviewed each week, or more frequently if necessary. Hold a family meeting, at which time adjustments can be made easily and other problems—a member not doing his part, the patient's constant complaining, a recurring schedule conflict—can be quickly addressed.

Because no one wants to leave the patient alone, members feel compelled to rearrange their lives so they can be at home. Providing enough coverage may mean family members will have to ask for leave from jobs, or at least negotiate with their employers for permission to shorten the workday, be able to leave work quickly, and occasionally work at home.

PATIENT LIVES ALONE

When a patient lives alone, family members often move into the patient's home, leaving jobs and other families temporarily behind. Following is an account told by the cousin of this unusual family. It says everything necessary about what can be done when caregivers make up their minds to be present.

> Margaret lived alone, and her children must be given credit for coming home to help her. One left graduate school, one took a leave from his medical residency, another left a carpentry job. They were valiant beyond words through the very long and hard seven weeks. If only every dying person could be assured of that much love. Direct involvement helped them get over their fear of her, and I know it saved them from regret. The three of them took turns being in the room with her, doing laundry, sleeping, cooking. If one was harried, the other two pushed him out the door for a run or a movie. It was very long, and they were wonderful.

Stories about family members and friends rallying around a patient to enable her to stay at home are very characteristic of home care, and those who reorganize their lives for this purpose are very precious.

ABSENT FAMILY MEMBERS

Some members of the immediate family cannot or choose not to drop what they are doing and be on hand. Some may not be asked to do so. These "absentee" members are in touch by telephone or infrequent visits. While such relatives will often do their best to make some contribution, their absence can result in a lot of guilt and resentment on both sides.

My brother called frequently and offered to help, although he lived some distance away. We both knew it was very difficult for him to come, but his constant concern was an enormous source of strength.

This woman later expressed deep resentment that her brother hadn't visited in the last few months of their mother's life so that she had been left alone with responsibility for care. When asked about his staying away, her brother explained, "I felt she didn't want me there, that it would be just one more person underfoot, and I guess I was happy to duck out, too, because I was somewhat afraid to go."

It is not unusual for caregivers to resent absent family members. Explaining the patient's condition to someone on the telephone takes time and emotional energy, and a sense of frustration often results from not being able to convey satisfactorily what is going on. Distant relatives create an added strain since they themselves are grieving and may feel helpless. Troubled about what to do or say, everyone is overly sensitive. Faced with such conflicts and feelings, it is not unusual for the caregiver and the callers to feel even more isolated after trying unsuccessfully to communicate by telephone. When family members are not close by, everyone should rally as best they can, relay information, and be open about shared concerns and confusion.

If a friend or close family member lives at a great distance and seems to be waiting to make the trip until the funeral, encourage him to come soon while the patient is able to be aware of his presence.

One daughter who lived two thousand miles away telephoned frequently and managed a few days' visit. Our son flew from Berlin to spend five weeks with us, and this gave my husband untold pleasures and warmth. They had memorable talks. Neither of them was here when he died, but that wasn't really necessary. Spending time to create memories was what they needed.

Having a visit with the patient when he is still alert, whether or not he is able to converse, gives the visitor a living memory of intimacy and an opportunity to resolve past conflicts and express love. This is less likely to be true if the person dying is so ill or medicated that communication and clarity are difficult. Visiting while the patient is requiring a great deal of care has the added benefit of supporting the caregiver, even giving her a break.

KEEP TALKING

The cornerstone of a family's success in dealing with any crisis is the ability of individuals to speak openly about emotions. In home care, that openness is critical for the mental health of everyone concerned.

"When I tell people how I feel, I feel better," said the eleven-year-old daughter of a woman dying. A wife whose husband has cancer recalled, "When we began to talk openly, we came to appreciate the life we had and each other, and this made all the difference." The fourteen-year-old son of a dying father admitted, "Once we talked as a family about his cancer, I felt less lonely."

Avoiding open conversation about the fatal illness of a family member is, sadly, quite common. Even though a patient's children or spouse may have the best intentions of trying to save her from further anguish or others from grief, the effects of keeping feelings under the table are extremely harmful. A sixteen-year-old boy told the story of his family when his sister was dying at home.

> There were five of us children at home. My sister was there, in bed, in pain, doing what we all thought were really gross things, but my parents refused to talk about it. We weren't allowed to have friends over, and no other family came. Even her friends didn't visit. We were completely isolated and I felt ashamed of her.

Openly crying and expressing fear and even anger are preferable to the possible denial and inevitable isolation that the patient and family members suffer when they cannot talk, or feel they are the only ones suffering. Showing feelings and dealing directly with each other about reality may seem "messier," but the result will be a firm foundation of truth and peacefulness. Full expression of feelings means forgetting old judgments about being "appropriate" or "overreacting." Constant change, separation, development, growth, and loss are all normal parts of family life, and learning to live with them is important for each person. In home care, individuals are strengthened as they express grief and anger, acknowledge love openly, even talk about past conflicts with the person dying. Many people say that being able to express feelings and in fact say goodbye, while it is terribly sad and difficult, is one of the privileges of knowing in advance that someone is dying; it provides the opportunity to conclude the relationship rather than be wrenched from it.

CHILDREN

When a parent or sibling in the home is dying, a young child will rather quickly recognize on some level the unhappiness in his surroundings. Gloom will affect his mood, and he should be told something specific as soon as it is feasible. "Daddy is very sick, and the doctors and I are doing everything we can to make him cozy." At a later point the explanation should be, "He is very sick and may die soon, and that's why we are all so sad." Although what you say may not be fully comprehended, you need to keep real information in the open, so the child knows what is the cause of trouble in his surroundings. Children tend to take responsibility themselves for what they do not understand, and it is important that they be constantly informed and then reassured that they are loved and included. Early discussion, as substantive as possible, is important groundwork for the time when you must finally explain, "You remember I told you Daddy was awfully sick and might die. I'm very sad to tell you that Daddy did die last night."

Children who have a prior awareness of death may have an easier time when a family member is dying. The death of a pet, a television personality, or a prominent national leader gives the child a reference. To prepare a child to experience loss, talk about a death she has experienced, making sure to call it "death" and not "sleep" or some other indirect word.

By the age of three, or perhaps younger, children can grasp some idea of death if helped to translate details into their own understanding: "The dog does not need food any more." "No—the cat doesn't pee." A favorite television star who dies doesn't sleep or play or get sad or happy anymore. Try to allow some time to pass before replacing a pet or lost object. A child can easily learn to think that if she or a parent dies she can be replaced immediately, too. Allow the child to experience missing someone or something and to develop memories.

If the person dying is a brother or sister, older siblings will generally want to know details. Talk specifically about the disease; don't just say it's a cold. Make sure they understand it's not contagious and that they needn't worry about their own health or catching it. Children may also experience guilt; most have at some point "wished death" on their sibling. Assure the child that his anger was natural and not the cause of the illness, that he does not have to "make up" for those wishes but can show simple caring today. When a child appears to resent special attention given a sick sibling, talk to him about the patient's needs and solicit his help.

When a parent is involved in care or is dying, and the other parent cannot be present all the time, a young child needs someone in the family or a close friend to be her steward, to have clear responsibility for her. This is not to "banish" her to a "substitute mother" or any such variant, but to provide her at all times with a loving companion whose first concern is her care. Consistency is very important, so whoever volunteers should make a commitment to remain close by during the illness and afterward. When possible, the child should remain at home, sleep in her own room, have her own toys, and eat her accustomed foods. If in doubt, err on the side of familiarity and routine. She needs to have whatever stability can be provided.

Children will also probably appreciate being confided in and given chores. Giving them special assignments ensures that they feel responsible and special themselves and draws the family together. Including children in care, conversations, and planning is beneficial for the patient as well. Even older patients derive great joy from children's freshness and vitality. At St. Christopher's Hospice near London, patients routinely visit the child care room and playgrounds for children of staff members. Children rarely suffer from such contact, unless adults with them are exhibiting anxiety or difficulty and are not talking openly about it. Parents who think children should not be exposed to illness are usually taking care of the child in themselves who is still afraid of disease.

A child's behavior may become trying as he expresses his feelings, deals with the change in family life, and grieves the loss of companionship. He may be fearful or angry when people leave him even for an evening, and may have problems with sleeping, toilet habits, playing, and schoolwork. Be sure to inform his teachers and other parents close to him about what is going on in the family so they can assist with extra understanding and suggestions. At any point, the child may become so difficult or be so obviously in pain that help may be required. Seek a family or child counselor when you feel the child is not responding to the care family members offer. How he learns to cope with this sorrow is vitally important to the rest of his life.

TWO-MEMBER HOUSEHOLD

When the family unit consists of only one person who is well and the patient, practical matters of home care may actually be easier, since many of the usual tasks required in larger families will not exist or will be simpler to carry out. However, special care and planning will be required just to maintain bare essentials of living for the two people, particularly when the patient requires full-time attention. One widow described how she had managed:

> Our apartment was compact and I could attend to the kitchen and cleaning chores without being out of earshot. Our daughter and other family came often, bringing groceries and other supplies. A neighbor brought our mail. When my husband slept I put laundry through the machine in the basement. I managed by planning my day carefully.

Though at first it may seem impossible, home care can even be managed successfully when the caregiver must be absent for part of the day. The examples below show how this can work. In the first, a young teacher cared for her mother while carrying a full teaching load.

> Mother and I had an incredible schedule. After the morning chores and meal, Mom fell into a deep sleep, and I would go to the university. I always drove to save the fifteen-minute walking time. I would get home by eleven-fifteen; Mom would wake up about then, have lunch and medications, and go back to sleep. I would return to teach or do office work, coming back by three-thirty, when she would

awake. Close friends and our priest had keys to the house in case of emergency, and they came on scheduled afternoons so that I could teach a late afternoon class. It actually worked quite well.

In the second, a free-lance writer organized her grandmother's care.

I was trying to keep up my work, and although I could be flexible, I still had to put in the hours at some point during the day. We had housekeepers who would come on a schedule to clean, cook, and help with care. My grandmother claimed they were "underfoot," which was her way of saying she wanted me to be there all the time. I just had to ignore the guilt that produced for me. Even so, transporting, scheduling, food shopping, arranging for the nurses, trying to be there when the doctor called, and communicating food preferences and instructions took a lot of time. Negotiating the personalities was a daily challenge.

No one has the perfect household for home care. Organization, adjustment, and determination are the only ways it will work.

Most families can handle more than anyone gives them credit for. Assuming that the family is in reasonably sound physical and emotional condition, caring for a dying member is a natural undertaking and well within its ability. Social workers, clergy, health care professionals, and hospice workers remind us that the family is durable and can even be strengthened by home care. Most also acknowledge that the characteristics most often used to measure the success of a family—occupations, education, religion, children, finances—are not necessarily relevant to predicting the success or failure of home care. The critical factors are the desire of the patient and her family to be at home and everyone's agreement and determination to have it work.

17
VISITORS
AND FRIENDS

In the course of home care, the presence of friends and associates can offer a great deal to both patient and caregiver. While people not in the immediate family often feel they have little to offer, such is not the case. Thoughtful attention from the whole realm of acquaintances is invaluable during the patient's illness and after he dies. Visitors can be welcomed into the home, even on the most difficult days. Some caregivers say they hesitated to have anyone come when the patient was very ill, or when emotions in the household were very high. They regretted keeping people away at times when they could help most. Don't worry about upsetting visitors. Welcome them and let them decide whether they want to come and how long they will stay. Here is how one caregiver put it:

Visitors need to know first of all: "We need you; please come." Don't hesitate to call old friends, tell them what is happening, and say, "You are welcome to come. I know it's hard for you . . . You don't have to, but we would love to see you." Let people know the patient is dying, and don't decide for them in advance that they don't want to visit. What they need to know, too, is that they are important to the family and represent a big caring world that we tend to forget in our homes.

Visits can be especially welcome when only one caregiver is on hand, to provide a fresh face and some objectivity. If the patient is withdrawn, resentful, or confused, having to rise to the occasion of a visitor often helps to orient him. Visitors can not only read to the patient, play card games, or share a hobby, they can also help to provide a break for the patient and caregivers in their usual patterns of acting and thinking.

Families have had good success with setting visiting hours or having a flag system, such as turning on the porch light when visitors are welcome. It's generally easier on the patient and the company if several people are present; if a visitor should want privacy, she can easily ask for it.

Remember that the patient does not have to see everyone who wants to visit, and he should always be asked before a visitor is admitted into the room, even if he agreed to the idea a few hours earlier. Moods and physical comfort constantly change, and he should always have freedom from making the extra effort of entertaining company. This holds for even the closest friends, relatives, and the boss.

The family and caregivers should realize that most visitors will be frightened or nervous about seeing the patient.

I knew I was going to see Marie but I was scared to death. I didn't know what to do once I got into her room. I didn't know how to look, how to step, or should I stand or touch her, what should I say? If I talked about mutual friends, would that make her sad? Should I just chatter about my work and the thunderstorm? What if she were silent, or cried, or talked about dying? I didn't know what she would look like; how could I keep from staring horrified at her?

An infrequent visitor can easily be overwhelmed by the smells and sounds of the patient's room. Symptoms or deformities from the disease may make physical closeness difficult. Many are afraid to touch the patient.

BEING A GOOD VISITOR

What can a visitor be told so that he is more comfortable? The following guidelines will offer some suggestions, and can make stopping by more pleasurable for everyone.

- Don't stay too long; a few minutes spent with the patient is fine. While longer visits are possible, they should probably be restricted to close friends, who can sit quietly or help the caregivers with tasks.

- Remember that this is not the time to try to change anything about how the patient or family members behave or interact. Help the principals to preserve relationships they have; try not to intervene even though you feel you can see more clearly than they. Keep quiet about what you would do if . . .

- Don't feel you have to entertain or make a speech or present a gift. You are the gift. If appropriate, bring an old record or photograph album to share.

- Accept the patient's environment as it is. Her bed and room are probably the way she wants them. If you sense there is something she would like changed, offer to help.

- Begin by saying hello. Tell the patient you are sorry she is ill; then listen. Don't be afraid of silence; remember that the patient is not in the same active, verbal world she was in, so that even a few minutes of sitting quietly together can be immensely beneficial. See what she wants to talk about, what she asks about. Pick up on clues. Often the patient needs only an attentive listener.

- Look the patient in the eye and talk directly. Ask if you can help with anything; ask for a specific task. Make sure you can fulfill whatever the commitment entails.

- Talk of your life, feelings, work. Don't avoid talking about future plans, even if the patient will be unable to participate. He still wants to know what's happening around him.

- Be yourself. If in the past you have argued politics or joked with the patient, do that now. Admit you are anxious, if you are.

- If the patient requests information about her illness, ask her what she knows or why she is asking, or suggest she discuss it with the visiting nurse, doctor, or caregiver.

- If the patient talks about dying itself, or despair, anger, pain, or loneliness, sit it out and listen. Don't let him feel you will visit or stay only if he is cheerful. He needs to talk about his fears and needs others to sympathize and understand. Share your own feelings, so he knows you are really there.

- Try to avoid comparing the patient's problems to those of others. It doesn't matter if someone else has "something" similar. Respect confidences, of the patient and of others.

- Don't give medication unless specifically asked. Be cautious and modest in offering advice about treatment or care. Remember, the patient's comfort is the goal. Make a suggestion if it is appropriate, and then step aside. Pressuring or laying blame is not helpful.

- Be physical if you can. Hug, touch, stroke, hold hands. An embrace often conveys more than words.

- If the patient is tired or embarrassed, or needs to have a treatment that is obviously awkward, or somehow implies that she wants to be alone, accept the hint.

- Take along some small project—a checkbook to balance, a letter to write, handwork—so that silences can be natural and the patient can doze off without concern for entertaining you.

- When you leave, say, "I've enjoyed being with you. May I come again?" Whether or not you have had a conversation, or the patient has said anything "important," the visit has filled some hunger she feels for friendship, hope, and outlook. She is comforted by your presence.

- Be cheerful and accepting. Everyone in the patient's immediate vicinity is sensitive to both the condition of the patient
and the quality of care. They need support and much encouragement.

Many visitors come with an agenda or feel the patient has one—to
settle a memory, make a commitment, receive approval for some
decision. Be attentive to it. Ask for privacy, listen and respond, be
direct and clear.

> I wrestled with the problem of how to say goodbye. I wanted the right
> words to come at the right moment. I wanted to be forgiven. I would
> visit each day, hoping for the inspiration, courage, or a moment when
> she would be awake when no one else was in the room. Finally, I
> opened my mouth. I spoke, she listened. When I stopped, I thought I
> would be rewarded. But no great absolution came. I was crushed. I
> realize now that by being there I was affirming our relationship. My
> guilt over something I had done years ago was not important to her.
> Dying erases the petty offenses.

Remember that if you come with a request or an old guilt to
alleviate, it may be perfectly clear to you but not be understood by
the patient, whose mind is on his own matters. Say what you need
to say and trust that it has been heard as best as the patient can hear.
You need to say goodbye and thank you, and this can be done very
simply.

AFTER DEATH

During the initial period of shock and numbness, friends can be
encouraged to help those most affected by the death by sharing the
responsibility for organizing the funeral arrangements and burial,
legal and financial matters, care for children, and household chores.
In addition, sympathetic "outsiders" can offer objectivity, to reassure survivors that they needn't take on all the decisions or problems immediately. Help with good advice and the many tasks to be
done, beginning with making thorough lists, can also be an invaluable service.

Friends must be aware that grieving is not a rational process, and that for each person it has quite different manifestations. Many of us have preconceptions about proper grieving or correct behavior for a widow, and now is the time to drop them. You may observe extreme activity or inactivity, anger, guilt, and other behavior you think does not make sense, but it is that person's right. Some survivors show no feelings at all for long stretches. Remember that the human system will take on only what it can, and no more; there is no schedule or prescription for "getting better" or "getting over it."

In helping someone cope with grief, the most useful role a friend can play is just being present and attentive. This will not always be very easy. Don't be put off by anger, which can occasionally be almost terrifying. The person grieving may not be "rational" in any usual sense for a long time. He will react impulsively to those around him. Nothing anyone offers or says to him will be right, and many of his interactions will just seem to make his mood swings greater. He will be highly sensitive to real or imagined slights or judgments. Friends may be frightened by the intensity of his need and suffering; some, and even some members of the family, will stop wanting to listen or to talk about the dead person. The very best you can do, the greatest gift they can offer, is simply to listen, without any investment in trying to make the person feel better or to help her reach some conclusion. Her recuperation lies in her willingness and support you and others can provide for expressing her emotions. In this way, you help her to drain off some of the power of her feelings, making way for healing to begin.

The following are some general guidelines for helping someone suffering a loss.

- Don't try to remove the pain, correct his formulations or memories, or solve his problems.

- Don't force the person away from her concern with basic survival; gently offer activities and perspective.

- Don't diminish someone's pain by telling him of someone else's.

- Be accessible; physical presence, including eye contact and touching, is the greatest comfort.

- Don't judge expression of feelings.

- Listen to the stories over and over again; if you don't, she will think you don't care.

- Help him talk about unpleasant memories as well as good ones.

- Don't ignore physical symptoms; a visit to a physician can be good for confidence.

- Show her in various ways she is important to you and others.

- Offer practical help.

- Give him permission to be cheerful and have a good time when he seems to be unable to allow it himself.

- Remember that Friday nights, Sunday afternoons, holidays, anniversaries, and even certain times of the day are more difficult than others. Ask if and how the person would like help with these occasions.

You can learn these guidelines and then use your own intuition about what is specifically needed. Add to this what you can learn by reflecting, "If someone wanted to help me come to terms with a loss, even with this loss, what would I want said and done?" Being a good friend to caregivers and survivors is a great gift. Your care and concern remind them they are not alone, and this connection to the human family will make all the difference.

18
BEING
WITH A
DYING PERSON

Caregivers often find it easier to manage all of the necessary details and strenuous physical effort than the other crucial dimension of care: sitting, talking, and listening to the dying person. Do not be dismayed if you are unsure about *being* with the dying person. Caregivers, by the very nature of their taking home care responsibility, are people of action. They want to help and see results. Sitting still and listening are very difficult, yet your mere presence probably has more to do with the patient's comfort than anything else you can offer.

I needed to have people around me and to help my friends understand they didn't have to go away out of fear as many people do. We talk about my dying and they keep calling, being there for me. I vacillated between feeling as though I were a statistic and not alive or human but already dead, and feeling I might be the one in a million who would survive. I got a lot of information about the kind of cancer I have and talked with doctors about treatments and expectations. Finally I decided to stop treatments and just live it out. It helped to find out how the disease would progress and how I would probably die. I was reassured to know that chances are I'll sleep more and more and then lapse into a coma. Knowing I'll die makes me see there are no magic answers out there for me, so I can relax, let people help and be with me, and live each day the best I can.

This patient illustrates the various stages of a dying person's response to her prognosis and how much she depends on people—their support, information, and acceptance—to come to her own terms for living out the next weeks.

While being with the patient will mean helping her come to her own understanding of her imminent death, you will also participate in all the other things on her mind. She is still very much alive, with all the trivial and serious preoccupations we all have. Of course, she has a clearer idea than the rest of us when she will die, and physical symptoms do not allow her to wander too far from this awareness. But she is not and need not be thinking continually about her dying, and caregivers need not either. Today is what counts for the patient, and she needs to have the cooperation of those around her occasionally to forget her dying. She can have a sense of humor, waste time, and argue over trivial matters if she wishes. Do not try to make a saint out of her or minimize the importance of everyday matters. In other words, don't discount her or her various moods. As one social worker advised trainees in a hospice program, "Don't kill her off ahead of time."

So how should you be with a dying person? Be gentle and slow, be reliable, be honest, be permissive. These guidelines from nurses who work with dying patients sound easy. How could you possibly miss? You can't. But no matter how hard you try, "mistakes" will be made. You cannot always measure your own words, and you can *never* control the patient's reaction. When you do or say something that hurts, just apologize and keep going. If you give the patient a chance to get angry or to say, "That's okay, I understand," so much the better.

Knowing generally that there are pitfalls—as indeed there are in any relationship—in caring for someone dying can help you avoid them. The illness is bound to create confusion, even in a stable relationship. Most of the awkwardness will diminish with time and a lot of honest talking. Begin by admitting your sadness and discomfort with the condition of the patient and by admitting your fear of saying or doing something wrong. Listen and try to accept the patient as he or she is, rather than trying to change what can't be changed.

WHERE TO BEGIN

Even though the patient may not consciously think about her dying all the time, the knowledge and feelings about dying pervade everything she says and does. As home care begins, be aware that the patient is, to greater and lesser degrees, grieving her dying. What is going through the person's mind? At various times she may be thinking, "What is dying like?" "How can I be assured the best care?" "What happens after death?" "How can I keep control of what is happening to me?" Other patients devote a lot of mental energy to self-recrimination: "If only I hadn't smoked . . . If only I had seen the doctor sooner."

Many patients will also have had a friend who had the same disease and suffered a great deal, or will have heard of someone who had a similar procedure that didn't work, or who was misdiagnosed.

> My grandmother had a friend who had died from cancer; she had heard horror stories about the pain. Also, she had her own fears from growing up in a generation that equated physical well-being with a daily bowel movement. When she became constipated, terrible associations arose for her. I guess I learned that it's the little things that count. We need to find out what they are.

Because any number of imaginable fears plague a sick person, it is very helpful to be open to references and encourage talking about memories so that they can become a little less vivid, or perhaps can even be successfully put to rest by the doctor.

General anxiety about the disease and dying are magnified for the patient each time a symptom recurs or another activity becomes impossible. Under such circumstances, even when secure in his own bed, with caregivers and family in place, the patient's greatest fear is of being alone, abandoned to die, and losing control of his body and actions.

I am uncertain, completely *uncertain,* about tomorrow or even one hour from now. I am afraid of pain, especially excruciating pain that won't let go. I am afraid of the feelings of unreality I get. I am afraid of waking up with amnesia. I am afraid of never being able to wake up completely. I am afraid of my next bowel movement. I am afraid of what will happen to me. I am afraid because I don't know what will happen. I am afraid of hospital trips, operations, medicine. I am afraid because I am no longer in control of my life. I am now powerless and unable to do anything except try to love, to keep my heart open.

As the patient reveals her specific fears, reassure her by words and action that you and others will stay with her and are committed to her comfort.

GUIDELINES

More than anything else, patients resent being treated as children. They want to be in charge of themselves and not be "taken care of." Even though you have the best intentions in offering help, let the patient know he is the boss. He should be encouraged to get up and sit in a chair or take a short walk, select his food, make a telephone call, shave himself, and do anything he can on his own. One patient summarized what he wanted from his family:

If you take on my work, you confirm my helplessness. I don't want to get away with self-pity. If I let go of my responsibilities, my guilt will increase and you will feel resentful at the burden you have taken on. So let me be who I am. I don't want to remake myself to keep in your favor; I don't want to feel I am falling short of your expectations of me. Don't spare me any information about my disease or about those I love or about how you are. I want to be present in my life as long as I am here. Be gentle but be truthful and direct.

Ask the patient at every point what he would *like* to do. Constantly create conditions in which he can make choices, do something himself, and be rewarded and recognized for his own actions. Reassure him: "It looks just fine." Ask him to do something for you and thank him. If he takes on something but doesn't carry it out very well, don't comment on it. If he didn't shave his right cheek, whose whiskers are they, after all? However, if the patient seems frustrated or it is clear that he would welcome some help, offer it.

Overzealousness in your attention to the patient can actually have a destructive effect on the patient's attitude. A patient who is dying may adjust to her limitations more rapidly than her caretakers. The unfortunate development of the "sick role," which can be created by both patient and caregivers, can be short-circuited if the parties involved make a conscious effort not to play into it. People around a dying person tend to treat him differently, no matter how hard they try to be "normal." Because the patient is weak and vulnerable, he is likely to take on behavior that fits more and more others' perceptions of his fragility: he becomes childish, even weaker, and incapable of making choices. Caregivers who have begun by being overprotective now find that they resent all they must do. Again, remember that even if they resist at times, patients *want* to manage themselves.

> I needed someone here to help, not to do. It's hard to have anyone see my weakness, but I need a friend here to read to me, or just sit. In the midst of all this activity and people telling me this or that, I need a confidante who will be quiet and keep me safe and listen to me when I want to talk. It is so comforting to have someone who will say, "Will you tell me about it?"

In your conversations, try not to underplay your own life and future plans. Within the bounds of good judgment and timing, don't hesitate to talk about events in which the patient cannot participate. The patient is nourished by observing activity and is not harmed by some degree of sadness about what she may miss. Be sensitive enough to stop when you think she has had enough. More often than not, you will be surprised at how much the patient can enjoy.

You can also help by keeping in mind that both you and she will occasionally forget the disease is not her fault. She may even think the disease is punishment for past actions. Try not to lecture, blame, or scold her, even when in her own periods of self-loathing or anger she may provoke you to do so. If she's having a day of self-recrimination for whatever reason, try not to feed into it. Be gentle and kind in little ways, giving her a treat with the next snack, reading her favorite short story, or inviting a special friend to visit.

Try to establish boundaries for what you can and cannot provide. On some days you may think the patient wants you to do everything and even doesn't mind taking advantage of your pity or guilt. Whether or not this is true, the burden of acting this way will probably soon become too great for the patient to carry. If you have been allowing yourself to be manipulated, both of you may end up being quite angry at yourselves and each other. Set reasonable limits and stick to them so that she can ask freely, knowing you are not afraid to say no.

Don't talk behind the patient's back or whisper in the room. Respect his right to know everything and also to be private if he wishes. He may ask to be alone with a member of the family or with the doctor, and, of course, this request should be accepted. Similarly, if you need to have privacy, leave the room.

As a way of managing all the responsibility you've taken on, it will be very tempting to try to organize the patient. "Now is the time to read letters. I'm going to serve you some ice cream in a few minutes. I'd like to comb your hair now." But keep in mind that the patient may not want to be so thoroughly scheduled. Her world is quite small—her bed, medications, family, and meals—and her sense of timing is probably slow and variable. In order to keep you happy, she may be afraid to complain or to resist your efforts. If so, she is bound to express her frustration indirectly by experiencing pain or by becoming depressed or angry at someone else. Try to ease up on the schedule as much as possible, still retaining whatever order you need to keep the household running smoothly.

Much has been written in the last decade about the benefits of a positive attitude toward disease. The patient may fall victim to some variant of the stiff-upper-lip mentality present in our culture. In fact, many people *do* experience the power of a positive mental attitude in turning around a downward spiral of emotional or physical illness. Yet too much pressure to keep up a fighting spirit can place an unnecessarily heavy burden on the patient.

While encouraging the patient is a responsibility of caregiving, be sensitive to crossing the line into goading or insisting. Positive thinking is to be encouraged, but it should not be accomplished by pushing a patient beyond her abilities or at the cost of her feelings.

LISTEN AND ACCEPT

One of the most important services a caregiver can provide is to be a good listener. Listening to a dying person means first of all being flexible enough to set aside or at least to reconsider the small and large courses of action on which you or the family may have set your minds. The patient has her own serious wishes.

My grandmother kept saying she wanted to go back to France, to die there and be buried with her father. The family didn't really want to listen to that. My grandfather was buried in this country, and they thought it was more appropriate for her to be buried with her husband. Besides, it would have been difficult to move her. She was bedridden; she had only a few weeks to live. It would have taken a lot of arranging.

My family exerted influence on her—I can see that now—to stay here. If she said she was tired or in some pain, they would use that as a chance to remind her of how difficult it would be to travel. Finally she said she thought it really best that she stay here. But the wish never left her; she kept saying she wished she could die in France.

Listen well enough to know what is a passing whim and what is a serious matter. Ask the patient how much she needs to have the request fulfilled, if you cannot tell from what is said. Acknowledge that you hear the request, understand it, and will do the best you can to satisfy it.

Learn how to respond when he wants to talk about his illness or asks for help in dealing with it. When we ask someone how he is, we tend to be at a loss if the response is anything but, "Fine." More information than that and we learn not to get into that mess again. But the answer to "How are you?" is the whole point when someone is dying. Whether or not you ask, in the course of any conversation the patient will probably refer to his emotional, spiritual, or physical health. You may naturally think, "I want to get out of here," "I want to change the subject," "How can I cheer him up?" You may think you have failed if he is saying these things. You may say, "Don't say that," or "You don't mean that," or change the subject.

Practice saying, "How are you feeling?" or to understand further, "Is there anything I can do?" and then keeping silent. If the patient needs help articulating feelings, be willing to say, "It isn't easy to live this way, is it?" and be still. Try to sit and listen, allowing silences, and respond only when the patient has finished speaking. Accept what the patient says as her truth. Understand what she really needs or wants. Explain what appears to you to be true, tell her what you feel, even when you feel hurt, stressed, or helpless. Gently correcting an important fact or giving your interpretation is just fine.

If he needs help, tell him—and mean it—that you will see what can be done, and keep him informed of what you find out. Even small requests that may seem silly to you probably carry a lot of meaning. Eating a special food, wanting to see a certain friend, asking to be informed of a particular noise in the furnace, and other such queries are important in the patient's frame of reference. Since she cannot tend to these matters on her own, especially if she is bedridden, a patient must depend upon responsive people. Leaving her hanging, even when you imagine she has forgotten a conversation, is likely to be interpreted as desertion.

People who are dying are often extremely sensitive to indications that they are in the way or that they are not what they once were. Help the patient know that whatever he has been or is now is just fine, and that he continues to be valued by those around him. Do what your instinct and knowledge of the patient tell you will "speak" your acceptance of him. A thoughtful action, a small gift, or a back rub may be even better than words. Allow the patient to feel and do what she is and wants without fearing disapproval. As the patient becomes more accepting of herself, others will have an easier time accepting her.

Perhaps the most difficult task most patients undertake, and it occurs instinctively, is reviewing the past. It can be painful for the person and for everyone nearby. Few if any shortcuts are possible in this very natural process of coming to terms with people, events, and possessions that have been important. Ideally, what results is a degree of self-acceptance and serenity few people in the thick of their lives experience. Reliving early events breaks the bondage of guilts and fantasies. To help facilitate this process, caregivers can be available and ready to talk. Let the patient work his way through the past, and don't discourage the expression of strong or negative emotions. You may gently correct the record, but arguments over "That's not how it really happened" are only useful if they will relieve mental anguish. Untying old knots and recalling accomplishments will slowly allow the patient and her family and friends to feel peaceful.

When you have what you sense has been an important conversation with the patient, take a moment to review it. Look at the transitions from subject to subject and whether you feel each was fully discussed. If you feel uneasy or angry after an intense talk, chances are you may see work still to be done. You may have cut off the person, or not allowed full expression of an idea. Go back to the subject when the next opportunity arises.

TALK ABOUT DYING

As improbable as it may seem, a caregiver can get so involved in the demands of the daily routine and concern for the patient's emotional comfort that he can miss or put off the need to acknowledge that the person is dying. If the caregiver is intimate with the dying person, not talking directly prevents important work for both. Several years after his aunt's death, this sensitive nephew was still mourning his missed opportunity. While he had allowed her to talk about her feelings and concerns about dying, he did not want to trouble her with his own.

> I wanted to talk about some important things—about the family and what she wanted done with particular things—but I was afraid she would get discouraged if I acknowledged that she was dying. My whole focus was to keep her comfortable and it's all I could think about. My friends were really wonderful and helpful, but I wish someone had said to me, "You need to step back and see the overall view, so you can talk with her about what you need to."

Whether or not someone speaks about her dying, chances are very good that, to some degree, she is thinking about it. In time she will probably want to discuss it, in her own way. Engaging in this conversation when the patient is ready will provide her much relief. Give her the right to choose her own words, and talk only to the extent that she wishes. Establishing yourself as a good listener will give her the security of knowing that she can come to you.

The patient will probably approach the subject without saying outright that she thinks she's dying. She may not talk directly because of her own fear or worry that she will be shut off. Or she may not be ready to follow exactly where her thoughts are leading, and so will introduce the topic with a general statement like "I don't seem to be getting any better." If you ignore it or say, "Of course you are," then the patient will probably withdraw into herself. But if you reply, "It must be hard," or "Are you worried?" then she has a chance to think out loud and express herself. You have in effect created an opening for her that she may use now or later.

Let the patient direct the conversation and stop it now if he wishes. If instead he asks a question you don't feel qualified to answer—such as, "What does this new sore on my cheek mean?"— be sure you let him know you will either get the answer yourself or will bring someone who can respond to speak with him. The patient may target you purposely, knowing you aren't qualified to reply, as a first step toward the truth. As he becomes more sure, he may ask to talk directly with his physician. If when you respond to a question the patient is silent or changes the subject, don't press him to talk further. He may just have been testing or exploring, wondering if his fear is well-founded or if he is being taken seriously.

If the patient asks directly if he is dying, ask him why he asks, does he think he is, or how does he know, did someone tell him, and what exactly did the person say? Take the patient's lead. Reassure him that he is very much alive now, which gives everyone much pleasure, and that there are ways to ease any pain he might anticipate. Ask about his fears and discuss them; tell him you will seek answers to questions. Use the words and phrases he uses, supporting him in his own knowledge so he knows he has company. The worst thing that could happen is for the patient to feel that he is the only one who knows—which he would translate as "cares"— he is dying.

Both before and after a serious acceptance of her condition, the patient will probably react as we all do to a crisis by various stages of denial, anger, and disbelief. "This can't be true . . . This can't be happening to me." Powerful emotions recur, overlap, and even coexist. She may think she is over her anger, for example, but it arises again. Everyone grieves differently, so do not expect a logical progression from one emotion to another, or even think that the patient necessarily must experience what someone else did. Don't be afraid of a natural despair. These awesome feelings will pass and probably create calm, even reduce physical pain. The patient is already "upset," whether or not he shows it; letting these feelings out, even though it may be uncomfortable for you and cause the patient some anguish, will probably be very beneficial. Talking and expressing "overwhelming" feelings have proven useful over and over for people in crisis. If the patient's emotions are too much for you to bear alone, or seem to get stuck and not provide relief, seek help from a member of the clergy or a counselor.

Many dying people will also ask "Why?" and will reach out for assistance in understanding "Why me?" "Why life at all?" or "Why suffering?" Whether or not the patient has a religious faith, he may seek spiritual answers to these questions. The reality of dying forces many patients to look for meaning beyond the here and now. Some seek help to understand their own theology and notions of God and immortality. Others find that their trials put existing faith to a test. Wanting to be touched in some permanent way by others in their lives, they need to know what importance they have had and what they have meant to their loved ones.

We can each be ministers as these questions are raised, and need not be thrown by the language of despair or of "religion." While we can be sensitive to these struggles, each person must resolve matters for himself. Listen well, and offer to help with whatever needs to be done. Since often spiritual concerns are accompanied by guilt—at least initially—suggest that the patient take an inventory of both "good" and "bad" actions of her past and then share it with someone she trusts.

If the patient wants to talk about God, or heaven, or her soul, she is probably not asking you to give her answers, even though the thoughts may come out as questions. If called upon to answer, you can simply say, "I don't know . . . This is what I think when I raise that question for myself" or "I have never thought about that." Say whatever is true for you.

My father reviewed his life and felt a lot of sorrow for not having been loved as he wanted by his wife. He felt he'd given up more in the marriage than he had received. He asked me, "Do you think I can have a loving woman in the next life?" I said, "Since we don't really know what happens after we die, I think we get to choose what we want to have. I hope you will plan on all the love you can imagine." He smiled and said he thought that was "just right."

If you are ill at ease or feel unqualified to discuss matters he raises, ask the patient if he wants to pursue the question with someone else close to him or a member of the clergy.

In coming to terms with death, a dying person, without meaning or wanting to, will use the same defenses and behaviors—as unpleasant as he and you may know them to be—that he has used throughout his life, and probably to an even greater degree. He may become manipulative, or depressed, or bossy, or sarcastic. Denial is a common defense. A patient may not want to talk about her illness and may prefer to act "normally," planning for a future that will not exist. She should be allowed to do so, even though it may be painful for those around her. If denial is how she has coped throughout her life, this is not the time to try something new. She must be respected for fighting with what she has. Dying people often maintain some level of hope, and they should. Hope is necessary for everyone.

If the patient loses interest in the world, becomes self-centered, hypochondriacal, and increasingly dependent and infantile, remind him of specifics true today (what he is able to do, who is visiting, what you will serve for lunch), but try not to confront him or get angry with his behavior. Talk about real events and conversations that will ground him in reality, and continue to behave in caring, supportive ways. When the patient speaks of what others must be feeling, that they must be tired of needing to wait on him, or tired of having him around, continue to provide evidence that you want him in your day.

Finally, in her own time, and usually as the last major effort, the patient will come to accept her life and relationships and publicly acknowledge her dying. Sometimes this follows a final resolution with a person who has been troubling the patient for some years. It is not unusual for a patient to hold off her dying beyond the anticipated time in order to tie up a loose end in her past or a relationship with someone close to her. Frequently the struggle is obvious

—narrated in the patient's dreams or restless worries or in ways she "acts out" with others. As this final work goes on, simply offer all the support you can, help with specific requests, and trust the natural process. Many observers say they can see when the resolution comes and that it is followed by peacefulness and increased withdrawal from day-to-day events. The patient has finished her life work.

PERSONALITY CHANGE

While fortunately most dying people remain themselves, with perhaps only a bit more or less of qualities always present in them, a few can undergo—for several hours or days, or for the duration of the illness—a quite drastic transformation. You may possibly be faced with the extremely confusing and painful experience of being with a patient much changed in personality. Depression, pain, physical changes from the disease, medication, brain deterioration, and other factors may cause new and probably unpleasant behavior. She may be petulant, hysterical, passive, belligerent, creating fear and anger among those around her; she may try to climb out of bed, scratch her face, pull her hair.

One night Ann struggled for nearly twelve hours with the arrangement of a lamp next to her bed. She couldn't manage to move it and didn't know where it should go. She stayed up all night working on this problem. It was frightening for her son, who came the next morning to find her exhausted, having not eaten for almost a day, and extremely anxious. During this episode she hung up on several friends who called her because she was fixated on this problem. We all tried to remember this was the disease, but we kept forgetting, since it was she who was doing these hurtful things—like a wolf in sheep's clothing. It was later conjectured that this was caused by a chemical imbalance, or possibly a tumor growing in her brain.

When you observe changes, contact your physician because a change in medication or another simple solution may be immediately available. When a patient's behavior becomes unmanageable, a mild sedative or mixture of drugs may be required or advisable. It is not worth the strain on the patient, the caregivers, or the family to withhold a dose of a calming drug. This can be done without substantially affecting his ability to be "himself" and can be reduced or eliminated when he is lucid.

A caregiver can also help when a patient begins to show signs of personality change by focusing yourself and him on his old self, his sense of humor, what interests him, and simple memories and events. Pick up on the clues he gives you of his old self and ask him questions about hobbies, work, or travel that you know he has enjoyed. When you cannot hold on to these threads, try to maintain some distance and to be angry at the disease, not at the person who is its captive. Even when the "acting out" is an aspect of the person's "normal" behavior, or an amplification of it, remember she is probably not in control of it. She is a victim of her illness.

Even patients who do not change as a result of their illness may occasionally seem depressed, unappreciative, or distant. As they approach death, most people step part way out of their lives, beginning to disconnect themselves from people and activities they love. Caregivers notice the distance and may feel hurt by it. We have to let them go and resist the temptation to call them back or resent their separation. For the patient's sake and for ours, we must allow this natural and gradual parting.

Home care offers a unique opportunity to surround the patient with tangible evidence of her value to others and to focus attention on what today offers. Make it easy for her to enjoy what has always been important to her. Caregivers and others are well justified in "spoiling" the patient. If her favorite color is pink, buy her a pink nightgown. If he loves basketball, get a television or a book of photographs of the sport. If she likes show tunes, bring in the stereo and play them. Play a game of listing the five things she loves to do most, and then see how they can be done in some way today. Help him to review his life positively, looking for memories of successes and skills he enjoys using, people he cares about. A vigorous effort to be grateful for today does wonders not only for the patient but for everyone around him as well.

19
SOME
HARD CHOICES

The range of moral, legal, ethical, religious, and social questions that may be raised for a patient as health declines, and for caregivers in the course of providing care, can be hugely complicated, so complicated that any attempt at reaching an immediate decision about an issue when it arises is almost impossible. To avoid choices that survivors will later regret having made, think about these questions now. Advance planning is also recommended so that if at some future point the patient is unable to speak for himself, those who participated in conversations with him will have an easier time making appropriate decisions.

Many of us have already thought about what we would choose to do or have done in the final stages of a terminal illness: "When I get that bad I want someone to pull the plug"; "I don't want any life-prolonging measures"; "When it's time I want to go peacefully." Because so much is being considered today about new pain-control methods, "good" death, hospice care, and euthanasia, people are being given the chance to investigate choices they never knew existed relating to illness and dying. Exploring the growing range of alternatives either alone or in conversations with friends or family can help the patient and caregivers think through the available options and how they reflect the patient's and family's desires.

For example, a person used to be considered dead when he stopped breathing. But with today's sophisticated medical technology, the definition of death has become problematic. Someone who would otherwise die can now be kept alive by machine: while part of the body may be "dead" (the brain, most typically), the sum of the parts can be maintained in a condition of living. Dialysis machines, intravenous feedings, and oxygen may in fact be doing nothing but keeping the organism alive, without improvement. To make matters more complicated, discontinuing such care or choosing not to receive it may be in effect suicide if the patient makes the decision, or a sentence of death if caregivers decide.

Medical ethics used to be a matter for doctors, but now both technology and greater consumer involvement generally in health care oblige everyone concerned with terminal care—patients, families, hospital staffs—to consider ethical problems. Despite the complexity, a new understanding of these issues is emerging: social attitudes are changing, legal responsibilities are becoming clarified, and individual choices are becoming easier to make and act upon. The result is that we are far less likely than past generations to rely on other people or institutions to make choices for us. Fewer people are willing to say, "Let the doctor decide."

This chapter raises some of the many tough issues that families, caregivers, and patients confront in the course of a terminal illness. Reaction to them will depend on many factors, including timing, individual ethics, religious background, and the particular mix of people participating in the discussion. No attempt is made here to solve these problems; rather to offer some perspective and the sense that many other people in this circumstance worry about similar issues. Since the topics raised here are extremely sensitive and complex, you may want to study the subject further or consult with people in any of the disciplines (medical, legal, religious, and others) concerned with ethics of terminal care. Lectures and workshops on these subjects can be found in many communities.

PATIENT FIRST

Begin your thinking about the various difficult decisions you imagine will arise or those that may face you today with this question: Have you and others caring for the patient done everything possible to create an environment in which she wants to live? We should always ask, "Have I met my responsibility to ensure her comfort, provide stimulation, and allow all reasonable independence? Does she know she is loved and has she real opportunities to be useful; is she consulted and included in household and personal matters? Are those around her cheerful, and encouraging delight and playfulness?" An environment in which everyone is gloomy and the patient has no sense of value to anyone is not going to allow her a fair chance to want to live.

One of the unique and important benefits of being at home is that the patient and family are in control of the patient's total environment. From the very beginning, the patient is involved in choices about what is done for her, and no second-guessing or assumptions need to be made about her wishes.

The key to considerations given to treatments and care should be "What are the dying person's wishes?" This may sound simple, but it is frequently forgotten in the course of providing care. It is essential that the dying person participate in all decisions, even when they may seem either inconsequential or too large for someone "in that condition." It is through these choices, both simple and serious, that life goes on, and taking them away quickly erodes the dying person's control over her life.

As caregivers, we are challenged to ensure the patient's independence. Dying is very individualized, and dying people will take responsibility in different ways. Some will subscribe for a time to the notion of the redemptive power of some amount of suffering, for example. Others may prefer to be "knocked out" completely.

Encourage the patient to make choices for himself, even though he may seem to want to delegate responsibility to others. Patients tend to be quite dependent upon caregivers and tend to do and say what will please them. They may make a decision to continue or terminate a treatment based on their sense of what their families want. Resist the temptation to decide for the patient, as if you knew best or better than he what is right and good for him.

From the position of being in good health, it is easy to say that we hope no one will prolong our dying: "I don't want to live beyond the point when I can no longer enjoy my life, my family, and my friends." "I see no reason to suffer when there is no hope of relief." "I don't want to be a burden to myself or to others." "If I were in pain, I would want someone to put me out." While the patient may have said these things at one time, she may feel different now. Once a person actually faces death, the attitude may no longer seem as obvious or rational. A terminally ill patient has gradually grown used to living another kind of life. It may be diminished in physical activity and future possibilities, but it is his life today. Most people have experienced this phenomenon to some degree. If you have given up smoking, you can recall that it is only once you stopped that you realized not everyone smoked. In the case of terminal illness, the change in perspective can allow a patient to become accustomed to disease, discomfort, and even pain. A dying person may be "too" unhappy or uncomfortable in healthy people's terms, but he still may prefer this state to being dead. Many people with chronic painful or debilitating conditions say they make this choice every day.

Actually, patients now have legal protection with respect to the course of their treatment. Under the doctrine of informed consent, no medical procedure may be performed without a patient's knowledgeable permission. As discussed earlier in relation to the patient's rights in obtaining informed medical care, it is an intent of this doctrine to encourage open discussion among the physician, family, and dying person. The terminal patient must be fully informed not only about the nature of his disease but also about whatever medical efforts are being taken to prolong life. The physician is liable for failure to make proper disclosure of the prognosis and treatment alternatives to the patient. If the patient expressly forbids a lifesaving procedure, her decision cannot legally be ignored, and the physician is not subsequently liable to malpractice charges for abiding by the limitations imposed by the patient. If the physician feels that, because of the patient's physical and mental condition, disclosure of certain information would unnecessarily harm the patient, he can recommend treatment without sharing that knowledge. On the same grounds, the physician can choose not to tell a patient that she is dying. However, if that judgment is challenged, expert medical testimony will be required to establish that the decision to withhold information was appropriate. If the dying person lacks the legal competency to decide on treatments, the doctor must turn to the closest family member or, if necessary, to a court-appointed guardian.

One frequent decision is the extent to which the patient would like to be medicated. While most people can be comfortable and still in touch with the people around them, many people in the last days need pain medication in dosages that can depress the functions of lungs and heart and also cause heavy sleep or long periods of little awareness.

In Elisabeth's last week, decisions needed to be made. She was eighty-three and she said she had lived a long life and was tired and "ready to go." She had made it clear all along that anything to prolong her dying was against her wishes. She had said repeatedly that she wanted to die, she was ready, her life was over. But the doctor retained a measure of control which made us all frustrated and angry. Even though she constantly complained of pain, he withheld medication on the basis that it might put a strain on her heart. This seemed an insane precaution.

As we have said repeatedly, comfort is the most important goal in terminal care. If in achieving comfort the body is weakened, remember that this is not the intent, and, although it is perhaps regrettable, reducing the body's functioning is appropriately considered secondary to easing the patient's symptoms.

Even though committed to allowing the patient freedom of choice, some families become concerned about choices the patient makes. For example, some patients are vulnerable to treatments and quackery touted as a new or quick or experimental solution. Some quack medicines are quite expensive and create more pain; others are harmless. The placebo effect by which a person feels better even though nothing has happened physically is real. Even though the patient makes a "crazy" decision, if it helps her feel better for a time, fine. While doing everything possible to use conventional methods to produce comfort, offer support for all solutions to pain. Whatever works, works.

Another complication to such choices arises from the power plays sadly common in families. All too often the person who is providing care, the priest who has come each day, or someone else intimately connected with the patient who understands his wishes is shouted down or overshadowed by a son who flies in for the weekend to pay respects and "have a talk with the doctor." While the relative has every right to say, "I want everything possible done for Mother," he is too far removed from the reality of the patient's life as it is today to make the appropriate choices. Even the doctor may cave in to a dominant personality. The result can be terrible bitterness within the family, and a tragic change in the care plan. To prevent such misunderstandings, make every effort to keep communication open among those who, even though not involved immediately, might have some concern or say in decisions about care.

THE TOUGHEST QUESTION

What do you do when the person says she's ready to die but her body is still alive? One of the most awesome dilemmas a caregiver may face is a request by the patient to help her end her life. Here is the way the question was put to one caregiver:

A month before she died, when she had clearly completed her own work—renewed her will, said goodbye to friends, settled with her sons and their wives—she asked me to buy her a new nightgown and asked the doctor to "please let me go." He responded that such things were not in his power. Later that evening, she asked me to see if there were enough sleeping pills in the medicine chest "to make me go to sleep and not wake up." She couldn't get out of bed to get them herself. I told her I couldn't do that. She asked me why. I could not answer.

Several more such requests were made of me, her two sons, and the doctor during the days that followed. Each in our own way recoiled from the plea. Her pain persisted, increased. Her humiliation grew as she became more and more dependent on us. She said she was "disgusted" by my necessary involvement in toilet matters. She cried with the frustration of being forced by disease and weakness to lose control of her life.

The tumor was growing, encroaching on her trachea, throat, esophagus, and tongue. She could feel the ugly boils and ridges on her left cheek. She could smell her own decay. It wasn't until after she died that I thought I should have given her request more consideration. Maybe I could have done better than respond with my own pat morality.

The complicated moral choice presented in this story is not uncommon. While a thoughtful caregiver knows that independence and self-determination are to be respected, and would want these very values revered if she were the person dying, she may draw the line at helping a patient die, out of conscience or fear of legal retribution. One husband admitted, "I refused to help my wife commit suicide because I was frightened that I might be accused of murder. I believed that my wife had a right to take her own life, but I wouldn't help."

Everyone must make his own conscious choice as to whether he can oblige a patient in the wish to die. We will not attempt to propose guidelines or pros and cons for deciding or even pretend to have answers ourselves. Of course in addition to your own various considerations, state and federal laws, legal interpretations, and medical ethics codes must be dealt with and are constantly being challenged and revised. You are wise to consult with a lawyer, a physician, and any organization such as the American Civil Liberties Union that keeps current on what could be the risks of making a choice to help someone die.

One response to expressions of wanting to die, and the most successful way to prevent them, is to devote attention to comfort. Look at the sources of despair and see what might be done to counter them. Patients who are in pain, whose surroundings are miserable, and who are not feeling accepted, loved, and in control of their lives will naturally have feelings of not wanting to live. Sufficient pain medications, help in settling affairs, intimacy with people the patient loves and who love her, all work to keep life full, peaceful, and comfortable.

THE RIGHT TO DIE

For most people, the issue of "the right to die" will not involve the question of "killing" the patient or allowing him to take his own life, but the right to allow the body to die when it will. At some point, with or without medication and treatments to extend life, the body will naturally wear out. Encroachment of the disease, slow deterioration of body systems, and effects of malnutrition, dehydration, and other chronic complications gradually add up.

Unlike the case of a patient choosing to die in response to the pain or anxiety of terminal illness, the final decision of a patient to die in peace when her body wears out tends to be undramatic, just the natural letting go when the patient senses her body offers little or nothing to hold on to. Here are two typical examples of how this occurs:

> When we first brought Grandma home from the hospital we talked about what to do if she stopped breathing. We needed that conversation because I am a nurse and I had to know what they expected me to do. Grampa, Grandma, and the rest of us agreed not to reverse the natural process. I asked them if they wanted me to call the rescue squad or get her to a hospital and they were all firm in saying no.

> Mother knew her lungs were filling with fluid and decided she would not be tapped to drain it off, only to lie comatose in a hospital bed. She had sifted and sorted through all the information she'd gotten from the doctor about what could happen. She had consulted her own God against this event and had come to her own terms. I came to appreciate the strength and unbreakable will under Mother's sweet, soft Southern surface. "It comes down to destiny," she said. "I'm glad to be lying down before it." She chose to surrender to her own dying, and we all respected that decision.

However strong the patient's intentions regarding ending treatment, a number of issues complicate them. While the patient above made a clear choice, the decision about lung drainage can be quite difficult. When a patient's lungs begin to fill, suction can be justified even when everyone elects no life-extending services, since this treatment is a means to promote comfort. However, it may have the side effect of extending life. To complicate matters, labored breathing may actually be less of a problem for the dying person than for those observing him. It may even be less painful than bedsores or a spreading tumor. Being aware of anticipated symptoms and their usual treatments—and then weighing what each means to the patient's general comfort—will help you make choices consistent with the goal of terminal care.

Since most people do not die specifically from the disease but from its accumulated side effects, often there are many opportunities to accept or decline a treatment on the basis of what provides the most comfort. In the case of the patient whose lungs fill or who develops pneumonia, the greatest comfort may be achieved by allowing these conditions to progress, especially if your physician anticipates that they mean the patient will "die in her sleep" or experience some other peaceful drifting away. Pneumonia has long been referred to as "an old man's best friend" for that reason.

When and whether to stop or refuse treatments are matters of individual choice, and increasingly such choices are not contested. At home, allowing the patient to drift away without intervention is usually what the doctor, patient, and family agree upon early in caregiving. Experience reveals that although these may be hotly debated issues among people not involved in terminal care, most people engaged in home care know intuitively what is the right decision to make. Dr. Saunders of St. Christopher's Hospice outside London offers these standards for appropriate treatment:

Terminal care includes the making of decisions concerning the correct treatment for an individual patient. There is a time for giving dexamethazone to a patient with a cerebral tumour but there is also a time to withdraw it. We have to concern ourselves with the quality of life as well as with its length and with the pressures imposed upon a family when we are maintaining what has become only a travesty of life. There are patients for whom chemotherapy gives great benefits but there are others for whom it becomes increasingly irrelevant, producing more side-effects with diminishing returns. We must learn when to withdraw such treatment.

There are other manoeuvres which should never be undertaken. There are time [sic] when the treatment for a haemorrhage is not a blood transfusion with its attendant alarms but instead an injection and someone who stays there. There are infusions which should never have been put up; feelings of thirst can be relieved by the right use of narcotics. It is far better to have a cup of tea given slowly on your last afternoon than to have drips and tubes in all directions.

Again, we sometimes need to make decisions concerning the use of antibiotics and other measures for the very old or the very ill who develop pneumonia. There are ways of relieving the dyspnoea, cough and any other distress which do not prolong further a life which has come to its close. These are not "untreated" patients but rather those who have received the treatment relevant to their condition and so often to their wishes.

Much has been written on what is dignified, appropriate, humane, or good for the dying. For the majority of families, decisions about treatments are most often made in stages. As each symptom occurs, the dying person, family, and physician consider the value of various treatments. Gradually, most of these decisions mean rejecting drugs and treatments that merely keep a failed system in enough balance to function.

Because legal considerations are less limiting today, more options are available to take control of the course of dying. Many states have enacted "right-to-die" legislation, which authorizes a competent person to execute a document directing physicians not to prolong life artificially, through medication or mechanical means, in the event the person becomes terminally ill. Physicians who follow the wishes expressed in these documents are legally protected, unless they act negligently. Even in states that do not have such laws, most courts now recognize that a competent person has the right to refuse medical treatment, even though that refusal may hasten her death. Find out what is allowable in your state by contacting your local bar association, legal aid society, or civil liberties union chapter.

Drawing up a document that makes explicit the patient's wishes is particularly important in the event that the patient reaches a point of illness where he can no longer speak for himself. Disputes among family members, or between family and the doctor, can be defused or prevented by producing evidence of the dying person's wishes.

The Concern for Dying Council has prepared a Living Will that can be used by individuals to make their intentions clear in advance of terminal illness. It is reproduced here, and copies may be obtained by writing to Concern for Dying, 250 West Fifty-seventh Street, New York, New York 10107.

To My Family, My Physician, My Lawyer and All Others Whom It May Concern

Death is as much a reality as birth, growth, maturity and old age—it is the one certainty of life. If the time comes when I can no longer take part in decisions for my own future, let this statement stand as an expression of my wishes and directions, while I am still of sound mind.

If at such a time the situation should arise in which there is no reasonable expectation of my recovery from extreme physical or mental disability, I direct that I be allowed to die and not be kept alive by medications, artificial means or "heroic measures." I do, however, ask that medication be mercifully administered to me to alleviate suffering even though this may shorten my remaining life.

This statement is made after careful consideration and is in accordance with my strong convictions and beliefs. I want the wishes and directions here expressed carried out to the extent permitted by law. Insofar as they are not legally enforceable, I hope that those to whom this Will is addressed will regard themselves as morally bound by these provisions.

A number of specific statements may be inserted above your signature to include additional provisions you may desire, such as:

1. a. I appoint _____ to make binding decisions concerning my medical treatment.

   or

   b. I have discussed my views as to life-sustaining measures with the following who understand my wishes:

   _____

   _____

   _____

2. Measures of artificial life support in the face of impending death that are especially abhorrent to me are:
   a. Electrical or mechanical resuscitation of my heart when it has stopped beating.
   b. Nasogastric tube feedings when I am paralyzed or unable to take nourishment by mouth.

   c. Mechanical respiration by machine when I am no longer able to sustain my own breathing.

3. I would like to live out my last days at home rather than in a hospital if it does not jeopardize the chance of my recovery to a meaningful and sentient life or does not impose an undue burden on my family.

4. If any of my tissues are sound and would be of value as transplants to other people, I freely give my permission for such donation.

The council advises that you make the best use of this document by taking the following measures:

1. Sign and date the will before two witnesses, who should not be blood relatives, or beneficiaries of your property will. (This is to ensure that you signed of your own volition and not under any pressure.)
2. Give your doctor a copy for your medical file and discuss the provisions with him to make sure he is in agreement.
3. Give copies to those most likely to be concerned "if the time comes when you can no longer take part in decisions for your own future." Enter their names on bottom line of the will.
4. Above all discuss your intentions with those closest to you, *now*.

If you decide to prepare a Living Will, and your doctor does not agree with your intentions, find another doctor. Make sure to discuss the will and file a copy of it with your lawyer, especially if you anticipate disagreement from anyone in the family.

The issues raised in this chapter are for some the most challenging and painful of home care. Although you can rationally consider choices about death and dying now, remember that acting on your decisions will not be simple when the time comes. No matter how many books you read, or conversations you have, or workshops you attend, the options are still extremely trying and sad when the circumstances are real ones and the person is you or someone you love. What is most important for caregivers to remember is that the patient is in charge of her own care and thereby rightfully takes responsibility for choices and their outcomes.

20
LIVING ONE DAY AT A TIME: FOR SOMEONE DYING

This chapter is addressed particularly to the person who is dying. By the time you read this book you will probably have experienced the initial shock of learning your condition. Whether you receive the news directly from the doctor, or come to sense that you aren't getting better, or hear people begin to talk of treatments not taking hold—whatever the scenario, the truth is devastating. How could this happen, what went wrong—with me, with my doctor, with God?

The early days of living with your prognosis are awful. You have your own natural feelings, compounded by a doctor's visit, a new ache or lump, a stumble, or a telephone call from someone who "doesn't know." Everything tends to trigger anxiety. Each experience—people, events, weather, your whole environment—will be full of reminders that you are dying. With every assault, you feel angry or depressed. Others' reactions are almost intolerable. You barely get settled in a degree of forgetfulness and something else happens to remind you. While initially you may feel little else but a turmoil of feelings and an overload of information about what you need to do, most people say the intensity of the feelings diminishes somewhat. You begin to sort out what is important for you to do and whom you want to have near you. You slowly adjust to your new life. It becomes easier to accept another restriction on your independence. Step by step, you may discover the paradox many have described that the closer they get to death the more they understand about how to live.

If you tried today to plan how to spend the rest of your life dying, you would quickly be overwhelmed. But if you try to focus your thoughts simply on how to live just for today, or even just for the next half hour, you will soon learn to take care of what you need in small, manageable increments. Some terminally ill patients describe the period before dying as the play for which life is a rehearsal: the last three months require all the knowledge, faith, and support acquired over a lifetime. "What is important to me is no longer courage, but communion," said one dying patient, who viewed her life as a series of obstacles to conquer. "Now it's not a matter of strength; any false illusions of power or seeking are over. I live in the present, and what I want is company."

DAY BY DAY

How does living a day at a time work? Each morning when you awake, spend a few minutes looking at the day ahead and what you would like to accomplish. Make a modest schedule of activities: three meals, two snacks, a radio program, a telephone call, a visitor, a conversation about a piece of furniture you would like to give someone. Structure the day to include an event that will offer a particularly fulfilling reward, such as sharing an intimacy or accomplishing a small but important task. Plan to do something nice for a caregiver or visitor, such as thanking someone for his companionship or asking a question about his life. Finally, try to arrange to talk to a loved one about how you are feeling, how angry you are, or how disappointed. Allow yourself to get deeply involved in that feeling with someone who will listen and support you. Be sure to tell the listener that her willingness to be there is important to you.

The details of your day depend exactly on what your heart tells you to do. Daily activities vary as infinitely as individuals do. Here are some routines as recalled by caregivers.

- We had breakfast listening to the morning news, followed by a bath and a change of bed. Then a nap, lunch, another nap, and usually a visit from a friend. I would read aloud to him, or we would "gossip" about our family or friends. We never ran out of talk.

- Mother slept a great deal, and when she was awake she would pray the rosary and visit with guests. Her eyes became too weak to read, and radio music was too much, so we would talk or just rest quietly. We always prepared menus together. She loved her mail.

- My grandmother first spent her days giving away her belongings and making lists of what she needed to have done. She spent a lot of time watching television and thinking quietly on her own. She enjoyed her grandchildren's visits and talked a lot about what she called the "happy times."

- My brother lived each day by visiting with his children. He had a priest friend who came every afternoon for a talk. When he could not speak, he kept up these visits by watching and writing notes.

- Mom wanted us to read her classical poems and short stories about dying; she said they helped her see her own life and death in a broader perspective. She said Shakespeare's sonnets made her feel less lonely. She spent hours napping and looking out the window. She was afraid at night because of times when she'd been alone and in pain, so we took turns being with her then.

What you do on any given day will also depend on how you feel and what you need to accomplish for your own peace of mind. Try not to take on the entire list of "shoulds" you may be tempted to inflict on yourself.

Try to surrender things you can no longer do, so you can get on with what you are able to accomplish. For example, walking may be extremely difficult. What is the goal of walking? To get to a chair where you can do some project? Instead of worrying about the walking itself, focus on what it is you want to do when you get there. Depending on your own energy or the availability of help, you can either do the task in some fashion where you are, or ask for help in moving to the chair. Choose the simplest ways to do tasks you consider necessary. Don't exhaust yourself through stubbornness; set reasonable goals. If you must undertake a challenge, do it with confidence and humor, but learn to accept what you cannot change.

You can also learn from what others in your stage of life have done. Many value the general guidelines of Make Today Count, an organization started in the early 1970s by cancer patient Orville Kelly. Determined to help himself and others to live with "life-threatening" illness, Kelly made the following suggestions, which have since helped thousands of patients answer the question, "How do I live each day?"

1. Talk openly about the illness and your struggles. You can't make life normal again by trying to hide what is wrong.

2. Accept death as part of life.

3. Consider each day as another day of life, a gift from God to be enjoyed as fully as possible.

4. Realize that life never is going to be perfect. It wasn't before, and it won't be now.

5. Pray, if you wish. It isn't a sign of weakness; it is a source of strength.

6. Learn to live with your illness instead of surrendering yourself to dying from it. We are all dying in some manner.

7. Take an active role in putting your friends and relatives at ease. If you don't want pity, don't ask for it.

8. Make all practical arrangements for funeral, will, etc., and be certain your family understands your wishes.

9. Set new goals; realize your limitations. Sometimes the simple things of life become the most enjoyable.

10. Discuss plans and concerns with your family, including your children, if possible. Involving them is very appropriate, since they are each affected.

However you decide to spend your time, remember that you are not being judged on the success or failure of your strategy. Acknowledge the boundaries of a day. Begin and end each day with some recognition that you are grateful to be alive and have people you love in your life. Accept the fact that you have used the day to the best of your abilities; if you find yourself wishing you had said or done something differently, forgive yourself, plan to apologize to the person, and know that tomorrow is full of opportunities. No one is perfect and you have earned a good night's sleep.

YOUR FEELINGS

You are living face-to-face with the news that you are dying. Your whole life—as you have known it—has completely altered. Dying changes your relationships with people. Among other differences, you are probably experiencing for the first time since childhood that you are to some extent dependent on others. Because of what is happening to you, you will feel you are living on an emotional roller coaster. Here are several recollections by patients about the internal havoc they experienced:

We are all so complicated. I talk a lot and try hard to express my feelings, but I know I'll never be able to feel finished.

I resent having someone else in my house all the time. I want to tell her to get out of my kitchen.

Sometimes I want to go off to die. I'm embarrassed and I don't want to be around my family when I have bad times. I'm dying, but I'm still fun to be with, even though not all the time.

I'm really thankful for my husband and the care he takes of me. We have become quite close. But I hate being waited on all the time. I'm used to fixing my own food; sometimes it's hard to be hungry for his cooking.

It's the waiting that's most difficult. Why can't I die? Eating is just a waste of time, and I feel that everyone is standing around and there's nothing new to say.

In her classic work *On Death and Dying,* Dr. Elisabeth Kübler-Ross describes the emotional turmoil of dying as happening in stages: denial, anger, bargaining, depression, and acceptance. This model has deservedly become well known, as it is of great benefit in offering people the knowledge that their wide mood swings are natural and shared by others. While the "five stages" are a useful way of generalizing about typical feelings, you can avoid the temptation of anticipating them, adjusting how you feel according to them, or watching for an identifiable progression from one to another. You need not adhere to any schematic description of the emotional process of dying. Feelings overlap, ebb, and flow. Each person will experience exactly and only what she experiences, what is necessary and true for her.

The best advice is just to keep talking out every feeling as it arises—complaining, crying, raging—and to focus on what you *are* able to do. Learn as you read further what new activities might help direct your attention away from fear and anxiety.

NOURISHING INTIMACY

In thinking about what to do in the next days and weeks, most people say their strongest impulse is to cut away busywork, superficial relationships, and mundane activities. "I turn my full attention, with as much energy as I have in any given day, to what I really cherish," said one patient. Being with loved ones, reading, and thinking are treasured ways to spend time. Joan Erikson, artist and wife of noted psychologist Erik Erikson, says she has learned—in her experience working in creative arts with dying people—that what they want most is to "nourish the intimacy in their lives." A patient called it "rejoicing in what is most essential."

Mrs. Erikson speaks of creative work as a means to fulfill some of the desire for intimacy. Music, art, literature, crafts—whether we look or listen or play or write—involve us in a universal language, linking us as individuals to past and future. If you have the energy, try to pursue a daily creative task. If you have played an instrument in the past, pick it up for a few minutes and play some simple pieces; if you have little or no musical background, you may enjoy learning to play a simple instrument like the recorder. You may find satisfaction in crayons and coloring, sketching simple objects, paper-folding, calligraphy, flower-arranging, or writing poetry, all of which can be done on your lap or in bed, with minimal physical exertion.

Singing favorite songs, looking at photographs, seashells, fabrics, plants, and religious objects all feed the innermost feelings of belonging, caring, and warmth. Mrs. Erikson advises that you look at some object you love and ask yourself what it suggests to you. Is there anything to write about, talk about, or draw? Simple creations made with clay or colored pencils can help link you with a memory. You may even give your poem or drawing to people who love you and explain to them what you are depicting and why you want them to have it.

Another way to achieve simple pleasures and hold attention to feelings and people who matter to you is to share thoughts and wishes with family and friends. Chances are, many people are literally or figuratively standing on one foot, then another, waiting to be invited closer to you in any way. Reach out physically, too. Hug friends and hold hands, and ask to be held. If part of your body is too painful to be touched, let people know, but invite other contact. You need to be desired and needed in ways important to you. For some, this may include sexual activity. People's experience with sex during illness varies widely. Some say dying gives a freedom that heightens excitement and increases the desire for sex. Others find that as part of closing out their lives they want to move away from physical intimacy. Your interest in sex will also depend upon how your body feels and what part sex played in your life prior to your illness.

In whatever ways you can, attend to the instinct to spend your time carefully. Invite people around you to give and receive love. No matter how "independent" you have always been or even want to be now, welcome the impulse to draw close to people. As one patient said, "What I feel is the need to gather around the fire with my three closest friends and just stay there, sitting, talking, and being quiet together."

YOUR RIGHTS

While you may in some ways want to lie back and let others make decisions and deliver care to you, even tell you what to do today, taking the backseat in your life will probably not feel right generally. Within the boundaries of your physical limitations, many choices and opportunities for taking direct action still exist. You may be a victim of your disease, but the disease is only part of you and you need not surrender more than its share. You can insist on exercising your many human rights.

You have the right to privacy. You have the right to demand information about your illness and what treatments are possible, and assurance that whatever is necessary for your comfort will be done. Ask for help in controlling pain: you have the right to undisturbed sleep and to comfort. Show that you intend to be actively in control of your own comfort and of the degree of alertness you will surrender for it. You are entitled to financial and legal help. You have a right to control as much as possible the day-to-day matters of your existence: foods, medicines, visitors, and how to spend your time. You are entitled to feel and express feelings, no matter how unpleasant they are to others. You have a right to develop spiritually in whatever direction you choose. Above all, you should not feel hesitant to expect others to do all they can to help you live and die in dignity and peace.

An effective way to keep your rights in focus is to tell your family early on that you do not want to be shut out but prefer to stay as much as possible in touch with the household. Encourage them to include you even though it may occasionally be inconvenient to them or difficult for you. Ask them to share vacation plans you won't be able to participate in. Tell your wife you want to see the new dress she bought, your son that you want to hear about what his boss promises for his career. Time has not stopped since you learned that you were dying. Like most patients, you will probably prefer to remain in the flow of life, which includes an orientation to the future.

State clearly to all those who may be involved what exactly are your wishes regarding funeral arrangements, disposition of your possessions, and anything else you feel should be noted. Be specific. Select someone who can speak for you if you are unable to speak or not competent to represent yourself adequately and forcefully. Have a heart-to-heart talk with your physician about what turns your disease is liable to take, and what if anything you want done about them. Review issues that may arise as your disease progresses by reading Chapter 19, "Some Hard Choices." Study the Living Will and, if you wish, sign it and give copies to the doctor and members of your care team.

You have selected a sympathetic and like-minded physician. You are blessed with attentive and commanding caregivers who will provide and seek for you appropriate medical care. But even so, establish yourself as the decision maker early in home care so that no questions will be left to chance or guess.

LIFE REVIEW

Life review is a natural process. Your instinct may be drawing you to recall the past, to organize it into a pattern of memory. Older people, without being urged, recall events and people in their past, even things they would choose to forget. Similarly, people who are dying often find themselves living close to memories. You may be surprised to remember an event in the distant past better than what you did yesterday.

Take opportunities to reflect on your life, particularly on people who are important to you. Understand that you have always done the best you could do at any point in time, even when you feel you made mistakes or errors of judgment. If there are people you would like to apologize to or thank, do so. As you take an inventory of your past, be grateful for the good things, people, and events that have happened in your life, for the opportunities you have had to be useful to others. Ask for help in accomplishing what will bring you peace with these memories. You may want help in locating a person from your past, making out a check to repay an old debt, or writing a letter to an old friend. A grandmother asked her grandchildren to read aloud poems she had written.

One caregiver wrote the following observation of her mother's methodical way of organizing the past:

I watched her accept the news of her dying by carefully reviewing and closing aspects of her eighty-three years. She began to summarize, to itemize, to instruct. In this manner, she said goodbye to the furnace, the dishwasher, the gutters—all of which had been constant sources of stress—and to her 1966 two-door sedan with its intermittent engine rattle. She stopped asking for the checkbook balance. One morning she dictated to me the disposition of her most valued things. ("The pewter and glass should be divided between the boys, the Pembroke table to Laurie—it is her great-grandmother's"—and so on.) She asked me to read her A. A. Milne's "Lines and Squares" poem which she had read us as children. She asked me to call friends and tell them what the doctor said. She asked several to visit, but stated the limits: "Don't let him stay too long. He tires me so." She taught me a prayer her mother had taught her. She struggled in dreams and conversations to reassure herself that one son was "fine," meaning, "I don't have to worry about him," and that another "is on his own—I've done all I can," meaning, "I'll never be able to feel completely at rest, so I must give up." By the end of a month, the process was complete. She lived another three weeks, but minute to minute, focused on her own self. She'd done the work she needed to free herself from others. *This not unusual story illustrates the range of review work a patient will undertake.*

Some of what you remember may not be pleasant or easy to accept, and anxiety, confusion, anger, and guilt may arise with it. Working out these conflicts in an artistic activity, such as drawing or writing, has proven successful for many. Some need solitude; others need conversation. One patient spent days rereading old letters from her mother and husband, answering each one in her mind.

Patients often have the need to give their memory to others. If you carry information about people or events that only you know and you feel it should be passed along, write it down, tape-record, or tell someone about it. One patient counted as one of her most important acts the day she spent with her niece and nephew, telling them about her brother, their father, who had died when they were babies. A grandmother told her granddaughter about a folder of old letters she had hidden in the house. A man who was president of his company agreed to have a documentary film made of his life and dying. It is natural to want to be remembered and even to have control over what others remember about us. The facts themselves are important and so is your point of view about events.

Knowing you will die soon offers the chance to come to a conclusion with your life and people whom you care about. Self-consciousness is very natural and even necessary for this work to be accomplished satisfactorily. Take the time you need to review and terminate what you can.

Accepting your prognosis and then taking control of how you are treated and how you want to spend each day is made bearable because of the people in your life. As you review your past and important relationships, it is natural and even necessary to say goodbye to many of them, as one patient said, "to close the circle." A few people will stay at your side until the end and these are usually the ones to whom you cannot say goodbye. Let them know you need them. Rejoice in selecting these few people who will always remain with you.

21
PRACTICAL MATTERS

Meg called it closing the circle. She reviewed her will, divided her possessions among her three sons, gave all of her clothes except two nightgowns to the Salvation Army. She said goodbye to all the people in her memory, by telephoning them or writing letters. Seven of us were asked to stay with her to the end, and to carry out her wish to be cremated and recalled in a simple memorial service. I had the feeling we were the ones to whom she couldn't say goodbye.

While some have a natural impulse to settle their affairs, others experience great difficulty and need help with the many practical matters that must be determined when someone dies. Further, because of weariness, distaste, and grief, family members tend to put off discussing such matters among themselves or with the patient. Yet there are decisions to be made and most are best done in advance. You need to consider: legal and business formalities, disposition of possessions and of the body, funeral services, and who should be notified when death occurs. Such planning may strike some people as insensitive, but there are a number of compelling reasons for undertaking it.

First, serious legal entanglements can be avoided. An estimated one quarter of Americans now die without leaving wills; many more die without telling survivors how and where they want to be buried. Second, families who have the strength and foresight to work out plans with the patient will be comforted later in the knowledge that they are carrying out her wishes. Third, since families often experience some upheaval and strife over who gets what, discussion about matters that might be difficult later is better held with the patient's participation. Although many caregivers feel the patient should be spared these worries, chances are she has been thinking about them on her own and would be relieved to take part in settling her affairs. If the patient hesitates to discuss these matters, ask if some objective outsider would make it easier—the family lawyer, a pastor, or a trusted friend. In cases where the patient is unwilling to talk with anyone about his wishes for a funeral and distribution of his things, you could say, "If you don't want to tell me or talk about this with us, then write it all down, we'll put it in a sealed envelope, and you can direct someone to open it when it is needed."

What are the practicalities that will have to be handled? The following outline, "Putting My House in Order," is an easy guide for what needs to be available. Section I details data required immediately after death; file the completed form in the general notebook or somewhere else known to others on the team who may need it. Section II provides information that will be necessary later and should be filed with the will and other valuable papers where some responsible person knows to go for them.

Sit down with the patient and fill out the forms, asking questions as you go and making notes about where missing information is available. Specifics required to complete the form will ease the task of discussing "difficult" subjects, including funeral arrangements and burial. This inventory will guide you to know what notifications are necessary, including the lawyer and executor of the estate, and insurance companies. Someone—you or a recruit who is not awed by such details—will want to check all life and casualty insurance and death benefits, including social security, credit union, trade union, and fraternal organizations. In addition to regular benefits, they may provide income for survivors or cover burial expenses. All debts and installment payments should be studied; some carry insurance clauses that cancel the debt upon death. As you review all these matters, you can make notes about what must be done and when. Doing this work now is not pleasant, but it will be even more difficult later.

CONFIDENTIAL

Personal Data of_____

Use a separate form for each individual.

PUTTING MY HOUSE IN ORDER

Foreword

This form is published by the Continental Association of Funeral and Memorial Societies, Inc., 2001 S St. N.W., Suite 530, Washington, DC 20009 for use by its member societies and their members.

The following factual data is to provide survivors with a guide for attending to the legal, tax, funeral, obituary and other matters after your death. Omit items that do not apply. Additional sheets may be added to complete information. This form should be brought up-to-date at each important change that occurs and reviewed at least once each year. Revisions can be more readily made if pencil is used in filling in the items subject to change.

This is **NOT A WILL** and does not govern the disposition of your property after death as that is the main purpose of your **WILL**. You may wish to consult your attorney and arrange to execute a will in event you have not done so.

Section I contains information that is **needed immediately** and should be kept where readily available in case of need. Section II contains items needed later and should be filed with your Will and other valuable papers.

* * *

SECTION I   Keep this sheet readily available.

The person named below has consented to help in making arrangements after my death and to comply with my wishes: (usually a close and trusted friend, perhaps your Executor).

Name_____Phone_____

Address_____

I am a member of the following memorial society and I wish to have my remains cared for through arrangements that have been made by them:

Society's Name_____Phone_____
For prompt assistance after my death call:

Mortuary_____Phone_____

Address_____

DATA FOR DEATH CERTIFICATE: The doctor in attendance is officially required to prepare and file a death certificate. The following personal data is usually required:

Name_____
              First   Middle   Last

Address_____
                            Street

City	County	State	Zip Code

Resided in this location since (state year) City_____: County_____; State_____
Residence is: Inside city limits–Yes____: No____ On a farm–Yes____: No____
Sex: Male____; Female____   Color or race____Place of Birth:_____

Marital Status: Never Married____ Separated____ Widowed____
Married____ Divorced____ Remarried____
Date of Birth:_____
Citizen of what country:_____My Social Security No. is_____
My Father's full name_____
My Mother's maiden name_____
Served in U.S. Armed Forces? Yes____: No____ State War and dates_____
FUNERAL ARRANGEMENTS: I prefer: Cremation____Burial____Bequeathal____

METHOD	TYPE	PLACE	NAME & LOCATION OF PLACE:
Dispose of cinerary	Urn in niche ____	columbarium ____	_____
(cremated) ashes by:	Urn burial ____	cemetery ____	_____
	Urn entombment ____	mausoleum ____	_____
	Scatter ____	(where permitted)	_____
Body to receive:	Earth burial ____	cemetery ____	_____
	Entombment ____	mausoleum ____	_____

If niche, lot or mausoleum is owned or otherwise provided list details separately.
TYPE OF SERVICE: Memorial (body not present)____; Conventional (casket open____, closed____;
FOR: Friends and relatives____; Private____; Other_____
AT: Church____; Funeral Home____; Our Home____; Other_____
NAME & ADDRESS OF   If church show denomination
PLACE TO BE HELD:_____
TO CONDUCT SERVICE: Soloist,
Clergyman, or other:_____ if any_____
Favorite hymns/music_____
LIMIT EXPENSE TO: Minimum____; Low Average____; Average____; Immaterial____

REMEMBRANCES to church or favorite charity. To those wishing to aid the "Memorial Way" movement you may name Continental Association or your local Memorial Society.
Send remembrances to:_____

MY SAFE DEPOSIT BOX is Number_____, in_____Bank,
_____Branch, in_____, key is located_____
Contents of box belonging to others, explain:_____
Name others that have access to the box_____

LAST WILL & TESTAMENT: I have no Will:____ On (date)_____I executed a Will;
Location of my Will is_____

(Attach the following data on separate sheet or sheets)

OTHER INFORMATION FOR NEWSPAPERS: Time lived in this community, occupation, employers, organizations of which you are a member, schools attended and degrees or honors received, military service showing honors or decorations, other items of interest as well as names of those that would survive you as of this date. (Don't be bashful, tell about your life, it will be a big help to your survivors.)

PEOPLE TO BE NOTIFIED: (List names, addresses and phone numbers).

PROFESSIONALS THAT ASSIST ME: (Show profession, name, address and phone).
My attorney, accountant, banker, investment counselor, life insurance agent, casualty insurance agent, auto insurance agent, doctor, dentist, etc.

FAMILY DATA: Date and place of marriage to present spouse; domicile on date of marriage to present spouse; children by present marriage: (Name, sex and birthdate, if children married state married name also). Previously married? Yes——; No——. If yes, indicate following: termination date, by death, divorce, annulment; name of former spouse (before marriage to you); children by former marriage (Name, sex and birthdates–if children married state married name also).

BUSINESS OR OCCUPATION: (If retired show former occupation.) Business or Industry; business address, if in business for yourself show your employer Social Security number, if any.

HEIRS: Next of kin, devisees, and legatees (only five principal ones required). Show their names, relationship (if related) and complete addresses.

END OF SECTION I–Additional data is filed with my valuable papers in Section II.

Additional copies of this form may be obtained from either of the following sources by enclosing 40¢ per set; 3 sets for $1.00 with your request.

Continental Association of Funeral
and Memorial Societies, Inc.
2001 S Street N.W., Suite 530
Washington, D.C. 20009

Signature————————————————
Address————————————————

Date compiled———————————— My phone is————————————————
(change as revised)

CONFIDENTIAL

Personal Data of_____

This form is for an individual or couple. Use H for Husband; W for Wife, where applicable.

SECTION II   Keep this section with your Will and other valuable papers.

YOUR WILL: Everyone should have a Will, if you have not made one we urge you to do so promptly, and then bring it up-to-date as conditions change, it avoids much delay, expense and doubt. It also provides for you to distribute your estate in the manner YOU desire. You will obtain satisfaction and be aiding the cause of the nonprofit "Memorial Way" movement if you are able and include in your Will a bequest either to the Continental Association or your local Memorial Society.

SURVIVORS DEATH BENEFITS: Many death benefits are unclaimed as the survivors are not informed of their availability. Some of the sources are listed below, check the ones you are entitled to receive. Details as to source and amount where known.

Social Security lump sum benefit_____; most covered workers are entitled to benefits under varying conditions. Is your job normally covered under State Workman's Compensation Insurance?_____ Employers'?_____; Fraternal organizations?_____; religious groups?_____; trade unions?_____; death benefits included in life, health and accident insurance policies? _____; other possible sources _____ Are you currently covered under Medicare? Yes_____; No_____.
    Veterans of U.S. Armed Forces in certain cases are entitled to death benefits. Are you a veteran of the U.S. Armed Forces? Yes_____; No_____. If yes, state your service serial number _____, branch of service _____Dates served_____, peace time_____; war time_____; Are you now receiving a service pension? Yes_____; No_____. If yes, is pension for disability_____; length of service_____; other_____

* * *

The following items make up a check list of the information your Executor, Lawyer, Accountant and family will need answers to after your death. Many items will not apply to most persons. Where they do apply to you a sheet should be made up with the information and attached to this form on all items to which your answer is Yes or which need space to explain in detail.

RENTS, PENSIONS, ANNUITIES: Do you own any property upon which you receive or are entitled to rent or royalties? Yes_____; No_____. If yes, describe your property rights, lease, contract or royalty source and basis or amount of income derived.

SOCIAL SECURITY BENEFITS: Do you now receive S.S. Benefits for Old Age?–Yes_____; No_____; Survivors?–Yes_____; No_____; Disability?–Yes_____; No_____; If Yes–state monthly amounts $_____. Do you contribute toward a pension fund (through your employer) other than for Social Security? Yes_____; No_____; If yes, explain. Do you now receive an annuity from your employer or insurance company? Yes_____; No_____ If yes, show Company, address and amount. Did you contribute toward the above annuity? Yes_____; No_____ Is any continuing annuity payable to spouse or other survivors? Yes_____; No_____ Where are policies or contracts located?_____

OUT OF STATE PROPERTY: Do you own property in any other state or country? Yes_____; No_____.

GIFTS AND/OR TRANSFERS: Have you made any gifts or transfers of the value of $5,000 or more during your lifetime without an adequate and full consideration in money or money's worth? Yes_____; No_____.

TRUSTS: Have you created any trusts or any trusts created by others under which you possess any power, beneficial interest, or trusteeship? Yes_____; No_____.

LIFE INSURANCE ON YOUR LIFE: Show name of insuring company and address, also name and address of local agent, policy numbers, face amount, beneficiary, who pays the premiums and location of policies. Explain any policy loans you may have.

HEALTH AND ACCIDENT INSURANCE: Same general data as for life insurance.

AUTO INSURANCE AND CASUALTY CONTRACT: Same data as for other insurance and also show what property the insurance covers or what other risk covered.

REAL ESTATE: Separate property owned by married persons should be clearly indicated. Jointly owned property (other than with spouse) should be indicated and fully explained giving names, addresses and interest of each joint owner. For each parcel of property show: description of property, deed in name of _____, location of deed, date acquired, how acquired? Purchase_____; gift_____; other_____. Cost_____. Mortgaged–Yes_____; No_____. Leased–Yes_____; No_____. If real estate contract still owing show name, address and balance owed to contract holder.

STOCKS, MUTUAL FUND SHARES OWNED: Show number of shares owned, type of shares, name of company or mutual fund, your mutual fund account number, certificate numbers, location of certificates and name of your broker and the brokerage company he represents.

BONDS AND DEBENTURES: Same general data as for stocks and add face amount of the bond, interest rate, and type of bond or debenture.

MORTGAGES AND/OR PROMISSORY NOTES OWNED: Show original amount, date made, name and address of maker, collateral, interest rate, location of documents, assignments or co-signers, etc.

CONTRACTS TO SELL REAL ESTATE OWNED: Full price, down payment, date of contract, name and address of purchaser, interest rate, location contracts, balance as of what date $_____ ___/___/___

CASH- CHECKING-ACCOUNTS: Show name and branch name, and address of bank, your account number, list names of other signers on account.

CASH ACCOUNTS WITH CREDIT UNIONS, SAVINGS BANKS, SAVINGS & LOAN ASSOCIATIONS: Show name, branch and address of each depository, your passbook number, type of deposit, rate of interest currently paid, other signers on the account, location where passbooks are kept. Explain any interest of others in any balance.

MISCELLANEOUS PROPERTY OWNED: Check only the items you own or in which you own interest and give full details. Interest in a copartnership_____; interest in life insurance on life of another_____; interest in an unincorporated business_____; debts owed to me by others_____; amounts due me from claims_____; rights_____; royalties_____; leaseholds_____; judgments_____; remainder interests_____; shares in trust funds_____; farm products_____; growing crops_____; livestock_____; farm machinery_____; autos_____; other_____

LIABILITIES: Check only the items that you owe as of this date: Real Estate mortgages_____; Real Estate Contracts_____; Notes Payable_____; Bank Loans_____; Credit Union Loans_____; Finance Company Loans_____; personal loans from friends_____; personal loans from relatives _____; time payment accounts (where not paid in full each month) _____. On all of the above liabilities checked indicate where the documents are located, and attach details.

LAWSUITS: Are there now pending any lawsuits against you? Yes_____; No_____. Explain.

CLAIMS: Are there any claims against you which you consider invalid? Yes_____; No_____. Explain in detail.

END OF SECTION II–Additional data is filed where readily available, in Section I.

Signature_____
Address_____
Date compiled_____ My phone is_____
(change as revised)

POSSESSIONS

Making gifts of various items of furniture, jewelry, and other objects of value helps patients demonstrate their care for special friends and relatives. Passing along various heirlooms establishes a sense of value and cohesiveness within a family. The simplest way to handle distribution of possessions is for the patient to make a list of all the things she values and to whom she would like to give them. If money or property is involved, however, the patient should consult a lawyer or legal advice agency and most likely make a will so that the disposition of property will be clear and uncomplicated for heirs.

A patient may prefer a more personal method of passing on her possessions, one in which she can take an active part. The dying mother of three teenage girls called on them to spread out all the valuable family china and glassware on the living room floor. As she lay on the couch, she helped them divide the treasures among themselves. "I gave away all my finery," she said. "It wasn't really sad, because I got to see the pleasure on their faces."

Try to encourage the patient to begin this work of distribution, because you cannot know what effect medication or the disease will have on his willingness or energy. The patient may want to put it off, anticipating family battles or even desertion by relatives he fears are hanging around only to get their share. While these are real concerns, the person dying can do his family a great service by allowing reactions to occur when he is alive, and not later, when they will be compounded by grief. Sad experience shows that families almost inevitably have trouble agreeing among themselves on equitable distribution of property. The patient is obviously the best person to make and explain bequests and can answer questions about them, hopefully minimizing future anguish.

In addition to family goods, family history is often "possessed" by the patient and can be passed along. Sorting through photographs and memorabilia, labeling treasures, and deciding who should be told what are activities as important as the distribution of the patient's "valuable" property. Not everyone will be interested in preserving family history, but the person dying deserves to have the past honored, and survivors are later often saddened at having broken family threads. One woman said she thought the hardest reality of her great-aunt's death was the loss of information stored in her head about their family. One mother of teenage boys spent the last six months of her life going through photographs and making picture-and-story books for each of them so they would know about their childhoods.

One particular benefit of being at home is that it is a natural setting for this work of disposition. Patients can be encouraged to talk about family stories, genealogy, and other information stored in their memories. Caregivers and visitors can even take turns making tape recordings or notes, asking questions, and writing up the history. Setting aside objects for particular people is so much appreciated by recipients that caregivers may want to help patients accomplish this work.

LAWS REGARDING THE BODY

Check with your funeral director, home care nurse, or some other reliable source regarding the state and county regulations concerning home deaths. A physician's certificate of death is always required, and will probably have to be signed in the home before the body is removed. Again, verify with your physician that he will be available to be in the home at the time of death or soon after. Depending on local laws, a medical examiner's certificate may also need to be completed at the time of death to verify such information as place of death; date, time, who was in the presence of the person who died; the next of kin and what relationship he or she is to the patient; the doctor's name and telephone number; and the probable cause of death. Other questions you may need to answer are the date the patient came home from the hospital, birth date, age and sex, what medications she was taking, what the predicted life expectancy was, and the address and telephone number of the closest relative.

Depending on your town or state, you may be able to avoid the unpleasantness of having the county coroner, police, or medical examiner come to the home to examine the body. Local regulations may allow you to contact the necessary officials prior to death, explaining that the person is dying, stating the diagnosis and giving the name, address, and telephone number of the physician who will sign the death certificate. If you make such arrangements, explain them to the funeral home if you use one, so that the police or coroner will not be asked to come to the home.

Ask about other laws some localities require. You may need to transport the body in a "funeral-type vehicle" driven by a registered funeral director. If you choose cremation, a waiting period of forty-eight hours may have to pass after death, during which the body may have to be kept at a funeral home. Embalming may or may not be necessary; in some states it is demanded only if the person died of a communicable disease or if the body is to be transported by plane, train, or truck. Try to ask questions that occur to you beforehand so that you can plan carefully and not have to deal with all this rather jarring information right after death.

AUTOPSY

When possible, the patient and family should decide in advance whether or not to have an autopsy. Unless your physician feels medical science can learn something about the patient's disease or treatment that will benefit others, you will probably choose not to undergo this procedure. The final decision in any case need not be the doctor's. Even if you do decide on an autopsy, you can change your mind at any point until it is performed.

If you choose to have an autopsy performed, find out in advance from the hospital or physician what procedures must be followed. Transportation will have to be arranged to have the body delivered to the hospital where the autopsy will be done. A physician may have to pronounce death before the body is moved from the house. After the autopsy, the funeral director can be instructed to transfer the body to the funeral home. In most cases, there is no cost involved in having an autopsy performed, or whatever costs are incurred will be covered by insurance.

DONATING ORGANS

Each year thousands of people who could have been saved with an organ donation die. Medical advances have made it possible to replace malfunctioning parts of the body as diverse as kidneys and the corneas of the eye. More recently, successful transplants have involved the heart, liver, skin, and bones. Any patient who is over eighteen years old (younger people must obtain parental consent) may donate organs, unless the reasons for death preclude their use. The decision to donate organs need not interfere with choices for care or remaining at home, but will require planning, since organs must be removed immediately after death. The removal procedure is performed in an operating room by a skilled surgeon using standard practices. Whatever arrangements are desired for the body afterward are the family's responsibility and can be carried out immediately following the donation.

The patient should discuss this decision with the family and physician to ensure cooperation. Donor cards or "pocket wills" are available from kidney or eye foundations in your state, or you may simply arrange the donation in advance with your doctor in the presence of two witnesses. The bequest does not have to be attached to the will and can be changed at any time.

BODY DONATION

Dissection of human bodies is an invaluable part of medical education; teaching and research hospitals depend on private donations as the principal source of bodies. In addition to or instead of organ donation, the patient may arrange to donate her body to a medical school. To make the gift, contact the school or hospital you wish to receive the body and follow its procedure. Normally, an Instrument of Anatomical Gift is supplied, to be signed by the patient and two witnesses. At the time of death, the attending physician, funeral director, or next of kin notifies the designated medical school. The funeral director will arrange for the school to receive the body and provide a burial permit and certified copy of the death certificate. Cost of transportation is normally paid by the medical school. When the studies are completed, which may not be for a matter of months, the school will comply with the donor's instructions regarding disposition of the body. The family may reclaim the body for burial in a family plot or for cremation.

It is wise to make arrangements for donating the body before the patient dies because coordination of all the parties involved can be difficult. Even with the best planning, delays can occur in transportation, processing of forms, or notification within the medical school, especially if the patient dies late at night or on a weekend or holiday.

FUNERAL ARRANGEMENTS

Since the time immediately after the death is filled with confusion and activity, many people find it useful to make funeral and burial decisions in advance, even such specific selections as funeral home, coffin or urn, and readings for the service. Some families resist working out details before the person dies, out of a concern that it signifies "giving up hope." Most families find that this subject is on the patient's mind, and if you ask for help in knowing what his or her wishes are, the patient will be relieved and pleased to tell you. Knowing and not guessing "what she would have wanted" provides solace for survivors.

Among the choices that have to be considered for funeral arrangements are disposal of the body, cremation, embalming, viewing of the body, and funeral and memorial services. Tell the patient you would like to discuss these matters when he is ready, and that you will find out whatever specifically needs to be known in order to make decisions and final arrangements. Find out what she wants to have done, and what if anything worries her. One patient said she knew "everyone was getting cremated now" but she was fearful about it, and so her family assured her she needn't feel guilty about "taking up space" and arranged for embalming and a burial plot.

I was so glad my husband and I had talked about what we wanted to do before he died. We agreed together that we would be cremated and the ashes of the first of us to die would be saved for the other so they could be strewn together over a beautiful hillside where we lived. We didn't want funerals, but a short service of music.

Once you know what the patient wants, you may need to find a funeral home. If the patient has a religious affiliation, contact an official of the church to make arrangements and ask for a recommendation of a funeral home. If you must choose one on your own, be sure to visit it and take a friend to help with questions about services and prices. Ask what is covered specifically in any "one price includes everything" arrangement. You are entitled to an itemized list of services. Some services, such as notification of newspapers and transportation of the body from the home, may not be included, so if you want them, inquire about their cost. Persist in obtaining prices for less expensive "packages," since funeral homes may not volunteer information about their full range of offerings.

Burial must take place in a designated cemetery; cremated remains may be scattered, depending on personal preference and local regulation. If you are buying a cemetery plot or are using a family plot, ask what fees are involved in opening and closing the grave or vault. Most states require the use of a "suitable container" for both burial and buried ashes. Consider whether a casket with a long-term warranty or elaborate padding is necessary and appropriate. Ask whether your state requires a vault in which the casket is placed, or whether the cemetery requires a liner. A coffin or urn made by a friend, or even a cardboard container, is often permitted by law. If you choose cremation, find out what the fees are and who is to pick up the ashes and when.

If you wish to avoid the details of arranging for the disposition of the body, you may be able to find in your area a company that will pick up the body, deliver the ashes to you or dispose of them as you wish, and handle all necessary legalities for several hundred dollars. Look in the Yellow Pages under funeral or burial societies, or contact the local chapter of the American Friends Service Committee. Another alternative is a nonprofit memorial or funeral society, usually staffed by volunteers, which will make arrangements with a funeral director for you. For a ten-to-twenty-dollar membership fee, you may be able to obtain services at half the usual cost. For names of societies, write the Continental Association of Funeral and Memorial Societies, 2001 S Street NW, Suite 530, Washington, DC 20009.

There are as many ceremonies and rituals for recognizing the death of a person as there are people who die. The patient and family should do as they wish; no "correct" ways exist to remember someone. If you have a religious affiliation, you may choose that tradition's form of service. Many other options exist. Burial may take place one day and a memorial service the next. You may want a private service with mostly family members or an open service for friends and the community. Some choose to have visitation with the family and/or deceased person in the home or at a funeral home. Some have written eulogies or music as a last tribute; some have a close friend read a poem or eulogy. Several families said they found it useful to tape the funeral service for people who could not attend and even for those who did, to hear later.

Another practical matter that can be settled in advance with the patient's help is preparation of a death notice. This generally includes the person's age, place of birth, occupation, list of survivors, organization memberships, and outstanding work or achievements. Later you can add the time and place of the memorial or funeral service and can suggest an organization to which contributions may be made. The death notice may be delivered in person or by telephone by the family or the funeral director to newspapers in your town and/or in the town where the person is known. (Many city newspapers will not accept notice by telephone except from an established funeral director.) Some families choose not to publish times of the funeral or visiting hours for fear that this leaves homes of the relatives vulnerable to theft. Be aware, too, that some businesses get their prospective clients from death notices.

As with so many other difficult aspects of home care and preparation for dying, the many practical considerations are simply a matter of planning and doing one task at a time. One caregiver said she learned to do "one hard thing each day." One of the joys of home care is that the patient can be involved as much as she wishes in all the various activities to be considered and completed.

22
DYING

Most of your time and energy over the last weeks or months has been directed at care and comfort for someone dying. Living with the demands and strain of this work surprisingly often blurs the realization that death will come. Many caregivers say that no matter how "prepared" they felt beforehand and even though, to some degree, they "wanted" death to come, when it happens, as one husband said, "the shock is incredible."

Caregivers and patients say they can tell death is imminent. Changes in body, mood, and even spirit are recounted in story after story of home care. An obvious signal—although when you are in the midst it's easy to miss—is that caregiving in the last days becomes constant. A minimum of two people in the home at all times will be most comfortable. Massaging, comforting, sponging, and simply being a presence in the room will become a twenty-four-hour activity and just too much for one person.

More than the need for around-the-clock attention, subtle and not so subtle changes are observed by caregivers and often patients themselves. By learning what some of these changes are and what may happen, the anxiety for everyone can be minimized. Because you have learned the value of preparation as you have provided home care, you know it will help you now, too. What are the emotions likely to be? What are the physical signs of dying? How can you help?

MOOD CHANGES

While you have probably already struggled with various moods and effects on the patient's behavior of disease and meditations, be prepared for wide emotional swings as death approaches. The patient's mood is now even more vulnerable to anxiety, grief, and the disease itself. Depression, anger, irritability, whining, and withdrawal are common. The patient may want to be alone much of the time, or only with selected people. In some extremes, the person may be so agitated that he will have to be restrained, either by command or by the use of physical restraints. More often, though, the mood swings take the form of conflicting messages. Within five minutes you may hear in succession "Go away . . . I'm hungry . . . Don't leave me." The patient's disorientation can be a terrible strain, and even frightening. Your instinct will tell you when the need for companionship and intimacy prevails, even when the opposite is expressed.

In the last few days my mother wanted to be held and hugged, then would send one of us from the room. She would tell me what she wanted me to do with my life, then tell me she loved me, and then would ask why I was standing there, didn't I have something I could go and do? One day, after chewing us all out for not understanding how she wanted her soup prepared, she said, "I'm thinking about all the people in the world who are dying. Why is it so good for me?"

While you are probably drawn to keeping a constant vigilance, this is nearly impossible for one person, and not even advisable. To maintain your own and the patient's care, you need to leave the patient alone occasionally. Most caregivers struggle with the guilt they might experience if they are out of the room when the patient dies.

I often thought of whether or not I would feel guilty if I came in from outside or woke some morning to find mother dead. I worried whether or not I would feel as though I had neglected her. But after praying about it and discussing it with the doctor and friends, I understood that I would not feel guilty. Her death was inevitable and had its own schedule and could easily occur at some moment when I was not near. She knew I was with her.

Keep in mind that death is a transition that may go on for weeks or even months. The patient is well aware of others' presence, whether or not literally at the bedside. Do not consider it a failure if you are not there.

Check in frequently with a touch and a warm word so the patient feels and hears the safety of companionship. Be specific in offering him alternatives; not "Would you like something?" but "Would you like apple juice or eggnog?" Help the person make connections with people and objects outside her own frame of reference: say, "Timmy would like to sing you a song"; "Aunt Molly called and said she is thinking about you."

If she is in a coma or drifting in and out of awareness, assume that she feels your presence and understands what you are saying. Consider as a parallel what it is like to be a small child who has not learned to talk or express himself. Holding and touching, speaking softly and repeating assurances comfort him. Hearing is usually the last sense to go when someone dies; if not your words, then your tone of voice will reach the patient. A doctor whose friend of many years was dying told how she comforted her: "Ann was comatose for the last few weeks. When I visited I would gather her up in my arms and sing to her. I know she knew I was there, and after she died I was so relieved to know we had shared our affection."

LETTING GO

As the patient comes close to her death, she may experience sadness, be haunted by dreams or snatches of memory, and be troubled by unresolved difficulties with people. Physicians tell of patients who lived weeks beyond the expected time in order to see a son or brother whom they needed to talk to in order to find peace. The dying person is trying to lay her life to rest. Try to help her talk out these problems, and assist her in whatever actions she feels she must take. Sometimes you can help release a paralyzing bond, depending on what it is, by reassuring her that the old quarrel has come to rest, or that you will be okay, or that someone she worries

about will be cared for. Assure her that everyone feels her endur-
ing love.

If the patient appears to be continually under stress or agitated,
simple exercises may help. Chronic anxiety is not only emotionally
cruel at this point, but it also intensifies pain. Calm the patient by
guided meditations, gentle music, rhythmic poetry, rocking, hum-
ming. He may have a technique of his own that you can recall for
him. Chanting, saying the rosary, focusing on a religious image or
photograph of a sunset, and holding a natural object such as a stone
or shell are all methods people have used to resolve and become
freed from internal struggles.

Remind the patient that she is not her body. Her physical being
is slowly giving out, but her spirit is very much alive, treasured by
others, and will continue to be. Encourage her to separate from her
worn-out body, to let go of people, places, things, ideas, and problems.

Try a simple meditation practice, developed by psychotherapist
Richard Boerstler of Cambridge, Massachusetts, to relieve the patient of the emotional and physical agitation that often accompany
dying. It can be used easily by patient and caregiver, even when
neither of them has had any experience with meditation. The basis
of the technique is breath control. Breath has been called the pulse
of the mind; by regulation of the breath, the mind is calmed.

Prepare the patient with this procedure.

- Set aside thirty to forty-five minutes without distractions.

- Make sure the room is warm and dimly lit.

- Patient should lie flat (no pillow if possible), eyes closed,
  hands beside thighs palms up, toes pointing away from each
  other; he should wear loose clothing and be covered with a
  blanket.

- Sit or stand in a comfortable position close to the patient,
  even with his shoulder; be calm, accepting.

- Lead the patient slowly and gently in relaxing his body, beginning with the toes ("Relax the toes"), moving to the
  ankles, knees, hips, stomach, chest, shoulders, neck, etc., to

the scalp, forehead, eyes, mouth, chin. Observe the patient as he relaxes.

Ah sound:

- Ask the patient to keep his eyes shut and to pay close attention to your voice as you make a "letting go" sound on each exhalation: *Aaaaaaaaaahhhhhhhhhh.* The patient may sound the *ah* with you if he chooses. Try to adjust the *ah* sound exactly to the patient's exhalations. Ask him to listen closely and to drop everything else from his mind.

Count:

- If the patient's breathing is too rapid for the *Ah* to be appropriate, ask him to count with you his exhalations, returning to "one" each time you reach "ten." Urge him to relax, close his eyes, and visualize large white numbers over his head as you both count. Watch his chest and diaphragm carefully to be sure that breath and counting are aligned.

Chant:

- As an alternative method, you can have the patient repeat a prayer or word, preferably on the out breath. You may join him in the chant, and others may relieve you or participate.

If one of these methods works to relax the patient, continue the practice frequently, and encourage the patient to use it when she is alone. Some have even used it at the time of death. Even if she is asleep, in a coma, or "clinically" dead, she probably senses sound and will be comforted by it.

PHYSICAL SYMPTOMS AND CARE

When death is imminent, families and caregivers who are not prepared are apt to panic. They call the hospital or emergency squad, everyone rushes around, and the person is roused from his bed, jostled in an ambulance, and processed through the emergency room. The truth is, a natural process is occurring, and it can proceed most peacefully right at home. Families who are informed in advance about dying realize they can manage without becoming desperate and that they have the option to call in a nurse or doctor if that would make everyone more comfortable.

Prepare for what dying looks like, what it feels like to die, and what the possible causes may be. By asking people with experience, you will get relief from your fears. Though such information may be painful or even distasteful, it will put you in control and reduce the damage your imagination can do. Caregivers say knowing "the worst" helps. Ask specific questions, because professionals and friends may either avoid the subject or not realize that you want to be informed.

What are some signs? These three stories recalled by caregivers show a range of experiences.

The last few days there were long periods between breaths, some moaning, eyes not really open, a film over one, then over both. She could still suck to take in water and medication. She knew we were there. We stroked her, talking, coaxing her to take liquid. At times she seemed too far away to know what we were doing. We weren't sure she had pain, but were advised to give her a low dose of sedative and of pain and antinausea medications.

Her speech went a few days before she died. She was saying something, but we couldn't understand and felt extremely frustrated. One of us was with her all the time, responding with simple, clear, calm references to her surroundings and how we loved her.

The last week was the hardest. He couldn't eat, refused water, and drifted into and out of a coma. One of us always held his hand and talked to him now and then. Every so often he would squeeze a hand to let us know he heard even though he couldn't talk.

While death is different for everyone, general signs can be seen for most people and you can be alert for them. Changes in breathing and voice, expression, skin color and tone, eyes, and general mobility will probably be evident. Senses diminish and gradually fail. Many people say that in the last few days or hours the patient was noticeably more peaceful. Others said the opposite was true.

The deterioration of body functions and changes in metabolism at the final stages of dying may cause a variety of symptoms. To prepare, review the following description of typical symptoms, adapted from the terminal care manual prepared by the University of Minnesota School of Nursing. Learn here how to care for the patient as she dies.

General agitation: The patient may be restless, need light and fresh air, and be extremely thirsty. She may not want bedclothes; she may sweat profusely. She will probably not want to be on her back, so help her by propping her up on pillows with lots of head support, or moving her gently from side to side. Sponge and massage her body carefully and give ice chips or sips of iced water. Salve her dry lips. Agitation at this point can be eased with medication and by reducing any weight on her body, by relieving her of personal and bed clothing. Although the need for most medications will probably decrease, withdrawing them completely may risk further distress.

Temperature: As the heartbeat slows down and becomes irregular, blood circulation will decrease, and the body's heat-regulating system may fail. The first parts of the body to be affected are usually the hands and feet, which may be cold, and either pale or bluish. The color of the face may become grayish and the lips blue. Some feel that no matter how cold the body itself is, the dying person is probably not aware of the cold. If she is conscious, you could ask if she would like to be covered with blankets, although many prefer almost nothing over them. The body surface may also become cool and covered with damp, cold perspiration. Lightweight cotton blankets or sheets will help to absorb perspiration and keep the patient dry. The covers should be loose and light; too many covers may increase restlessness.

Pulse: Blood circulation decreases. Foot and wrist pulses become so faint that they cannot be felt. The heartbeat may become very rapid and then slower, irregular, and less easy to hear. No treatment of any of these symptoms is necessary, and the patient probably will not be aware of them.

Digestive system: Muscles that aid the normal movement of the digestive system (mouth, throat, stomach, bowel) slow down. Offer fluids such as water, tea, or fruit juices, or ice chips to suck as long as the patient desires to drink and swallow. Avoid milk products, which tend to produce mucus. If he is too weak to drink from a cup or suck through a straw, small amounts of fluids can be given using a teaspoon, special feeding cup, syringe without a needle, or medicine dropper. Stop giving fluids when he is unable to swallow. Mouth care is especially important when the person is no longer taking fluids or is breathing through his mouth.

A buildup of excessive secretions in the mouth or throat can cause a gurgling or rattling that is very eerie and can be frightening to hear. It is probably not distressing to the patient, however, and turning her on her side may aid drainage. Some physicians prescribe a medication called atropine to dry up these secretions. Atropine is given by injection. If you fear that you will be troubled by the "rattling" and would like to consider medication, talk with the nurse or doctor. If you have been using a suction machine, discuss the use of it at this time. Suctioning is usually not needed, but it is wise to be prepared.

Muscles that control the bladder and rectum will also work less well, and the patient may have uncontrollable bowel movements or leak urine. Keep cotton or paper pads or diapers under the patient.

Respiratory system: Respirations may increase to 30 to 40 per minute (16 to 20 is the normal rate) and then become very irregular and shallow with alternating periods of no breathing. They will slow from 40 to 30 to 20 to 4 to 3 to 2 per minute, until breathing stops.

Move the patient into whatever position eases respiration, remembering that he must be well supported to be comfortable. If lying down, he may be placed slightly on his side with his head elevated and firmly held on a pillow. Especially difficult breathing can often be relieved by propping the patient with pillows or a backrest in a well-supported sitting position. Depending on the size of the person, cradling or holding her so that she rests against your chest may aid in shortness of breath, increasing security and comfort. Administration of oxygen may be necessary in some situations to help the patient who is experiencing "air hunger" or shortness of breath. Talk with your physician about this likelihood.

Central nervous system: Some patients are alert and mentally clear until the moment of death; others may become disoriented, semiconscious, or even unconscious for several hours or days. Consciousness is often retained longer than may be apparent to an observer. Speech may become confused and increasingly difficult to understand. Even though the patient has trouble communicating, she is probably aware of others. Touch and talk with her even though she may not respond.

Senses become dulled and are lost altogether as a dying person becomes comatose. Although it is not known at what point senses cease to function, we do know that when a patient is in a deep coma he is probably not aware of taste, smell, touch, or pain; hearing probably continues. Keep talking even when she appears to be unconscious; soothing music may also be desirable. Definitely avoid speaking in the presence of the person as if she cannot hear.

While it is not common, a patient may make involuntary movements, such as jerking an arm. These need not concern you. If you fear she will hurt herself, protect with pillows the part of the body that could be harmed.

Eyes: Eyes may become sunken or glazed. Pupils may become enlarged and then unchanged. Eye secretions can be cleaned with a warm, damp cloth. If eyes are bulging out, place a small damp cloth over them to provide comfort.

Pain: Although a patient may not be able to communicate during the last hours, you will know if he is suffering pain by signs of restlessness, moving about the bed, anxious sounds, or changes in facial expression. Prepare for this possibility by discussing it with the home care nurse, and determine what remedies are available. When a patient is in deep coma, she probably will not experience pain.

DEATH

As death approaches, the patient will slowly fade away. What does it feel like? Patients who are alert within several hours of death describe a feeling of weariness. They want to say goodbye and are not frightened or unwilling to leave. Family members experience the person as very far away. While most speculate that death is usually not painful of itself, they say some become frightened. Be with the patient as much as possible. Most people are unconscious at the time of death—in other words, most do actually "die in their sleep"—and drift into this state apparently unaware of what is happening. Only rarely does a patient experience shortly before death a feeling of choking or suffocating. You can prepare for this possibility by having a sedative on hand.

In the final minutes, certain physiological signs will be evident. Breathing becomes slower and then stops. The patient may struggle to take several breaths or make long exhalations and then stop the effort to breathe. Shortly thereafter you will feel that the heart is not beating. The usual signs of death are absence of breathing and heartbeat, loss of control of bowel and bladder, lack of response to shaking or shouting, eyelids slightly open, eyes fixed on a certain spot, jaw relaxed, and mouth slightly open. At the moment of death, there may be a projection of material from the lungs or bowels, for which you may be prepared with towels.

Each dying is different, and for those who have never experienced it, the following recollections shared by caregivers can help alleviate some of the mystery and fear.

My mother died very quickly. I was standing next to her, and we were discussing ideas about breakfast. Suddenly her left side began to tremble and she said, "Betty, something is happening." I put down the rail of the hospital bed and held her in my arms. We even talked a bit more. I asked her if she was in pain and she said no. I asked her if she was doing okay, and she looked at me, smiled, and said yes. Then she died.

At dawn my husband spoke up saying that he felt cold and strange. He asked me to call the doctor, explaining, "If he can help me, now is the time I need him." The doctor said he was scheduled to perform two operations and would come as soon as he could. I knew I could call his alternate, but I wanted to be with my husband, to get him warm. He complained of stomach cramps, which I suspected from previous experience meant a failing heart. I gave him a pill to ease the pain. His breath became labored and I dreaded the rattle, but it didn't come. I took his hand and said, "God, how I love you." He began, "I know, God how—" and lost consciousness. Six or seven long breaths later he died.

My daughter's breathing became slower and slower throughout the day, with longer pauses between breaths. Everyone in the household focused on the breathing and the sounds of breathing. I would sit in the room and try to read or stroke her; all I could hear was the breathing. Then I left for a glass of water, and when I came back, it was quiet. Her body was already cooler than my hand.

The night my husband died our two eldest daughters were on watch, each holding a hand beside the bed. He came out of his coma, completely lucid at 6:30 A.M., told the girls he loved them and to "tell your mother I'm with her and always will be." Then he smiled, looking out at the bright new day, and died.

Nana asked for the bedpan, and Grampa had trouble getting her on it. He realized she couldn't feel his hand on her leg. She said she felt "funny" and that her bowels were going to move. I knew that these were common precursors to death, and I asked if she felt any pain. She said no, and her pulse was strong but irregular. She had some water and asked for applesauce. We didn't give it to her because she had choked a bit on the water. My husband kissed his mother and told her he'd see her in the morning. I stayed with them, and about forty-five minutes later she cried out loud. I checked the oxygen line and it was clear. She gasped several times and Grampa was there patting her face and crying, "Oh no, my buddy . . . I can't lose my buddy." I took her pulse and she was gone.

As with any other situation, survivors will react to the death in their own individual ways. One will collapse in tears, another will reach out to care for those in obvious grief, and a third will self-assuredly try to organize the family. Some will bustle about, cleaning and straightening up; others will stand rigidly off to the side. One caregiver told how her sister, a nurse on a geriatric ward where many people died, broke into sobs, apologizing, "I shouldn't be crying, I'm used to death." Everyone does what he or she has to do. Forget everything you ever read or were told about what was appropriate behavior. If they help, resort to formulas like "She's at peace now," or "Thank God she's no longer suffering." But while clichés may be true, right now they may have the effect of trampling your emotions. Efforts to be reasonable or philosophical are not at all necessary, and may only delay the cleansing power of expressed, unbridled feelings.

If a nurse or doctor is not present in the house at the time of death, call one immediately afterward. The nurse can confirm death, but a doctor is legally required to certify it. Call a friend or family member right away if you are alone. Don't wait to compose yourself or clean up; you need company. If you feel uncomfortable, stay on the telephone until someone arrives. When the person first dies and is still in the house, most people experience a huge silence, stillness, or absence. One caregiver spoke of being so frightened by the quiet once her grandmother died that she played loud chords on the piano while waiting for others to come. A thirty-year-old son described his experience.

> I held her for a minute and then put her down. I became scared. I had never seen anyone die and I couldn't quite believe it had happened. I even talked to her once thinking maybe she wasn't really dead. I couldn't reach the doctor. I called my neighbor, and she came, and we prayed a bit next to Mom. She helped me make telephone calls. Many people began arriving. I couldn't have made it alone at that point. I was so grateful for the people.

NOTIFICATIONS

Call the physician within an hour after the person dies. If the medical examiner or coroner must be notified, ask the physician to make this call for you. If there is to be an autopsy, or if the body or organs are being donated, call the hospital or medical school, tell them the patient has died, and arrange for transportation. You can wait to call the mortician or to remove the patient from the home. If you have made funeral arrangements in advance, notify the home when you want the body to be transported; if you have not, call a funeral home to begin making arrangements, or ask a member of the clergy or a friend to do so for you. Begin to call family and friends to let them know the person has died. If you don't know the plans for the funeral, try to provide them with a number to call, such as that of the funeral home or of a family friend, since you may not have the energy to make all those additional calls yourself.

The visiting nurse or another responsible person should make arrangements to remove any borrowed equipment from the home. Unused medications may be returned to the pharmacy or flushed down a drain. Other notifications can follow, using checklists developed by referring to Chapter 21, "Practical Matters."

SAYING GOODBYE

My mother came to our home when we knew she was dying, and she was wonderfully attended by my wife, me, and her grandchildren. Three of our youngest children slept each night in sleeping bags under her hospital bed. She was literally surrounded twenty-four hours a day by love. A few minutes after she died we untied two heart-shaped helium balloons my son had tied to her bed and all went outside, said a prayer, and let them go. When I explained to her youngest grandchild that they would float up and eventually burst in the atmosphere, she said, "Yes, and all the love will float out and fall all over the world." We all went back inside to say goodbye.

Families and friends have often remarked that one of the benefits of death at home was that they did not have to separate immediately from the person who had died. In hospitals, the family is often requested to leave the room soon after death so the body can be prepared for the funeral home. At home, families are in control of how long they would like to remain with the body. This final separation is very difficult, and making it on your own schedule allows each person the time needed to say goodbye. Many families allow several hours so that children can be brought home from school and any friends and relatives who wish may come to pay their respects.

Everyone should be encouraged to do whatever helps. Touching or holding the deceased person, praying, and washing or dressing the person can be encouraged. Some will want to be alone; some will want to be accompanied.

We all gathered around the bed, grateful that he was at peace. We held hands and said a prayer of farewell. Each of us told a favorite funny thing Dad had said. There were no tears then.

This can also be a time of great closeness among those who have been involved in or touched by the caregiving. Praise and thank people who have helped; reminisce about the last few weeks. Someone in the household may need special attention in order to be able to acknowledge the death.

I went downstairs to the living room and I saw Grampa on the couch. I felt I could actually see visions of the past flashing in front of his eyes as he wept. I wished I could help. Instead, I just stood in a daze as tears streamed wet down my face. I walked over to him and sat down. I tried to think of some profound comment to make on death. But I had nothing to say, much less anything profound. I reached out and wrapped my arms around him. Grampa and I just rocked sorrowfully back and forth on the couch. I kept telling him that I was there and that I loved him. That was all I could think to do. Then we went upstairs together to say goodbye to his wife of fifty-three years.

When representatives of the funeral home arrive, direct them to the patient. Some people prefer not to accompany them or to watch the patient handled by them. They will put the body in a bag or some other covering and will probably carry it out on a stretcher.

The men in black suits arrived at the front door, and I was frightened at first. I was so dazed by exhaustion and grief that I had forgotten who they could be. When they carried my mother down the stairs and out the front door, zipped up in a big black sack, I had the overwhelming feeling that *we* should have been the ones to leave. It was her house, after all. What right did I have to remove her?

When the body leaves, the bed, room, and house will seem very silent and empty. Medicines, sheets, soiled clothing, humidifier, and equipment glare at you. The room where so much has happened, particularly in the past several weeks, is now hollow. You may feel all you have is loss. There are no shortcuts or cures for grief. For the present you may just as well go for a walk, breathe deeply yourself, review the gift you have given and received, and express your gratitude for the experience and the relationship. Put one foot in front of the other even if you don't want to.

A Note about Team Members

Do not overlook the many people who have helped with care who may not be close relatives or even related by blood, but who over the last days and weeks have become very close to the patient. Tired and grieving, they have been left by the one person who understood their commitment. Resentments that grow from being ignored by the family will isolate these individuals from the attention and emotional connections they deserve and feel. Include them in planning for the memorial or burial events. Encourage them to support each other and to stay in touch. A primary caregiver who cared for her aunt took her team members—none of whom was related to the patient—out for dinner the night after the death and invited them and provided transportation for them to come to the funeral and lunch that followed. The team got together every few months for several years after, and still has reunions. "We formed a permanent bond," she said.

23
GRIEVING

The first few days after the patient dies will be filled with activity, and for those who are exhausted by the last weeks of caregiving, even the smallest matters will seem a burden. Welcome help with the many practical problems and needs that will arise almost immediately. People will ask to be given tasks, and they mean it. Running errands, cooking meals, and providing child care are all ways they can help you. Family, church members, or close friends can take turns answering the door or telephone, keeping careful records of callers. Relaying information, handling inquiries, making deliveries, and shopping can help relieve the family. Welcome offers of meals, ask the neighbor to tend your garden, accept loans of cash if you are short. People who care about you will feel better if they are contributing something.

To some extent, the necessary activity will provide insulation against grief, but as is true of any injury, when the shock and initial attention end, pain quickly follows. Concern and care for survivors are the logical and necessary ends of home care.

Learning to live again after the death of a loved one begins with acknowledging the seriousness of grief. Survivors are prone to illness, accidents, alcohol and other drug abuse, recurrence of chronic disorders, depression, and suicide. Bereaved people are also more prone to losing jobs and spouses. The truth is, death is not as hard on the person who dies as it is on the survivors.

Each person's manner of coping with death is different, and each person's grieving and emotions will be unique and should not be confined or determined by "appropriate" standards of behavior. Since you have lived each day with the gradual dying of someone you love, you have probably already experienced much of the grief from this loss. You have felt anger, denial, depression, and many other emotions associated with grief. Now the work is to identify symptoms of grief and learn to care for them. While everyone's "grief work" is different, learn general principles by reading here the experiences and advice of others.

WHAT DOES GRIEF FEEL LIKE?

When death comes, many caregivers experience immediate relief. The house is quiet; the sounds of labored breathing, the vaporizer, and whatever else has attended the patient are silenced. You can stop listening. The focus of the last weeks is gone. But soon most people feel empty, a huge void in their lives, and generally aimless and numb. These feelings are soon joined or replaced by confusion and overwhelming, mixed feelings.

> The next morning the telephone rang, construction continued on the building next door, Pepsi was delivered from the market, and I went to work. Cruel and comforting, the continuity. My life continues past the dead body, bearing words and memories, emptiness and uselessness. I carried all that information as I went through the motions of my day. I sent flowers to the doctor who had stayed with us through the long days and nights. What else could I do? Show up for life; pretend to be alive.

More than anything else, grieving is like extreme growing pains; it is a process of learning how to live over again in a new context, and with the presence of loss. A person who is grieving has had a familiar constellation shattered and must re-create another self in a new one. Especially when the loss involves a spouse, the survivor can often feel a complete loss of identity. No amount of platitudes or moralizing or interpreting can accomplish this enormous task of self-renewal.

The intense feelings associated with grief also contribute to a heightened sensitivity. Survivors can become acutely conscious of irreducible truths about the swiftness of life, the impermanence of relationships, and the worthlessness of most activity. If this awareness becomes an obsession it takes a toll on the survivor's ability and willingness to get on with life.

Since grief is so powerful and painful an emotion, many people wonder whether or not the feelings and actions are "correct" or "healthy."

> If there is one thing I learned when my grandmother died, it was that you can't make rules about how to grieve properly. I wince now to remember how judgmental I had been when I heard about a son who played golf the day of his mother's funeral or when a friend didn't even go to her brother's wake. I did what I needed to help my grief, and every mourner needs that latitude. I didn't bother being "correct": I just did the best I could. Somehow I knew the greatest "disrespect" would have been to throttle my grief for fear of being misinterpreted by others.

Panic over what are essentially natural reactions will make grief more difficult. Accept the fact that grief is terrible and also healing, and try not to judge yourself for any part of it. Be prepared to feel angry at yourself and the person who died and anyone else who gets in the way. You will be confused, shocked, anguished, depressed, withdrawn. You will lack any sense of self-worth or interest in people or activities, even those you used to love. You may lose your appetite, be unable to sleep, lose interest in sex or want more sexual contact than usual, and have either manic energy or none at all. You may separate yourself from others, or feel no one understands, or believe everyone is tired of your sadness.

Here are more of the common feelings of grief as summarized by professionals at the Boulder Hospice in Colorado:

- Tightness in the throat or heaviness in the chest.

- Empty feeling in stomach.

- Restlessness and looking for activity.

- Difficulty with concentration.

- Disbelief; maybe the death didn't really happen.

- Sensing the dead person's presence, hearing his voice.

- Aimless wandering, forgetfulness, not finishing things.

- Troubling dreams.

- Assuming mannerisms or habits of the dead person.

- Intense preoccupation with the life and possessions of the dead person.

- Furious anger at the person for leaving.

- Need to tell and retell details about the person and her death.

Usually survivors will also feel guilty about some aspect of their behavior during the last few days or weeks of the patient's life. Whatever the particular reason for regret—a last-minute hospitalization, not being there when the patient died, not understanding something he was trying to say—remember that you and everyone did the best they could at the time. Hindsight, the wisdom of time, and Monday-morning quarterbacking will only bring pain. You cannot change what happened. Someday what you regret now can be a gift of advice learned the hard way to someone else in a similar situation. For today, accept that you meant to do your best and you did no less than you were able to do.

Certain extenuating circumstances make survivors especially vulnerable: when other losses occur at the same time; if the grief of a previous major loss has never been fully acknowledged; if the death has been or is perceived as being sudden or unexpected; or if one feels or is socially isolated.

While the intense feelings and symptoms of grief—from depression to physical illness—may be themselves normal reactions to loss, they are frequently difficult for others to accept. Even close friends and relatives will meddle, with offers of advice, suggesting a vacation or some other "cure" that doesn't feel right. Others will react to the frustration of not feeling helpful by withdrawing, acting impatient or awkward, leaving the grieving person to feel abandoned. For the moment, someone grieving cannot play her usual role in the family, or among friends, and customary communication is difficult and unsatisfying. In a very real sense, no one *can* understand or help someone grieving. It is a path to be walked alone, but in the company of caring people.

WHAT HELPS?

Overcoming grief—integrating the loss and feelings into your life —depends primarily on staying connected to people, simple activities, and attention to what is real and true today. Structure the day with several "people events." Do not be embarrassed by holding on to whatever connection you need to the person who died. One woman did volunteer work at her husband's favorite charity. A widower chose to edit his wife's unfinished book. A daughter took up bridge so she could take her mother's place in a weekly bridge game. Holding on to the deceased person is frequently also done in very elemental ways, such as wearing the person's clothing or perfume. One widow reported that after her husband's death she had no appetite and thought she was assuming *his* loss of interest in food shortly before his death. Nothing is wrong with these coping methods. Eventually, letting go of them will probably offer you a sign you are achieving some freedom from the feelings of loss.

Many survivors discover the healing power of writing. Expressing your anger and frustration by scribbling down or banging out on a typewriter disconnected thoughts can help bring feelings to the surface. Some people try to put their relationship with the dead person in perspective by writing dialogues with him, finishing conversations. This activity may allow a degree of honesty that is not possible in talking with friends and will release you from the bondage of fantasy or wishful thinking. Painting, music, and pottery are other useful ways some find to express intense feelings directly.

To aid recovery, you can turn to competent professionals. Psychological support and monitoring can make every possible difference. Much excellent help—from books, support groups, or counselors specializing in bereavement—is available for people grieving a death. Since prolonged depression changes the way a person thinks, grief can become stuck. Mourning need not be a permanent condition; with help, you can turn away from what you cannot change and from grief behavior—such as isolating or always looking at what "used to be"—that locks in feelings of despair. The survivor can leave these habits and turn slowly, persistently toward a new life.

To care for yourself in this crisis, persist in a daily personal routine. Begin with the assumption that you will live through the day, ask for the strength to do your best, and then get into some form of action and continue to put one foot in front of the other. Action can take many forms: walks, movies, shopping, a new craft, baths, television, work, whatever keeps you occupied. Keep busy even though you don't feel like it, and when feelings arise, express them. Don't worry about being appropriate; take it out on the mailman or your best friend if either is handy. You can apologize later. Try to loosen the grip on your own pain, give up on efforts to "get under control." These "shoulds" will only make it worse. Develop a practice of being consciously grateful for something, anything: for a place to live and food to eat, for your children or friends. Even such simple disciplines will initially seem difficult, or impossible to carry out. Keep trying, because you need the safety of a minimal structure. Slowly each action will get easier.

Nothing you ever do is likely to be more difficult than what you are doing right now. Do whatever you need to get through the day, and be grateful for the extent to which it worked. Try what seemed particularly useful again tomorrow, and in this way slowly develop your own survival techniques. Just hang on as best you can so that time can work its wonders.

STRENGTH FROM OTHERS

For many, the greatest and hardest lesson of grief is the most obvious: other people and the caring they offer make an incredible difference. Somehow, force yourself to stay connected to family and friends. Pick up the phone when you feel terrible; say yes when someone offers to come over or asks you to coffee. Don't worry about what you will say or that the visitor will be bored by your sadness. Seek companionship in any possible way and worry about being a nuisance later. There's plenty of time for you to give back all the love you receive. Just for today, allow yourself to be carried along by the faith others have and offer.

Beyond immediate friends and family, as you may have learned in the course of home care, strangers quickly can become lifesavers if only we ask for their help. Many find solace in talking to others who are suffering loss and surviving. Read books by survivors. Participate in meetings of bereaved spouses and relatives. Most communities have special groups for parents of children who have died. Tell your story as often as you can, and listen to others tell theirs. Sharing experiences, getting out your own feelings among people who can identify with them, and hearing the hope and strength that others can offer are very healing.

Survivors of patients who contributed to this book describe here some of their experiences with grief, and what they learned.

At first, her death didn't seem difficult because Mom had lived longer than anyone expected, and we were able to share several months together. I felt good about having been with her and taken care of her. Shortly after the funeral, I got very angry at the rest of the family, who I felt deserted both of us and now wanted their share of her things. I didn't want her house to be sold, but they insisted. Sometimes I would just sit and cry: why hadn't she made them promise to carry out her wishes? I finally talked with the lawyer, who said it was unfair, but there was nothing to be done. Slowly, I just got up and on with my life.

I don't mourn my loss of her so much as I do her own loss of time. She had been very depressed for years and was finally making some healthy changes in her life when her illness began. I try to remember that she wouldn't have been sure enough of herself a few years ago to organize us all to care for her at home. My friends help me to take heart in the fact that in her dying she was strong and dignified. More than that, she brought the family together, and after our three months sharing caretaking, I feel much more comradeship than ever before with my brothers.

Grief has given me compassion for others. It makes me understand how important being there for bereaved people is. I used to have a terrible time calling or writing anyone who had a loss. Now I know it helps and is appreciated. I always thought I would be in the way. Today I am grateful for these "intrusions" of caring. They jar my despair. I am forced to see I have many reasons to live.

Despite every kind of preparation, I was devastated by Betsy's death. I feel that I will never fully recover from it, but perhaps grief is like that. I don't mean that I don't have a normal life, but I can't get close to anyone like that now. My immediate reaction to her dying was to think, "Nothing matters . . . everyone dies anyway." I am greatly helped by old and new friends, but I still feel abandoned by one of her closest friends, who turned against me when she died. Death really rattles people, and I'm particularly devoted now to those who've stayed by me even when I pushed them away.

CHILDREN GRIEVING

Young children cannot understand fully what has happened to the person who has died. A child is apt to be frightened and guilty, fearing the same thing will happen to him, or that he may in some way have caused his sister's or father's death. He probably even has the evidence for his blame, such as a fight months earlier, or a time he disappointed his parent. A child whose parent has died probably fears the surviving parent will die too. Since the child is surrounded by sadness, he will add to his sense of responsibility the feeling that somehow others' happiness depends on him. Since he will inevitably fail at cheering everyone, his feelings of failure will grow way out of proportion.

How should the adults nearest the child behave? What does the child need?

- The child needs to be reassured that those he loves are staying with him. If you are caring for him, he may ask if you are sick or if you will die. Say you don't think it will happen for a long time and you will be there to care for him for many years. Say that someone will always care for him and do the things that Mommy or Daddy used to do, or play with him as his brother used to do, although we will all miss the person for a long, long time.

- The child needs to know that she can be sad, see tears and be comforted when she cries herself. Say that we will be sad for a while and that's okay.

- Don't let the child be too good. Some will try desperately to make up for all the disappointment by trying to be perfect or happy or invisible.

- Gently help the child by being honest and sincere. Be with him when he is crying and answer questions.

- Give the child all the patience and attention you can, no matter how annoying she may be or how painful it is for you. Chances are it will make all the difference to both of you.

- Learn to listen. Don't interpret anger and denial as insensitivity. Ask open-minded questions such as "What makes you say that?" "What do you think? Tell me more."

- Be aware that the child may take on some symptom of the patient. For example, if the parent had a colostomy or some bowel complication, the child may well experience confusion with her toilet training, or even develop a seemingly unrelated behavior.

- Make every effort to relate the loss to the child's experience. For example, remind him how he loves Spot even when Spot is not here. Talk about how he cares for a favorite toy, which he can think about even when it's not with him. Ask him to recall memories of warmth, security, and making the hurt go away. In this way, learn what might be a comfort.

- Help her to acknowledge her own life by staying with usual routines and returning soon to school.

- Volunteer that there is nothing fair about what has happened, nor is there anything he can or could have done about it.

- Learn about her pain by asking, listening, and observing her general behavior and interactions with her friends.

Children may at times appear to be ignoring the truth by watching television or playing. They may say Mommy will feed me, knowing full well she cannot. Remind the child that Mommy would have liked to but cannot and explain why. Children will be more obvious than adults in their denial and gently correcting misstatements is important.

Children grieving require special attention, which will be hard to give. Not only are adults engaged in their own terrible pain, but they tend even in normal circumstances to have difficulty being consistent in allowing children their own feelings. Many adults simply prefer to think children are too young to understand and that their sense of loss is better ignored. Resisting this natural fear and instinct will prevent children from becoming isolated in their grief, a situation that can cause a great deal of emotional damage.

The degree to which a child is affected by the assault death makes on normal emotional development depends largely on how important adults help him recognize, talk about, and live with his feelings. Everything can be gained by simply listening to the child, listening without "knowing all along what he will say" or "knowing what he feels like" or some other preconceived knowledge that prohibits true empathy. While there may in fact be usual responses and stages of grief for children, avoid categorizing the child or his feelings.

> It's hard on all of us, being without a mother. If our children ask a question, I answer it. My seven-year-old spends weekends with my mother, who gives him undivided attention. My friends also take the children. We all talk about their mother and are as simple and honest as possible. My thirteen-year-old is awfully angry and stays in her room when we don't hound her to join us. Our social worker is helping all of us to know how to talk to each other.

Death for children is so complicated and important in their development that you should not hesitate to seek help for them and encourage them to talk and seek help from peers, parents of their friends, and others. Many wonderful books are available for children on the subject of death. Seek counsel from teachers, clergy, and therapists. Inform all adults with whom the children have contact that there has been a death in the family and that you can use their help. Ask them to inform you of anything worrisome about the child's behavior, or if they have any thoughts about how the child could be helped. She has a long life ahead, and it is very important to give her all the emotional support she needs now.

SURVIVAL

After the initial period of suffering the loss of a loved one, most survivors begin to experience the person not so much as "dead," with all the memories of how she looked and what the last weeks of her life were like, but more as part of their familiar and cherished history. Memories become less anguished and begin to serve as resources, part of each individual's constitution.

My husband was a violinist, and fine music was religion to us. Even after four years, when I feel alone and grief overwhelms me, I can put on a recording of Brahms' violin and piano sonatas and the beautiful music we shared brings him back.

While at first nearly everything you see and touch and remember is painful—the car the person drove, clothing or jewelry, her political views and magazine subscriptions, a flash memory, old family friends, a favorite writer, the arrangement of a closet, a brand of canned peas—slowly objects, ideas, and friends from the life you shared become small, secure stepping-stones to a new life.

24
EPILOGUE

How do we and so many others survive terrible, seemingly unendurable loss? How is nature constantly made new? Rivers that have been polluted cleanse themselves over time. Abused children can become sensitive, caring adults. Alcoholics and chronic depressives can emerge day by day into hopeful, useful, and giving individuals. How do hopeless people become serene? I struggle for the words to describe a process I experience in my own life, which brings me gradually out of the darkness into light. My own grief has been transformed in writing this very personal book. But how? And what now gives me the confidence to let it go and walk forward, leaving these pages to be scattered about where I hope others will benefit from them?

Once in a very dark hour, not long before finishing this book, someone I was given the grace to trust sat with me and spoke in a soft, sure voice about sunrise. He said the sun would come up tomorrow whether or not I believed it would, or watched for it, or wanted to wake to it.

Healing is a gift of the universe—it both simply happens and is won by the innate human ability to put one foot in front of the other, even when we do not believe in the future.

We naturally look to recovery as a return to former "happiness," as if pain is of no value and to be forgotten. But while we may imagine this is what is best for us, human experience has more to offer. In order not to miss the real treasure buried in our survival, we must, as the poet T. S. Eliot urges us in *Four Quartets*, "be still, and wait without hope/For hope would be hope for the wrong thing." Life no longer is simply a quest for happiness. We can come to recognize we have been enriched in ways we could not have imagined. We rejoice in texture, compassion, turbulence, and in the hard-won confidence in our strength.

My own grief has brought me to see what otherwise I never would have sought: thousands of sunrises in nature and human hearts, giving me confidence to rest when it's dark and let go when it's time to be finished.

BIBLIOGRAPHY

GENERAL

"All About Home Care: A Consumer's Guide." National Home Caring Council, 235 Park Avenue South, New York, New York 10003, 1982.

Alsop, Stewart. *Stay of Execution: A Sort of Memoir.* New York: Harper & Row, 1973.

Baulch, Evelyn. *Home Care: A Practical Alternative to Extended Hospitalization.* Millbrae, California: Celestial Arts, 1980.

Brim, Orville G., Jr., et al., eds. *The Dying Patient.* New York: Russell Sage Foundation, 1970.

Davidson, Glen W. *The Hospice: Development and Administration.* Washington, D.C.: Hemisphere Publishing Corp., 1978.

Fulton, Robert. *A Bibliography of Death, Grief, and Bereavement, 1845–1973,* 3rd ed. Minneapolis: University of Minnesota Center for Death Education and Research, 1973.

Hamilton, Michael P., and Reid, Helen F., eds. *A Hospice Handbook: A New Way to Care for the Dying.* Grand Rapids, Michigan: Wm. B. Eerdmans Publishing Co., 1980.

Hooker, Susan. *Caring for Elderly People: Understanding and Practical Help.* Boston: Routledge & Kegan Paul, 1981.

Howell, Mary. *Helping Ourselves: Families and the Human Network.* Boston: Beacon Press, 1975.

Irwin, Theodore. "Home Health Care: When a Patient Leaves the Hospital," Public Affairs Pamphlet No. 560. Public Affairs Committee, 381 Park Avenue South, New York, New York 10016, 1982.

Kübler-Ross, Elisabeth. *On Death and Dying.* New York: Macmillan Publishing Co., 1969.

————. *Questions and Answers on Death and Dying.* New York: Macmillan Publishing Co., 1974.

————, ed. *Death: The Final Stage of Growth.* Englewood Cliffs, N.J.: Prentice-Hall, 1975.

Kutscher, Austin H., and Kutscher, A. H., Jr. *A Bibliography of Books on Death, Bereavement, Loss and Grief: 1935–1969.* Brooklyn, N.Y.: Center for Thanatology Research and Education, 1969.

Lack, S., and Lamerton, R., eds. *The Hour of Our Death.* London: Geoffrey Chapman, 1974.

Lamerton, Richard. *Care of the Dying.* New York: Penguin Books, 1981.

Langone, John. *Vital Signs: The Way We Die in America.* Boston: Little, Brown & Co., 1974.

Murphy, Lois B. *The Home Hospital.* New York: Basic Books, 1982.

National Cancer Institute. Free materials on care, nutrition, coping. Write: Office of Cancer Communications, Building 31, Room 10A18, Bethesda, MD 20205.

Pattison, E. Mansell. *The Experience of Dying.* Englewood Cliffs, N.J.: Prentice-Hall, 1977.

Pearson, Leonard, ed. *Death and Dying: Current Issues in the Treatment of the Dying Person.* Wolfe City, Texas: University Press, 1977.

Rossman, Parker. *Hospice.* New York: Fawcett Book Group, 1979.

Sargent, Jean V. *An Easier Way: Handbook for the Elderly and Handicapped.* Ames, Iowa: Iowa State University Press, 1981.

PHYSICAL CARE

American Red Cross. *Family Health and Home Nursing.* New York: Doubleday & Company, 1977.

Jamieson, R. H. *Exercises for the Elderly.* Verplanck, N.Y.: Emerson Books, 1983.

Prudden, Bonnie. *Pain Erasure.* New York: Ballantine Books, 1982.

A CHILD IS DYING

Baker, Lynn. *You and Leukemia: A Day at a Time.* Philadelphia: W. B. Saunders Co., 1978.

Grollman, Earl. *Explaining Death to Children.* Boston: Beacon Press, 1967.

———, ed. *Concerning Death: A Practical Guide for the Living.* Boston: Beacon Press, 1974.

Gunther, John. *Death Be Not Proud.* New York: Perennial Library, Harper & Row, 1965.

Gyulay, Jo-Eileen. *The Dying Child.* New York: McGraw-Hill Book Co., 1978.

Kushner, Harold S. *When Bad Things Happen to Good People.* New York: Schocken Books, 1981.

Jackson, Edgar. *Telling a Child About Death.* New York: Channel Press, 1965.

Martinson, Ida. *Home Care for Dying Children: A Manual for Parents.* Minneapolis, Minnesota: University of Minnesota, 1979.

Schiff, Harriet S. *The Bereaved Parent.* New York: Crown Publishers, 1977.

Sharkey, Frances F. *A Parting Gift.* New York: St. Martin's Press, 1982.

Sherman, Mikie. *Feeding the Sick Child.* Department of Health, Education, and Welfare Publication No. (NIH) 77–795. Available through the American Cancer Society.

Troup, Stanley, and Greene, William. *The Patient, Death, and the Family.* New York: Charles Scribner's Sons, 1974.

Wolf, Anna. *The Child's Attitude to Death.* New York: Child Study Press, 1973.

HOW TO BE WITH A DYING PERSON

Abrams, Ruth D. *Not Alone with Cancer: A Guide for Those Who Care; What to Expect; What to Do.* Springfield, Illinois: Charles C. Thomas, 1974.

de Beauvoir, Simone. *A Very Easy Death.* New York: Penguin Books, 1969.

Boerstler, Richard W. *Letting Go: A Holistic and Meditative Approach to Living and Dying.* Watertown, Massachusetts: Associates in Thanatology, 1982.

SOME HARD CHOICES

Behunke, John A., and Bok, Sissela, eds. *The Dilemma of Euthanasia.* Garden City, N.Y.: Anchor, 1975.

Downing, A. B. *Euthanasia and the Right to Die.* New York: Humanities Press, 1970.

Veatch, Robert M. *Death, Dying and the Biological Revolution.* New Haven: Yale University Press, 1976.

Williams, Robert H., ed. *To Live and to Die: When, Why, and How.* New York: Springer-Verlag, New York, 1973.

LIVING ONE DAY AT A TIME

Johnston, Jennifer. *The Christmas Tree.* New York: William Morrow & Company, 1982.

Kavanaugh, Robert E. *Facing Death.* New York: Penguin Books, 1972.

Lerner, Gerda. *A Death of One's Own.* New York: Simon & Schuster, 1978.

Mannes, Marya. *Last Rights.* New York: New American Library, 1973.

Sarton, May. *A Reckoning.* New York: W. W. Norton & Co., 1978.

Snow, Lois Wheeler. *A Death with Dignity.* New York: Random House, 1974.

West, Jessamyn. *The Woman Said Yes: Encounters with Life and Death.* New York: Harcourt Brace Jovanovich, 1976.

PRACTICAL MATTERS

It's Your Choice, the Practical Guide to Planning Funerals, ed. American Association of Retired Persons (write AARP, 400 So. Edward Street, Mount Prospect, IL 60056).

GRIEVING

Agee, James. *A Death in the Family.* New York: Bantam Books, 1967.

Grollman, Earl A. *Living When a Loved One Has Died.* Boston: Beacon Press, 1977.

Jackson, Edgar N. *When Someone Dies.* Philadelphia: Fortress Press, 1971.
———. *You and Your Grief.* New York: Hawthorn Books, 1962.

Lewis, C. S. *A Grief Observed.* New York: Seabury Press, 1973.

Moffat, Mary Jane. *In the Midst of Winter: Selections from the Literature of Mourning.* New York: Vintage Books, 1982.

Morris, Sarah M. *Grief and How to Live with It.* New York: Grosset & Dunlap, 1972.

Tatelbaum, Judy. *The Courage to Grieve: Creative Living, Recovery, and Growth Through Grief.* New York: Harper & Row, 1980.

Westbert, Granger E. *Good Grief.* Philadelphia: Fortress Press, 1977.

GRIEVING FOR CHILDREN

Buck, Pearl. *The Big Wave.* New York: John Day, 1973.

Center for Attitudinal Healing. *There Is a Rainbow Behind Every Cloud.* Tiburon, California: Center for Attitudinal Healing, 1978.

Coburn, John B. *Anne and the Sand Dobies.* New York: Seabury Press, 1964.

Fassler, Joan. *My Grandpa Died Today.* New York: Behavioral Publications, 1971.

Hunter, Mollie. *A Sound of Chariots.* New York: Harper & Row, 1972.

LeShan, Eda. *Learning to Say Good-Bye: When a Parent Dies.* New York: Macmillan Publishing Co., 1976.

Miles, Miska. *Annie and the Old Times.* Boston: Atlantic Monthly Press, 1971.

Viorst, Judith. *The Tenth Good Thing About Barney.* New York: Atheneum, 1971.

INDEX

Advocacy, patient, 33, 56–58, 72
Aging, Office for the, 22
Airway secretions, 148, 279
Alcohol, 161
American Cancer Society, 22, 86, 172–73
American Heart Association, 22
Anemia, 133, 142
Atropine, 279
Autopsy, 267–68

Bathing, 125
Bath supplies, 92–93, 125
Bed, patient's
  accessories, 89–90
  dimensions, 87
  furnishings, 88, 116–17
  items surrounding, 91–92
  mechanical, 87–88
  placement in home, 116
Bed care
  changing clothes of bedridden
    patient, 117
  changing position of patient in bed,
    117–18, 120
    drawsheet for, 118, 120

making bed with patient in it, 117,
  (figure) 119
Bedpans, 95–96, 121–22, 125
Bedsores, 122, 126, 130, 145–47
  preventing, 87, 126, 146
Behaviors to avoid during caregiving
  being the boss, 77
  rigidity, 77
  standing apart, 77
Bereavement counselor, caregiver as,
  34
Bleeding, 144
Blue Cross and Blue Shield, 22
Body
  disposition of, 269–71
  donating, 268–69
  laws regarding, 266–67
Body mechanics, principles of, 120
Breath control relaxation, 275–76
Breathing difficulties, 147–48
Burial, 270–71
Burnout of caregiver, 65, 78, 184–85

Canes for walking, 96
Care
  aggressive
    discontinuing, 38–40

vs. palliative, 7–8, 16–17, 38–40
continuity of, 49
emotional vs. medical, 61
ensuring consistent, 105
guidelines/plan for, 40–41
home. *See* Home care
instructions (figure), 103
palliative, 16
    defined, 7, 139
physical. *See* Physical care
terminal. *See* Terminal care
Caregiver
burnout of, 65, 78, 184–85
changing attitudes of, 8, 11
communication between physician
    and, 16
detachment of, 193–95
emotional support for, 191
experiencing blurring of time, 104–5
fears of. *See* Fears of caregiver
information needed by. *See*
    Information needed for home
    care
listening to patient, 226–28
long-term effects of caregiving on,
    64–65
mental states indicating stress of
    abandonment, 187–88
    guilt, 187
    hurt and embarrassment, 188
    odd person out, 188
    suffering servant, 187
    waiting, 187
needs of
    advocacy, 72
    companionship for patient, 73
    emergency support, 73. *See also*
        Emergencies, medical
    financial help, 72
    housekeeping, 71–72
    night care, 71
    supplies, 73. *See also* Supplies
    support at time of death, 73, 78
    telephoners, 72–73
    transportation, 72
outside, advice for, 34–36
overstressed, 64–65, 76–78
overzealousness of, 224
physical care for, 191
physical limitations of, 28
primary, choosing, 19–20
qualities needed for, 19, 25, 26–27

relaxation necessary for, 113
relief for, 36, 48–49
resources available to, 13–14, 70
roles of, 32
    bereavement counselor, 34
    information source, 33
    patient advocate, 33
    soothsayer, 34
    standard bearer, 32–33
    team captain, 33
self-care for. *See* Self-care
spending time with patient, 221–22
    guidelines for, 223–25
stresses on, 184–85, 196
    signs of stress, 185–86
supporting patient's wishes, 14–15,
    77, 223–24, 236
support of others required by, 20,
    64–65
support services for, 49
Caregiving
difficulties of, 27, 29–30, 36
impossible to do alone, 64–65
rewards of, 30
as way of life, 11
when death is imminent, 272–74
Chairs for patient, 90–91
Child, dying
continuity of care for, 178–79
death of, 181–83
eating habits of, 179
food preparation for, 179–80
hospitalization of, 177–78
informing child about illness, 172–
    74
medical team for, 174
pain medication for, 181
"Parents' Book on Leukemia"
    (American Cancer Society),
    172–73
parents of
    grief after death, 182–83
    marital problems after death, 182–
        83
    problems during illness, 170–71
    support for, 182–83
responding to behavior of, 176–78
responses to illness made by, 174–78
support groups for, 174
symptom control for, 180–81
Childishness of patient, 4
Children and home care, 209–11

needs of children after patient's death, 294–96

Chux, 116, 144

Comfort
importance of, for patient, 7, 9–10, 16, 18, 151–52, 162, 240
presence of caregiver important for patient's, 221–22
as purpose of terminal care, 48–49, 114–16, 238

Communication
within family, 208–9
physician-caregiver-patient, 16, 56–60
problems in, 58–60

Community organizations, 22
asking for help over the phone from, 70–71

Community resources supporting home care, 6

Compazine, 161

Concern for Dying Council, 243–44
Living Will of, 243–45, (figure) 244–45

Confusion/restlessness, 148–49

Consent, informed, 60–61, 237

Constipation, 123, 130, 136, 143–44

Consumer awareness prompting home care, 5–6

Continental Association of Funeral and Memorial Societies, 271

Cost of home care, 21–22, 72

Cramps, 144

Cremation, 267, 269–70

Curing
as goal of health care, 2
vs. caring, 2, 54

Daily care chart, 104–6, (figure) 107

Death
activities following patient's, 217, 287
assisting in patient's, 239–40
certification of, by physician, 182, 283
denial of, 231
explaining, to children, 209–10, 294–96
fear of, 181
as stimulant, 11
not as bad as fear of dying, 4
legal definition of, 235

natural, 6, 276–77
notice, 271
physical signs
after, 281
in final moments before, 281
of imminent. See Physical signs of imminent death
reality of, 11
support for caregiver at time of, 73, 78, 217–19. See also Survivors

Death Be Not Proud (Gunther), 111–12

Decadron, 163

Dehydration, 141, 179

Dental care, 123–24

Dental supplies, 93, 123–24

Dentures, 124, 140

Detachment of caregiver, 193–95

Diarrhea, 144

Disease. See Illness

Doctor. See Physician

Dying
acceptance of, 231–32
choices relating to, 234–35
getting the news, 1–2, 4, 197–98, 246–47
giving in to, 54
more feared than death, 4
personal meaning of, 32
physical signs of imminent death. See Physical signs of imminent death
proper place for, 4–5
symptoms of, 139–49
talking with patient about, 228–32

Dying patient. See Patient

Eating
chewing/swallowing difficulties, 134–35, 141, 163
feeding a patient, 138
food preparation guidelines, 135–37
for dying children, 179–80
high-protein foods, 133–34
importance of, 130–32
liquid diet, 130–31, 133, 135
and recovery, 131–32
supplies, 97, 135
taste-experience correlation, 132
treatments affecting, 132

Embalming, 267, 269

Emergencies, medical, 48, 67–68, 73, 75–76, 166

Emergency numbers (figure), 102
Enemas, 143
Erikson, Joan, 251–52
Ethics of terminal care
  deciding to let patient die, 235–41
  definition of death problematic, 235
  explore choices in advance, 234–35
  legal protections for patient, 237–38
    informed consent, 237
    proper disclosure, 237–38
  patient's wishes primary, 236–38
  prolonging life, 241–42
  the right to die, 241, 243
    Living Will, 243–45, (figure)
    244–45
Exercises
  breath control for relaxation, 275–
    76
  for caregiver, 191
  for easing pain, 159–60, 164
  foot, 124

Family
  absent members of, 206–8
  affected by home care, 196–201
  as basic unit of support, 69
  children in
    behavior of, 210–11, 294–96
    explaining death to, 209–10, 294–
      96
    involvement in home care, 210–
      11
  communication within, 208–9
  meetings, 200
  power play in, 239
  routines of, 204–6
  two-member, 211–12
Family service agencies, 22
Fears
  of caregiver, 27
    anticipating, 31
    about daily pressures of care, 29–
      30
    about home care, 24
    about medical needs of patient,
      28–29
    natural, 113
    about own death, 32
    about patient's pain, 151, 157,
      166
    about strength of relationship with
      patient, 30–31

of children
  about death, 181–82
  about hospitals, 177
  about pain, 181
of nurses, 49
of patient, 4, 9, 164
  about asking for painkillers, 158
  about dying, 156–57, 222–23,
    229
  about pain, 166
of visitors, 214
Fever, 144–45
Food. *See* Eating
Foot care, 124
Funeral arrangements, 217, 254, 257–
  58, 269–71, 283–85

Grief
  of children, 294–96
  diversity of, 217–18, 230, 287–89
  help from others for, 217–19, 292–
    94
    guidelines, listed, 218–19
  recovery from, 291–92, 297–99
  symptoms of, listed, 289–90
A Grief Observed (Lewis), 111–12
Guilt of caregiver, 273–74

Hair care, 94, 126
Hallucinations, 149
Healing, 298–99
Health care, home vs. hospital, 2
Health care professionals, self-care of,
  185
Health insurance
  coverage terminated to dying
    patient, 8, 21
  expenses covered by, 21, 86
Heartsounds (Lear), 111–12
  for home care, 21–22, 72
Help
  asking for, 68–71
    making a request over the phone,
      70–71
  needed after death, 217, 287
  requirements, checklist of, 71–73
  vs. control, 17
Helplessness of patient, 4, 57
Hiccups, 148
Home
  death at, 2
  defined, 8–9

difficult environment for physician, 56
preparing, for patient, 41–42
safety important in, 41–42, 83–84
Home care
alternatives to, 23
changing one's attitudes toward, 8
children and, 209–11
cost of, 21–22
difficult decision of, 22
for dying child. See Child, dying
effects on family of, 196–201
fear of, 24
flexibility of, 9–10
forced, 8
information needed for. See Information needed for home care
lessons of, 10–12
little things attended to by, 9–10
medical support for, 17–18, 20–21, 189–90
medication supply necessary for, 42
opting for, 4–7, 12–22, 24–25
practical considerations of, 7–8
social trends supporting, 6
success of, 18
supplies needed for. See Supplies
support of others for, 20. See also Team support for home care
survival rules
ensuring emotional support, 190
exercising, 191
using common sense, 190–91
transition period prior to, 37–44
in two-member family, 211–12
See also Physical care
Hopefulness of patient, 231
Hospices, terminal care in, 23, 67
Hospitalization
of dying children, 177–78
emergency, 166
nonmedical care during, 168
reasons for, 166
taking charge during, 167–69
Hospitals
acute care provided by, 7
as controllers of illness, 4
death in, 2
personnel in, 3
problems with, 2–4
routines of, 2–3, 9

terminal care in, 67
terminating treatment to dying patient, 7–8
visitors to, 3
House calls, necessary for home care, 46–47
Human bonds, between patient and caregiver, 4

Illness
attitudes toward, 3–4
blaming patient for, 3–4, 224–25
blaming physician for, 62
denial of, 4
fear of, 3–4
parents blaming self for child's, 171
personality changes during, 232
positive attitude toward, 225
reality of, 11
terminal
physical problems of, 56
transition period after learning of, 37–44
Independence
of caregiver, 69, 75, 77–78
of patient, 84, 127, 236
Information needed for home care
automobile mileage, 108, (figure) 108
care instructions, 103, (figure) 103
daily care, record of, 104–6, (figure) 107
emergency numbers, 102, (figure) 102
expenses, 101, 106, 108, (figure) 108
listed, 101–2
medical information from physician, 48, 52–53
medications given, 103–4, (figure) 104
offers of help, 108–9, (figure) 109
Information source, caregiver as, 33
Informed consent, 60–61, 237
Injections, avoiding, 97–98
Insomnia, 149
Instrument of Anatomical Gift, 268–69
Intimacy, nourishing, 251–52
Itching, 147

Journal, keeping a, 110–12

Kelly, Orville, 249
Kübler-Ross, Dr. Elisabeth, 251
  five-stage model on dying of, 251

Life
  caregiving as way of, 11
  daily
    altered by home care, 19–20
    disrupted by hospital stay, 3
  living one's own, 192
  physical limits to, 6, 241
  prolonging, 241–42
    by drugs, 158
  quality of
    in hospital, 167–68
    for patient, 7. *See also* Comfort
  review made by patient, 227–28,
    254–56
  sustaining, as goal of medicine, 54
Listening to patient, 226–28

Make Today Count guidelines, 249–50
Malnutrition, 130
Marijuana, for treating nausea, 142–43
Meals on wheels, 22
Medical care, increasing specialization
  of, 53–54
Medical ethics, 235
Medical support
  ongoing, during home care, 17–18,
    40–49, 66–68, 189
Medicare, 22
Medication
  administering, 97–98, 157–58, 161–
    65
  ample supply necessary, 42
  liquid, 98
  pain
    addiction to, 157, 162, 181
    adequate, 162–63
    administering, 157–58, 161–65
    alternatives to, 165
    drug mixtures, 161, 163
    preventive, 157
    side effects, 161–62
  pills, 98
  record of, 103–4, (figure) 104
  sedatives, 232–33
Memorial services, 271
Morphine, 157, 161
Mount, Dr. Balfour M., 158
Moving patient

from hospital to home, 38–43
from own home to caregiver's home,
  43–44

Nausea, 142–43
The New Diary (Rainer), 111
Nourishment
  inability to take in, 131, 141
  See also Eating
Nursing homes, terminal care in, 23

On Death and Dying (Kübler-Ross),
  251
Organs, donating, 268

Pain
  anticipating, 157, 161–62
  bone, 161
  defined, 155–56
  dividing into specific symptoms, 156,
    181
  emotional, 158–59
  exercises for, 159–60, 164
  management, 18, 49
    as goal of terminal care, 152
    in hospitals, 166
    satisfactory, 152–54
  medication. *See* Medication, pain
  preventive medication for, 157
  purposelessness of, 151
  understanding, 156–57
Palliative care
  defined, 7, 139
  medication for, 158, 160–62, 165
Palliative surgery, 165
Paraprofessionals, as asset to home
  care, 52
"Parents' Book on Leukemia"
  (American Cancer Society),
  172–73
Patient
  acknowledging dying, 231–32
  active vs. passive, 46–47
  adjusting to prognosis, 246–47
  advice to, 246–56
  advocacy, 33, 56–58, 72
  advocate, caregiver as, 33
  attitudes toward death, 237
  behavior of, 4, 231–32
  belonging at home, 8–9
  blamed for illness, 3–4
  blaming physician for disease, 62

changing position of, in bed, 117–18, 120
choosing home care for self, 14–15, 17
comatose, 274, 280
comfort of, 7, 9–10, 16, 18, 80, 82, 96, 151–52, 162
companionship for, 73
condition of, 15–16
creative work by, 252
denying illness, 231
dying, improved care for, 23
fears of. *See* Fears of patient
feeding, 138. *See also* Eating
feelings of, 250–51
final work of, 231–32
independence of, 236
learning to live a day at a time, 247–50
life review made by, 227–28, 254–56
listening to, 226–28
living alone, 206
medical support for, 17–18, 20–21, 40–49, 60–68, 189
moving, 38–44
needs of, 4–5
  nonmedical, 61
night care for, 71
participating in family routines, 204–6
passing on possessions, 265–66
personality changes in, 232–33
religious faith of, 230–31
resources available to, 15
reviewing the past, 227–28
rights of, 49, 60, 253–54
  the right to die, 241–45
room of, furnishing, 82–84
self-esteem of, 96
spirit of, 156, 168, 275
spoiling, 233
supplies for. *See* Supplies
talking with, about dying, 228–32
valuing, 233
Patient-caregiver relationship, 10–11
Patient-family relationship, 201–4
Pharmacist, 163
Physical care
bathing, 125
bed care, 117–20
for caregiver, 191

discontinuing painful procedures, 116
exercise, 124–25, 127–28
foot care, 124
hair care, 126
mouth care, 123–24
physician dedicated to, 168
sharing, with patient, 114
shaving, 125–26
should consider patient's habits, 115
skills required for, 113–14
skin care, 126
toilet care, 121–23
watching for physical changes, 128–29
Physical signs of imminent death, 272
central nervous system changes, 280
eye changes, 280
mood changes, 273–74
overview, 277–78
pain, 280
respiratory changes, 279–80
symptoms and care
  agitation, 274–76, 278
  airway secretions, 279
  digestive problems, 279
  pulse changes, 278
  temperature changes, 278
Physician
advice to, 61–63
  rules for terminal care, 62–63
angry at patient for not getting well, 55
behavior of, in hospital, 168
blamed for illness by patient, 62
confused about own emotions, 55
family, often not good caregiver to dying patient, 49–50
present at time of death, 73
problems with understanding, 58–60
responding to nonmedical needs, 61
responsible for proper disclosure, 237–38
selection of, 45–53
  guidelines for selection, 50–52
  preliminary questions to ask physician, 52–53
training of, 55
viewpoint of, regarding terminal care, 53–55
Physician-caregiver relationship, problems of, 46–47

Physician-patient contract, 2, 60–61
Physician-patient relationship, 55–56
Pills, 98
Placebo effect, 238–39
Pneumonia, 242
Possessions of patient, passing on, 265–66
Prednisone, 163
Preparing for home care, 37–44
Putting My House in Order, 258–59, (figures) 260–65

Records
    advantages of keeping, 101, 112
    keeping a journal, 110–12
    needed for home care. See Information needed for home care
Red Cross, 70, 85
Relationships
    patient-caregiver, 10–11
    patient-family, 201–4
    physician-patient, 55–56
Relaxation exercises, 159–60, 164
Religion, 230–31
Right to die, the, 241, 243
    legislation protecting, 243
    Living Will, 243–45, (figure) 244–45
Rules for physicians providing terminal care, 62–63

Safety
    home, importance of, 41–42, 83–84
    zone, journal as, 111
Saunders, Dr. Cicely, 153, 161–62, 242
Seizures, 145
Self-care
    of health care professionals, 185, 190
    importance of, 184–85
    living own life, 192
    saying no, 192–93
    survival rules
        asking for help, 188
        coping with boredom, 191–92
        ensuring medical support, 189–90
        learning detachment, 193–95
        managing time, 189
        organizing duties, 189
        physical self-care, 191

        setting limits, 192
Self-esteem of patient, 96
Self-pity of patient, 4
Shaving, 93–94, 125–26
Side effects
    of drugs, 161–62
    of illness, 242
Skin ulcers, 147
Social networks supporting home care, 6
Social Security Administration, 22
Soothsayer, caregiver as, 34
Spending time with patient, 213–14, 220–23
    guidelines for, 223–25, 215–17
Spirit of patient, 4, 156, 275
Standard bearer, caregiver as, 32–33
Stress
    list of stresses, 184–85
    mental states indicating stress, 187–88
    signs of, 185–86
        in family, 200
Supplies
    adapting existing equipment, 81, 85
    baths, 92–93, 125
    bed, 87–88. See also Bed, patient's
    bed accessories, 89–90
    bed and chair surroundings, 91–92
    bed furnishings, 88, 116–17
    borrowing vs. buying, 85–86
    chairs, 90–91
    dental, 93, 123–24
    eating, 97, 135
    furnishing patient's room, 82–84
        accessories listed, 82–83
    hair care, 94, 126
    importance of, 73, 80
    medication, 97–98
        ample supply necessary, 42
        See also Medication
    miscellaneous, 98–100
    shaving, 93–94, 125–26
    special equipment, 84–85
    suppliers of, 85–87
    toilet, 95–96, 121–22
    walking supports, 96–97
    wheelchairs, 91
Support groups for home care, 6
Support team. See Team support for home care
Survivors

guilt of, 290
help for
  from friends, 217–19
  psychological, 291–92
problems of, 287–89
reactions of, 282–86
recollections of, 281–84
Swallowing difficulties, 134–35, 141, 163
Symptoms
  airway secretions, 148
  anemia, 142
  bedsores, 126, 145–47
  bleeding, 144
  breathing difficulties, 147–48
  confusion/restlessness, 148–49
  constipation, 123, 143–44
  control of, in children, 180–81
  cramps, 144
  dehydration, 141
  diarrhea, 144
  dividing pain into specific, 156
  of dying vs. of illness, 139
  fever, 144–45
  focusing on, 156–57
  hallucinations, 149
  hiccups, 148
  of imminent death. *See* Physical signs of imminent death
  inability to take in nourishment, 131, 141
  insomnia, 149
  itching, 147
  listed, 139
  nausea, 142–43
  palliative care for, 139–40
  relief of acute, in hospital, 167
  seizures, 145
  skin ulcers, 147
  swallowing difficulties, 134–35, 141, 163
  thirst, 140–41

Tax-deductible expenses, 101, 106, 108, (figure) 108
Tea, herbal, 142
Team captain, caregiver as, 33
Team support for home care
  examples of, 66
  family and friends, 69–71
  hard work required from team, 78–79

help
  asking for, 68–71
  requirements for, 71–73
importance of, 64–65
organizational tools, 75–76
organizing team, 74–76
problem signs in team members, 76–78
professional, 66–68
remembering team members after patient's death, 286
selecting team, 74
value of team, 79
Terminal care
  comfort as purpose of, 48–49, 114–16, 238
  discontinuing treatments, 243
  ethics of. *See* Ethics of terminal care
  pain relief in, 157, 162–63, 165
  as self-care and self-management, 57
  See also Home care
Test period for choosing home care, 19–20
Therapeutic privilege, 60
Thirst, 140–41
Toilet care
  alternatives for immobile patient, 95–96, 120–21
  assisting patient in, 95–96
  constipation, alleviating, 123, 143–44
  helping patient to bathroom, 95, 121
  incontinence, handling, 122–23
  privacy during, 121–22, 143
  supplies, 95–96, 121–22
Transition period prior to home care, 37–44
Twycross, Dr. Robert, 153

United Fund, 70
United Way, 85

Veterans Administration, 22
Visiting nurses, 66–67
Visiting nurses associations, 22
Visitors
  fears of, 214
  guidelines for
    visiting patient, 215–17
    after patient's death, 217–19
  value of, 214

Visualization exercises, 160

Walkers, 96
Walking supports, 96–97

Wheelchairs, 91
Wills, 257
  Living, 243–45, (figure) 244–45
Writing, to overcome grief, 291